'In this challenging, accessible and important contribution to scholarship, Sally Findlow argues for a reconceptualisation of citizenship education, based on a powerful critique that draws on and synthesises political, feminist, ecological and multicultural perspectives and literatures. She is to be congratulated on bringing together discussions of citizenship education policies across schooling and higher education seeking to derive 'a model of citizenship that involves localism, stake-holding, cosmopolitanism and critical multiculturalism.'
Hugh Starkey, Professor of Citizenship and Human Rights Education, UCL Institute of Education, UK

'Sally Findlow extends the debate on what education for citizenship and social justice need to look like in our global age, beginning by critiquing citizenship education policy and practice in England, and highlighting tensions in the policies of the UK government, and in the professional and non-governmental organisations set up to support teachers in England. She extends her discussion to encompass a wide-range of international examples and her research on women, equality, and citizenship in various Gulf States. This is an engaging and sometimes provocative text.'
Audrey Osler, Professor Emerita and founder of the Centre for Citizenship and Human Rights Education, University of Leeds, UK

# Local Citizenship in the Global Arena

*Local Citizenship in the Global Arena: educating for community participation and change* proposes a reconsideration of both citizenship and citizenship education, moving away equally from prevailing 'global citizenship' and 'fundamental British values' approaches towards a curriculum for education that is essentially about creating cosmopolitan, included and inclusive, politically-engaged citizens of communities local, national and global.

Recent events have brought equality, voice and identity into fresh focus. While isolationism is futile, increased access to information about life elsewhere feeds anger at inequalities. Remote politics that ignore local needs for equality, voice and belonging in often bewildering global turmoil, don't work. Neither do forms of education that restrict their scope to risk-aversion, responsibilising and competition.

Viewing education as both problem and solution, Findlow argues in this book that today's climate of rapid and unpredictable geopolitical and cultural re-scoping requires an approach to and for citizenship education that both reflects and shapes society, paying attention to relationships between the local and global aspects of political voice, equality and community. Drawing on a range of international examples, she explores the importance and possibilities of a form of education that instead of promoting divisive competition, educates *about* citizenship in its various forms, and encourages the sorts of open and radical thinking that can help young people cross ideological and physical borders and use their voice in line with their own (and others') real, long-term interests. Successive chapters develop this argument by critically examining the key elements of citizenship discourses through the interrelated lenses of geopolitical change, nationalism, the competition fetish, critical pedagogy, multiculturalism, protest politics, feminism and ecology, and highlighting ways in which the situationally diverse lived realities of 'citizenship' have been mediated by different forms of education.

The book draws attention to how we think of education's place in a world attempting to ride the choppy waters of combined globalisation, localism, anti-state revolt and xenophobia. It will be of key interest to academics, researchers and postgraduate students in the fields of education, political science, philosophy, sociology, social policy, cultural studies and anthropology.

**Sally Findlow** is Senior Lecturer in Education at Keele University, UK. Prior to coming to Keele she had spent her working life (and some studying life) in Egypt, Kuwait, Bahrain and the United Arab Emirates.

# Routledge Research in Education Policy and Politics

For a full list of titles in this series, please visit www.routledge.com

The Routledge Research in Education Policy and Politics series aims to enhance our understanding of key challenges and facilitate on-going academic debate within the influential and growing field of Education Policy and Politics.

**Books in the series include:**

**Political and Social Influences on the Education of Children**
Research from Bosnia to Herzegovina
*Gwyneth Owen-Jackson*

**The Strong State and Curriculum Reform**
Assessing the Politics and Possibilities of Educational Change in Asia
*Leonel Lim and Michael W. Apple*

**Modernising School Governance**
Corporate planning and expert handling in state education
*Andrew Wilkins*

**UNESCO Without Borders**
Educational campaigns for international understanding
*Edited by Aigul Kulnazarova and Christian Ydesen*

**Education and Political Subjectivities in Neoliberal Times and Places**
Emergences of norms and possibilities
*Edited by Eva Reimers and Lena Martinsson*

**Using Shakespeare's Plays to Explore Education Policy Today**
Neoliberalism through the lens of Renaissance humanism
*Sophie Ward*

**Local Citizenship in the Global Arena**
Educating for community participation and change
*Sally Findlow*

# Local Citizenship in the Global Arena
## Educating for community participation and change

Sally Findlow

LONDON AND NEW YORK

First published 2017
by Routledge

2 Park Square, Milton Park, Abingdon, Oxfordshire OX14 4RN
711 Third Avenue, New York, NY 10017

*Routledge is an imprint of the Taylor & Francis Group, an informa business*

First issued in paperback 2018

Copyright © 2017 Sally Findlow

The right of Sally Findlow to be identified as author of this work has been asserted by her in accordance with sections 77 and 78 of the Copyright, Designs and Patents Act 1988.

All rights reserved. No part of this book may be reprinted or reproduced or utilised in any form or by any electronic, mechanical, or other means, now known or hereafter invented, including photocopying and recording, or in any information storage or retrieval system, without permission in writing from the publishers.

Notice:
Product or corporate names may be trademarks or registered trademarks, and are used only for identification and explanation without intent to infringe.

*British Library Cataloguing in Publication Data*
A catalogue record for this book is available from the British Library

*Library of Congress Cataloging in Publication Data*
Names: Findlow, Sally, author.
Title: Local citizenship in the global arena : educating for community participation and change / Sally Findlow.
Description: Abingdon, Oxon ; New York, NY : Routledge is an imprint of the Taylor & Francis Group, an Informa Business, [2017]
Identifiers: LCCN 2016025017 | ISBN 9781138859753 | ISBN 9781315716978 (ebk)
Subjects: LCSH: Civics—Study and teaching. | World citizenship. | International education.
Classification: LCC LC1091 .F49 2017 | DDC 370.116—dc23
LC record available at https://lccn.loc.gov/2016025017

ISBN: 978-1-138-85975-3 (hbk)
ISBN: 978-1-138-60962-4 (pbk)

Typeset in Galliard
by Apex CoVantage, LLC

# Contents

*Introduction* ix

1 The policy problem: Finding a meaningful frame of reference for citizenship education – the UK example    1

2 Locating citizenship: From the modernist education project, through regionalism to border crossing    21

3 Educating for citizenship as radical democracy    40

4 Education for community citizenship: Equality and critical multiculturalism    62

5 Education and protest citizenship    90

6 Feminist citizenship: Education and change in gendered societies    103

7 Ecological stakeholder citizenship: Educating for sustainability    121

Final thoughts: The educational mandate for boundary-crossing in an interdependent world    137

*References*    140
*Index*    157

# Introduction

We are now familiar with a range of 'globalisation' and 'citizenship' narratives, but the nature and role both of the 'local' and of education in our changing social landscape remain contested in various ways. The opening of borders to increased migration – of people, capital and ideas – has posed new questions about the interplay of global and local, and focused attention on the status of 'communities' and 'the national' in shaping and making sense of recent social, market and policy changes. These questions culminated recently in the United Kingdom in the form of two referenda, processes which uncovered huge inequalities – of share and outlook and forced us to acknowledge the swathes of traditional structures and balances that have been successively ruptured.

The challenges posed are many and often contradictory. While state power is being challenged in a range of ways, there are also calls for a reclaiming of 'the national'. Forms of competitive capitalism have produced such a pervasive fear of being left behind that few challenge it. The loss of stable community-based identity has produced new forms of racism. Competitively performative and censorial political and education systems require that we pay lip service to inclusion only to find that this means not equality but the enlisting of more people into the relentless pursuit of individual capital. Together, these changes combine to perpetuate unequal social systems rather than challenging or changing them. And despite agreement that this new way of thinking requires what has been labelled a 'critical education for citizenship' along with community mobilization, consensus evaporates when pushed on how.

Citizenship and education policies in the UK have of course been drawn together in various ways over the years, from the Crick Commission's focus on political literacy and anti-racism, through the Ajegbo Commission's on education for a multicultural national identity, the Parekh Commission's on managing cultural pluralism, and now the anti-extremism focused Prevent strategy/duty. But the tensions across these agendas and projects (equality versus diversity, global versus national or local, unity or pluralism) have not been satisfactorily resolved. Conceptually, there are several problems. First, there is not actually any form of education that is not 'citizenship education', and while the widely used phrase 'global citizenship' is persuasive on abstract levels, it is operationally meaningless. Ambivalence and over the terms 'national' and 'community' as place-based frameworks for citizenship contribute to this lack of coherence and relevance. And what of the right or responsibility of citizens to challenge policy and the power behind policy? Then there is a raft of important practical questions, such as: Does citizenship education mean educating for citizenship, or offering citizenship as a discrete subject to be studied in the form of 'Citizenship Studies'? How is it possible to train teachers, who have not studied 'citizenship', for either of these jobs? Is the best approach to creating 21st-century citizens through increasing knowledge of history and politics, by teaching 'citizenship' as a subject, developing skills, or through modelling and democratic governance? What would an ideal curriculum for the study of global citizenship would look like? In short, what these attempts do is reveal crises in both citizenship and education, each compounded by the other. Old assumptions no longer apply, teachers do not know what to 'do' with citizenship and in spite of successive commissions aimed at resolving these issues, there is a still pervasive lack of honest and coherent consideration of these questions at a policy level.

These problems have been reflected to varying degrees in recent literature spanning renewed interest in critical pedagogy, 'global citizenship', 'citizenship education', sustainability, and cultural citizenship and identity. Most of the latter take the form of practitioners' books about 'citizenship education', but there are also a number of books offering a broader sociological, historical or political science analysis of citizenship. This book shares theoretical and ideological touchstones with some of the most notable of these books. Like Ruth Lister's 1997 feminist deconstruction of citizenship, it explores the 're-localisation' of citizenship to allow real equality of participation, but with an added focus on the spatial or geo-political, as well as the gendered, aspects of inequality and hegemony. In terms of the action or activist aspect of citizenship, it draws on Craig Rimmerman's 1998 political science–grounded exposition of 'new citizenship' understood as a mix of "unconventional" politics and activism, but with an updated context and a different geo-political focus. Like Ralph Leighton's 2012 supposedly 'radical approach' to helping UK teachers, its centre is the idea of community action as citizenship. And like Tristan McGowan's 2009 discussion of 'a curriculum for participatory democracy', it looks at higher education through the lens of critical pedagogy and citizenship policy, but with higher education as part of an educational continuum rather than as a discrete sector and with a different geopolitical focus. From the (multi)cultural aspect of citizenship, it draws on Stephen May's 1999 exploration of 'critical multiculturalism' as well as Noel Noddings's 2005, US 'civics'-centred discussion of how to promote 'global awareness' in schools, and it places Nasir Meer's 2010 'critical race theory'—inflected discussion of British Muslim identity politics into a broader context of identity politics debates. It shares geopolitical assumptions with Avril Keating's 2014 critical discussion of European Union approaches to education for citizenship. It sees as central to citizenship education the same range of ideational, political, social, cultural and ecological debates discussed in James Arthur and Hilary Cremin's edited 2012 *Debates in Citizenship Education*, while integrating them more tightly – in ways reminiscent of Isin and Turner's excellent but overlooked 2003 *Handbook of Citizenship Studies*, whose historical, political, economic and cultural sweep it shares, particularly the focus on colonialism, globalisation and social change, 'radical democratic citizenship' and 'cosmopolitan citizenship'. The present book shares philosophical assumptions and this framing of citizenship, with the ways that Isin, Nyers and Turner developed it in their 2008 analysis, in *Citizenship between Past and Future*, of the many dimensions of citizenship as a "strategic concept".

Finally though, it is Nick Stevenson's 2011 exploration of the ecological essence of both political and cultural citizenship in *Education and Cultural Citizenship* that has most inspired the book's emphasis on the interdependence of cultural, political, social, ideational, environmental and educational dimensions of citizenship, which is what marks out this book's departure from existing citizenship education literature. This book is an attempt to capture the interlinked dimensions (social, economic, political and environmental) of current educational and citizenship crises, to explore the ways in which both are grounded in place and community and to consider a form of citizenship and education that might address the challenges of recent changes to who we think we are and what we think our role in the world is. While acknowledging the geopolitical diversity of the education~citizenship relationship, I argue that today's climate of rapid geopolitical and cultural re-scoping mandates an approach to educating both for and about citizenship that provides new narratives and structures while learning from old ones, is radical, critical and reflexive, looks both inwards and outwards and both reflects and shapes this dynamic society.

This reflexive theme brings us back to the book's other main focus: the importance of the 'local' – as perspective, contextual relativity, place and space and concrete experience – in both problem and solution, as a counter-perspective to undifferentiated or globalizing narratives. Thus, while this is not a book on urban geography, it focuses more than other citizenship education books have on the imagined and lived aspects of location and space (territory, resource, site and position) as central to these processes, relations and agendas, whose fluid nature makes the most meaningful way of understanding 'local' a relative one.

In using the term *local* in reference (depending on the context and focus of discussion) to country, city, community or institution, the book contributes to what can be called 'glocalisation' theory, situating discussion around both the existence and the transcending of imagined boundaries. In terms of both the concrete dimension and geographical specificity, location (or place) defines the context-specific diversity of education~citizenship links. Location and locatedness are equally central to identity and community, to resistance and oppression, and to equality and freedom. Yet while the 'spacial turn' has seen the introduction of a spatial vocabulary into the social sciences, this is deemed to have fallen short of the sort of "critical spatial lens" that illuminates how spatial configurations are "implicated in power, production and social relations" (Robertson, 2009, p.2 of online version). The present book attempts to develop the sociological significance of space by drawing explicit attention to its dimensions as it carves a route between intangible 'global' or 'flexible' citizenship and neo- or ethnonationalisms to argue for a model of citizenship that involves localism, stakeholding, cosmopolitanism and critical multiculturalism.

xii *Introduction*

Furthermore, while the book aims to contribute to a more productive alignment between the identity and ideas-shaping function of education and political structures, it does this through focusing on instances when these have been in conflict. For it is out of conflict, as I discuss (in the footprints of Gramsci, Apple, Giroux and Rancière), that new ideas and understandings emerge. I argue here that the process of geo-political re-scoping is cracked, and that it is these cracks that make collective policy critique / sub-politics not only possible but necessary. And that this, radical challenge to the ideological hegemony (action in line with real interests) rather than responsibilised self-authorship, is where education's focus in teaching and teaching about citizenship should lie.

These arguments are developed through policy critique, wide-ranging theory and concrete illustrations of the ways the education~citizenship relationship has developed in different places and at different times. Successive chapters concentrate on different (but interwoven) themes within this relationship: geopolitical change, critical pedagogy, community and critical multiculturalism, protest politics, feminism and ecology. Chapters consider, for instance, the competing priorities given to the construction of 'national' narratives, the interplay of identity and community, flexible and individualist forms of 'citizenship' and new, alternative or 'global' ideologies, revealing the gaps between lip service and experience and the ways in which citizenship and citizenship education are tied to place and to specific histories. It is intended that this complex and interwoven range of foci offer a nuanced contribution to understanding the education~citizenship relationship, grounded in the complexities of real events and experiences rather than reductive categorisation and spurious dogma.

Chapter 1, 'The policy problem', discusses recent searches for a meaningful and workable frame of reference for citizenship education in the United Kingdom. Critically reviewing evidence of uncertainty among education policy makers and professionals, particularly in the context of increasingly reductive and commodified educational structures, it analyses the uncertain place of 'nation' over a series of faltering pieces of official consultation, including Crick, Ajegbo, the Youth Citizenship Commission, and the emergence of semi-official citizenship education organisations.

Chapter 2, 'Locating citizenship', explores the problem and a range of solutions in geopolitical and spatial terms, in the sense of both relational and absolute locatedness, focusing on shifting relationships between citizenship, education, nation and community. Considering how far 'global citizenship' is undermined by the mixture of resurgent protest politics, grass-roots and political localism, transnational competitiveness, new nationalisms and separatist movements, it challenges ambivalence over the concept of 'the nation'. And it reviews the competing claims of the 'modernist education project' against 'global', 'new', 'alternative', 'active', 'feminist' and supranational 'regional' citizenship education discourses, before concluding what a climate of boundary shifting and 'glocalisation' means for the role of education.

Chapter 3, 'Education for citizenship as radical democracy', focuses on the ideational aspects of education for change, exploring relationships among education, political participation, critical literacy and protest politics. The twin principles of enlightened political participation and deliberative democracy have long provided the ideological bedrock of educational thought. Yet there have been increasing curbs on freedom of ideas and speech, a reductive, responsibilising and competitive turn in education and widespread assumption of 'youth disaffection'. This chapter discusses the educational challenges posed by this contradictory mixture, at the levels of for curriculum, pedagogy and structure, with a particular focus on relationships between state politics and sub-politics, and the meaning of educational 'safe spaces', 'radical' and 'radicalisation' in this context.

Chapter 4, 'Educating for community citizenship', takes up the structural and social aspects of the relationship between education and democratic citizenship. In a world where borders are being redrawn and crossed, the chapter looks through a citizenship lens at the politics of cultural diversity, language and inclusion, social marginalisation, free speech, racism and Islamophobia. It considers alternative approaches to social cohesion, from assimilation and various forms of pluralism to critical multiculturalism and cosmopolitanism, looking at how these are reflected across public discourses, educational frameworks and grass-roots community movements. Particular attention is given to the policy~education relationships that shaped the rather similar processes but different outcomes of the civil rights movements in the US and Northern Ireland, where Integrated Schooling, for instance, provides an interesting case study of state enactment of contradictory 'inclusive' principles in a conflicted climate.

Chapter 5, 'Education and protest citizenship', unpacks the implications of previous chapters to excavate the complex links between education, dissent and radical action for social and ideational change. Reviewing a series of educationally mediated challenges to political power, this chapter focuses on the revolutionary links between education, political consciousness and action that lay behind the civil rights movements in America and Northern Ireland, as well as more recent unrest in the Arab Middle East and the UK, weighing alternative ways of understanding these links – disenfranchisement, student consciousness or individualisation and disillusion.

Chapter 6, 'Feminist citizenship', develops the links among education, marginalisation and radical action for social change from an explicitly feminist citizenship perspective. It draws on material from the postcolonial Arab world context, where traditional autocracy and a long-standing association between feminine and local is balanced by equally longstanding traditions of political activism and where recent social change includes the mass higher education of large numbers of women, and especially from fieldwork I have conducted in the Arab Gulf. Against an analytical framework echoing that of Chapter 4, weighing (gender) neutrality, differentiation or pluralism, the chapter explores education's oftencontradictory role in both equipping women to challenge hegemonic structures while simultaneously impeding the exercise of freedom through the imposition of 'subject' status. Underscoring the contextual specificity of the education~radical citizenship relationship, discussion focuses on apparently inconsistent rhetoric between 'women are different' gender essentialism and liberal feminist demands for equality, and the ways that space is drawn into these processes.

xiv  *Introduction*

Chapter 7, 'Ecological stakeholder citizenship', considers the obligation on schools and universities to educate young people to take collective responsibility for the world and its future – from a predominantly but not exclusively spatial or environmental citizenship perspective. Challenging the marginalisation of Education for Sustainable Development (ESD) or Education for Sustainability (EfS) from mainstream citizenship discourses, it argues that EfS is not only, or even mainly, about the physical environment and using fewer resources, but also about equal sharing of those resources. Sustainability understood like this is a fairly radical citizenship agenda, despite its dilution into self-authoring household responsibilisation. But the radical nature of this agenda actually goes further, asking fundamental questions about the sustainability of development and competitiveness, per se – and the desirability of an interdependent world where everyone is in competition with each other. The ways economics, cultural intelligence and our physical environment are linked are at the heart of a concept of citizenship that is truly 'global', or grounded in an understanding of the world as a series of overlaid, interdependent flows – ecological citizenship. This view thus shapes 'stakeholder citizenship' in a particular way – less about competitiveness and voluntarism, but as collective ownership and responsibility for action. This final substantive chapter examines the educational mandate that flows from this position, arguing for an approach to educating that is not about equipping the young for competitive capitalism, but for a new way of thinking about their relationship with the world and other people that promotes collective and long-term good and causes no harm. Drawing on a range of examples, the chapter explores the extent to which such principles have been put into practice, and the barriers against this.

A brief 'final thoughts' section brings together these context-specific explorations of the education~citizenship relationship in a re-scoping world of unpredictable flows, shifting power dynamics and rampant boundary crossing, and makes the case for, first, a radical, ecological, stakeholder, critical multicultural and community-based form of citizenship located in but not limited to specific places/localities and, second, an approach to education as the space for radical thinking, for transformative learning grounded in the ideals of encounter, struggle, boundary crossing and risk taking.

# 1 The policy problem

## Finding a meaningful frame of reference for citizenship education – the UK example

A high-profile speech in 2011 by UK Prime Minister David Cameron invoked a now dated idea of citizenship by conflating it with "national identity" and "shared values", as he criticised "state multiculturalism". The government line was that this speech set out an approach to zero tolerance of 'Islamic extremism'. But what it actually did was engage in a particular form of traditionalist disparagement of values seen as alien:

> So, when a white person holds objectionable views, racist views for instance, we rightly condemn them. But when equally unacceptable views or practices come from someone who isn't white, we've been too cautious frankly – frankly, even fearful – to stand up to them. The failure, for instance, of some to confront the horrors of forced marriage, the practice where some young girls are bullied and sometimes taken abroad to marry someone when they don't want to, is a case in point. This hands-off tolerance has only served to reinforce the sense that not enough is shared. And this all leaves some young Muslims feeling rootless. And the search for something to belong to and something to believe in can lead them to this extremist ideology. Now for sure, they don't turn into terrorists overnight, but what we see – and what we see in so many European countries – is a process of radicalisation.
> (Cameron, 2011)

The speech provoked liberal revulsion in the UK, mainly for the rhetorical mixing of criticism of multicultural 'tolerance' with discussion of terrorism, which represented Muslims as an example of a demographically distinct community and thus part of the problem rather than the solution. On another level, its significance lies in how emphatically it flies in the face with that other prevailing message – that we are all supposed to be 'global citizens' now. The inadequacy of the construct is easily summarised: "Today there are growing cries for individuals to take up their roles as 'global citizens'. While these cries may be frequent, a common understanding of global citizenship is not" (Langran, Langran and Ozment, 2009:1). The prime minister's speech and associated comment captured a range of contemporary debates around roots, identity, inclusion, sharing, responsibility and voice, as well as the widely misused tag 'radicalisation'. They also underscore the importance of addressing links between these global phenomena and education.

## The 'global citizenship' project

The global citizenship idea is grounded in the powerful and all-encompassing rhetoric of globalisation, understood broadly as either the decline or weakening of nation-state power in legal, financial, political, social and cultural terms. By the first decade of this millennium, 'global citizenship' had become an educational buzzword in the English-speaking world. But so, to a lesser extent, had something called 'global education', grounded in the emergence from the 1970s of values-based educational discourses, holistic, participatory, democratic, integrating in their sweep of attention human rights, world peace, poverty, health and well-being until a moment in the 1980s when they coalesced:

> Global education encompasses the strategies, policies and plans that prepare young people and adults for living together in an inter-dependent world. It is based on the principles of cooperation, non-violence, respect for human rights and cultural diversity, democracy and tolerance. . . . Learners are encouraged to make links between local, regional and world-wide issues and to address inequality.
>
> (Osler and Vincent, 2002:2)

The overlaps and tensions between these concepts and agendas led to calls to "look beyond old barriers that have separated citizenship education and global education and to form a new global citizenship education" (Davies et al., 2005b: 66). They also coincided with policy awareness of the need to re-examine the 'point' of education, in terms of the ideal mix of 'neo-liberal' (preparing students to be part of the same economy), 'transformationalist' (inclusive and fighting against local social injustice) or 'radical' (preparing students to fight against the hegemonic imposition of power; Bates, 2012:268). One intellectual outcome was the imaginative construct of a 'critical education for ('global' or 'new') citizenship' that would be based on revisions of both unit of belonging or frame of cultural reference and education's role in preparing students for life in a supposedly borderless world (Ohmae, 1994). This would help students understand "the politics of difference" (Rimmerman, 1998:100), promote peace and inclusion (Noddings, 2005; May, 1999), and be framed around the kind of political critique that can "help students make the connection between their lives and their role as global citizens" (Langran et al., 2009).

But there have been consistent concerns about both the global and educational dimensions of this construct. The first is grounded in the legalistic objection that "there is no global state that could guarantee citizenship" (Bates, 2012:262). Thus, "outside of the unlikely prospect of a global state, there is no such thing as global citizenship" (Stevenson, 2012b:114). As a result, therefore, "[o]ften the concept of global citizenship is limited to the idea that we should 'care' about other human beings, the environment or disarmament" (Langran, Langran and Ozment, 2009:1). However, the impact of 'globalisation' on education has in many ways been the opposite of global emancipation. More often, "[g]lobalization foregrounds education in specific ways that attempt to harness education systems to the rapid and competitive growth and transmission of technologies and knowledge linked to the national competitiveness of nations within the global economy" (Ozga and Lingard, 2007a:70). This phenomenon, along with the reduction of school curricula to preparation for high-stakes testing which makes *relative* exam success of questionable collective value, is among the manifestations of what has been called the 'competition fetish' in education (Naidoo, 2011). And Robertson has attributed the limited educational purchase of global citizenship to an intrinsic flaw in the education rather than the globalisation construct itself: "There are neither adequate framings at the global or supra-regional levels . . . nor sites of legally institutionalized power that might enable a system of claims-making that does not privilege global capital at the expense of the global citizen" (S.Robertson, 2007:2).

Still as far as policy discussions of citizenship go, the role of national or other place-linked identities in a 'globalised' world is problematic. In the UK, while most policy actors try to avoid overt nationalism, it continues to pop up when the ostensible focus is on other things. The spectre of nationalism lay, for instance, behind David Blunkett's introduction of citizenship 'testing' and associated forms of 'citizenship education' including English language and British Politics and Customs. In 2002, Blunkett as Home Secretary proposed in a white paper the introduction of a written test on English, British politics and culture and British life for people (immigrants) who apply for British Citizenship. Preceded by lessons and followed, for successful entrants, by a special ceremony – designed to endow a symbolic value to being a citizen – it also harkens back to an older form of distinction between citizens and non-citizens. The 'Life in the UK' citizenship test was implemented in 2005. Although such institutionalised efforts to encourage national belonging are far from unique across the globe, it sits awkwardly against recently prevailing multicultural rhetoric. Yet for every critic there is also a more nuanced advocate of reclaiming the national in a reimagined national narrative.

Ongoing uncertainty about the place of the 'nation' is due partly to increased global mobility, which challenges the way it was once possible to connect citizenship unproblematically to place of birth or ethnicity, while complex and fragile geo impede attempts to establish a clear replacement framework for both bestowing and understanding the relationship between nation, community and identity. 'Nationality' is no longer a simple matter. Though we are *told* we are living in a globally dis-embedded world, instead we find three contradictory structures competing for legal, political and social allegiance. On one level, the boundaries of existing countries and 'nations' are disintegrating and re-forming along lines not exclusively shaped by ethnicity, but also recently shared history. Political and religious tensions that shade into neo-nationalisms provide various new or revived frames for collective identity and allegiance. Meanwhile, efforts have continued to build supranational unions with clout. The European Union is one of the most well known, but it is not the only regional unit of governance and strategic alliance developed as a way of managing economic competition, conflicts and diversities. Social and political unrest is a familiar response to such complex redrawing of allegiances. But the complex counter-narrative also includes moves for smaller, subnational autonomous units bestowing belonging and identity and local community revivals.

The widespread loss of autonomous and stable nation-state units has affected both policy-making and citizens' responses to this. While policy has to be framed around these tensions, perceptions of profound global instability amid increased international competition for resources are manifest in the questions people have asked about our local and global institutions. Political concern about social cohesion and migration in the wake of transnational terrorism and local riots is often attributed to lack of community, and has produced both media chatter and a raft of funded academic projects investigating young people's disillusion with institutional politics. One of the results is a series of linked commissions and widespread endorsement of global citizenship rhetoric, in which social policy merged with educational policy.

## The citizenship education project

In the late 1990s, concern about antisocial behaviour and decline in moral standards expressed in response to the high-profile racist murder of a black teenager Stephen Lawrence were met by a raft of policy reforms including the Race Relations [Amendment] Act 2000 requiring schools and other public bodies to address discrimination and promote race equality. But educational reforms were prominent among them. On 19 November 1997, following proposals in the education white paper 'Excellence in Schools', the secretary of state for education and employment pledged 'to strengthen education for citizenship and the teaching of democracy in schools' and to that end set up an 'Advisory Group on the Teaching of Citizenship and Democracy in Schools' chaired by Professor Sir Bernard Crick, a pre-eminent advocate of political education.

The commission's aim was "[t]o provide advice on effective education for citizenship in schools – to include the nature and practices of participation in democracy; the duties, responsibilities and rights of individuals as citizens; and the value to individuals and society of community activity." The intended scope included "the teaching of civics, participative democracy and citizenship, and may be taken to include some understanding of democratic practices and institutions, including parties, pressure groups and voluntary bodies, and the relationship of formal political activity with civic society in the context of the UK, Europe and the wider world . . . and . . . an element of the way in which expenditure and taxation work, together with a grasp of the underlying economic realities of adult life . . . ". The main outcomes of the group's work were expected to be guidance to the UK Qualifications and Curriculum Authority (QCA) in their review of the National Curriculum through "a statement of the aims and purposes of citizenship education in schools; a broad framework for what good citizenship education in schools might look like, and how it can be successfully delivered – covering opportunities for teaching about citizenship within and outside the formal curriculum and the development of personal and social skills through projects linking schools and the community, volunteering and the involvement of pupils in the development of school rules and policies" (QCA, 1998:4).

The Advisory Group sought to champion what it called 'political literacy' as the route to strengthen democracy, promote the rights of minorities and combat racism. But the report of 1998, known as the Crick Report, had many difficult balances to strike, such as seeking to avoid the emphasis on patriotism and good behaviour redolent of US policy and rhetoric while simultaneously deploying some of the language of US 'civics'. The 'citizenship learning outcomes' it recommended included a mix of activity, knowledge, skills and values: community activity; knowledge about political systems in the UK and around the world, about rights and responsibilities, about economic realities; an understanding of diversity, exclusion and sustainability; concern for the 'common good'; tolerance; a commitment to justice and human rights; and a whole raft of skills, including "mak(ing) a reasoned argument", problem-solving, the "ability to use modern media" and "to tolerate other viewpoints". (QCA, 1998:44; Fig 1, "Overview of essential elements to be reached by the end of compulsory schooling", p.44). And as a result of the Crick Report's recommendations, in 2002 Citizenship was incorporated into the English National Curriculum as a statutory subject for 11- to 16-year-olds, assessable by means of a General Certificate of Secondary Education (GCSE) examination at the age of 16. Though its remit was limited to compulsory schooling, the report recommended that citizenship education should not end at sixteen, and in due course an A. level in Citizenship Studies was established by the AQA (formerly known as the Assessment and Qualifications Alliance) education charity, covering the themes of "Identity, Rights and Responsibilities; Democracy, Active Citizenship and Participation; Power and Justice; Global Issues and Making a Difference" (AQA, 2013).

Yet the Crick Report was widely judged full of admirable ideals that were unworkable in practice. Ongoing confusion over the meaning of the term citizenship led to confusion over the role of education in its promotion. The DfEE (Department for Education and Employment) Advisory Group submitted to the commission its view that the consultation did "not provide a clear consensus on aims and purposes or a conceptual framework for education for citizenship, but that is not surprising since they were not asked to comment specifically on these matters" (QCA, 1998:18, 3.18). This lack of consensus should have carried a warning for the commission. Instead, the report's list of "essential elements" ended up reading rather like a list of schooling outcomes. Everything was included, despite cautions such as the British Youth Council's that the citizenship curriculum "should not cover, or at least not be dominated or distracted by . . . issues based on moral education, revolving around key concepts such as drugs, health education, housing and homelessness, careers development and employability etc." (QCA, 1998:20, 3.20). It was widely felt that the report had fallen into a series of 'traps', as a result of and in response to the social, political and cultural changes that had taken place since further projects followed. Prime among the shortcomings of both the mandate and the Crick Report itself was the way it had fallen into "the trap of presenting certain ethnicities as 'other' when it discusses 'cultural diversity'" (Osler and Starkey, 2001:292), while simultaneously failing to interrogate the geopolitical frame for whatever form of citizenship was envisaged.

## 6  The policy problem

More work was needed, and the Crick Commission was quickly followed by two more, explicitly addressing multiculturalism and identity. In 1998, the independent Runnymede Trust set up a commission on The Future of Multi-ethnic Britain, whose report is known by the name of its chair, Lord Bhikhu Parekh. Published in 2000, the Parekh Report outlines the challenges for "a community of communities of citizens", in which education is identified as the third of nine areas for 'immediate action', after 'coordination by central government' and the 'criminal justice system' and before the arts, health, employment, immigration, politics and religion (Runnymede, 2000:5).

The Parekh Report's analysis of distinct approaches was undermined operationally by not being grounded in the complex realities of multi-ethnic life, resulting in a fudged manifesto for a form of nationalistic pluralism or pluralist nationalism. Seven years later, the 'Diversity and Citizenship Curriculum Review' of 2007, known as the Ajegbo Report after its chair, Sir Keith Ajegbo, had the more focused Parliamentary brief to explore what the Crick Commission had been so reticent about: the extent to which British social and cultural history should be a pillar of the national Citizenship curriculum. The report's key recommendations were that "citizenship education works best when delivered discretely" (rather than through 'citizenship' classes), for greater conceptual definition including "strengthening treatment of issues relating to the 'political literacy' strand", increasing the number of initial teacher training places for Citizenship teachers, and for whole-curriculum planning across schools that might "develop ways of linking Citizenship education effectively with other subjects, with the ethos of the school, and with the community". It was further recommended that this holistic approach should include GCSEs comprising topics that "link Citizenship to other relevant subjects", with emphasis on identity and diversity, and "a number of joint GCSEs, for example, a joint Citizenship with History GCSE, a joint Citizenship with Religion GCSE, a joint Citizenship with Geography GCSE" (Ajegbo, 2007:11). Yet this report had a very limited impact and was criticised both for *too narrow* a focus on race and diversity and for "fail(ing) to adopt a critical perspective on race or multiculturalism or adequately engage with young people's lived experiences of citizenship within a globalised world" (Osler, 2008). It has since been archived, along with a note stating that "[i]t should not be considered to reflect current policy or guidance" (DfE, 2011).

Notwithstanding these hesitant starts, political attention to the education-citizenship relationship has continued. In 2008, the Youth Citizenship Commission was tasked by the government to explore what citizenship meant to UK youngsters and make policy recommendations. This commission included a range of people including academics, young people and members of the Political Studies Association (PSA), an organisation founded in the 1920s out of a commitment to the principle that politics big and small is everybody's business, which in 2007 had expanded into the specialist group Young People's Politics in response to New Labour perceptions of youth disaffection. When the commission ended, the PSA continued with this work through the more explicitly political project 'Beyond the Youth Citizenship Commission – Young People and Politics' (BTYCC). BTYCC was grounded in the perception that accessible citizenship policy rhetoric for young people was, when not confused, either overly passive (focused on good works for the community) or too focused on individual CV-building as a way of papering over cracks instead of focusing on actually changing things. Ongoing commitment to the education–citizenship policy project has also taken the form of citizenship education organisations, whose typically neo-liberal links with government have been opaque. Whereas the PSA's involvement with citizenship education has been greater at the post-compulsory level, the Association of Citizenship Teaching and the Citizenship Foundation have been more influential at school level, with mandates that straddle advising government, disseminating policy, and offering practical advice to citizenship teachers.

The Association for Citizenship Teaching (ACT) is the most 'establishment' of these. ACT was founded by Bernard Crick in 2001 as a registered charity and the following year became the professional subject association for Citizenship, representing teachers and others involved in Citizenship education. Its honorary president is still the Right Honorable David Blunkett. The association's mission is to "to support the *teaching* of high quality Citizenship and to promote wider public understanding of the subject . . . [and] research into the participation of young people in society" (ACT, 2015). However, while 'democratic society' features prominently in its broad conceptual sweep, ACT has consistently sidestepped actually defining citizenship. And since 2011, the organisation has moved more emphatically away from ideational aspects of the business and towards closer policy alignment by reporting on National Curriculum issues and providing resources. These resources include teaching and learning ideas and materials, membership services including education programmes, professional development, training and networking opportunities and a members' journal called Teaching Citizenship. ACT has also contributed to the government-funded Global Learning Programme (GLP), which was set up to provide training for staff in schools in what they call 'global teaching', with differentiated provision across the various UK nations. Its published goal is ". . . increased knowledge of the developing world and evidence of the skills to interpret that knowledge to make judgements about global poverty, its causes and what can be done to reduce it" (ACT, 2015i).

The evolution of the Citizenship Foundation, on the other hand, is reflected in an imagining of 'citizenship education' that is about justice, morality, politics, power and authority. More consistent with the political ethos behind the Crick Commission and the British Youth Council, the foundation, in fact, predates both and is more independent of government. The foundation was founded in 1989 as an offshoot of the 1984 joint Law Society and National Curriculum Council 'Law in Education Project' led by the solicitor Andrew Phillips (later Lord Phillips of Sudbury). It was a key pressure group in bringing citizenship education into the English National Curriculum, a cause at the time seen at least partly in terms of providing an education policy counterpoint to the disciplinary weight of History and Geography lobbies. Since then, its mission has shifted slightly from educating students about the role of law in democratic society to the wider one of promoting critical thinking and democratic discussion through a

8  *The policy problem*

focus on controversial topics and a range of projects including mock trials, youth parliament competitions and work with young offenders.

Despite these structural building blocks, in terms of actual impact on education, there is still a large disconnect. Although there is broad awareness that geopolitical change is impacting on education and will continue to do so, and despite vibrant policy debate and widespread use of the 'global citizenship' and 'citizenship education' mottos, citizenship education has little purchase on the imaginations of educational staff, pupils or the public in England. There is also uncertainty about continued funding, to the extent of a 2010 early Coalition threat to remove citizenship entirely from the National Curriculum, thereby returning the national curriculum to what it called "its intended purpose – a minimum national entitlement organised around subject disciplines" (Rose, 2011).

Warnings against the removal of citizenship from the National Curriculum underscored three things: the need to give young people tools for life, the patchiness of citizenship provision and that citizenship provision works best when integrated into the curriculum. These cautions came from a range of groups organised by the umbrella coalition Democratic Life, a coalition set up as a sister organisation of the ACT to support, maintain and improve the teaching of citizenship education but also with links with the Law Society, the Citizenship Foundation, the Public Legal Education Network, Amnesty International and the British Institute of Human Rights. They pointed out that "we cannot whinge about apathetic youth while not giving them the tools to engage with society" (Rose, 2011). Part of the evidence used to support their argument came from the Citizenship Education Longitudinal Study (CELS), begun in 2001 by the National Foundation for Educational Research (NFER) and commissioned by the Department of Children, Schools and Families (DCSF). The CELS was a nine-year study on the impact of citizenship education on the knowledge, skills and attitudes of young people and on how citizenship education was being delivered in secondary schools. On the basis of case study visits to schools and both longitudinal and cross-sectional surveys with pupils between the ages of 11 and 18, teachers and school leaders (approximately 11,250 pupils for the longitudinal survey and approximately 7,500 students for the cross-sectional survey), it found that citizenship education was patchy and uneven. It also found that the most successful approach was "where citizenship is embedded in the curriculum, has links to student participation across the school/college, and encourages links with the wider community". As for insights into young people's understanding of citizenship, they found that "students define citizenship as more to do with rights and responsibilities, and issues of identity and equality, than with political literacy and active participation in formal political processes" (NFER, 2010).

Although these were very mixed findings, the campaign eventually resulted in a reprieve: citizenship is on the reformed National Curriculum and the qualifications and examinations regulatory authority for England Ofqual rewrote the GCSE. Yet citizenship's place in the curriculum remains fragile. In May 2015, Ofqual announced that it was dropping citizenship as an A level option, following the AQA exam board's decision to withdraw the only citizenship A level currently on offer due to small numbers. Protest was unsuccessful, and the weight of funded and government sponsored work in the UK that is badged 'citizenship and youth' is beginning to coalesce around the narrower focus of political engagement, such as that coordinated by the PSA.

## Impediments to citizenship education

So confidence in citizenship education is undermined on both operational and ideational levels. Operationally, ideals of promoting 'global citizenship' and educating for political or social participation – or even life – are swiftly shattered by realities of tightly regulated and competitive state education systems with national curricula and little or no funding for this – certainly none to train teachers. Prime among the aspects that the CELS found needed further development were the availability of teacher training and, since teachers assigned to teach citizenship often have no specialism, "teacher confidence in teaching political literary topics" (NFER, 2010). Relief, then, that citizenship was going to continue was mitigated by caution:

> ACT hopes that the government will also ensure that there continues to be specialized training for those wanting to teach the subject, including in ITE. ACT stands ready to support the Department for Education in continuing to develop this subject through the curriculum revision phase and help teachers implement any changes to programmes of study in school.
> (Waller, 2013)

Meanwhile, citizenship education continues in the experience of young people in the UK to mean either training in workplace skills or, more often, Physical, Social and Health Education (PSHE). Despite the pains taken in the Crick Report to distinguish between Citizenship and 'broader PSHE' (p.20), these attempts actually muddied the waters and have resulted in citizenship often being relegated to the extra PSHE hour in the week – a repository for everything that teachers think pupils should know not otherwise covered in the curriculum or simply a timetable slot for dealing with 'any other business' means that secondary pupils remember this as the lesson when teachers would tell them how to behave well. Teachers continue to point out the need for the teaching of basic politics, with the caveat that it should be taught by teachers who understand politics and that it should not be mixed up with the teaching of (politically defied) 'values':

> [A] requirement to teach "fundamental British values" (FBV) that extends to all . . . falls within a broader strand known as spiritual, moral, social and cultural development (SMSC). The basic political toolkit – knowledge of voting systems, legislation, parliament and cabinet – is likely to get lost in this alphabet soup. And are students really best served by an ideological programme designed to inculcate specific beliefs, rather than one that explains the nuts and bolts of the constitution? . . . "Values – honesty and obeying the law and compassion and concern for others – that should be part of every child's experience of going through the school system. . . ."
> (Shariatmadari, 2015)

10  *The policy problem*

Mixing this fundamental educational job with the teaching of politics under the 'citizenship' umbrella means that "instead of it being taught really well by people who are qualified to teach government and politics, it's taught badly by physics teachers" (Shariatmadari, 2015).

Underlying this operational muddle is a deeper conceptual one. Instead of drawing critically from the literature to create well-defined corpuses of knowledge and associated educational aims, most attempts at constructing a citizenship education curriculum read rather like 'wish lists'. Alternative badges including 'active citizenship', 'new citizenship', 'alternative citizenship' and 'feminist' citizenship are simply name-checked in ad hoc and often incoherent ways. Inclusiveness is prioritised over coherence in the hope that some elements will stick and work, whatever 'working' means. The approach has been criticised for producing an absence of actual content in what was described in 2005 as "the worst taught secondary subject":

> [T]he Qualifications and Curriculum Authority, argued that citizenship education was "about promoting and transmitting values", "participation" and "duties". But the obvious question of "values about what?" was carefully avoided. Instead, its advocates cobbled together a "hurrah list" of unobjectionable and bland sentiments rebranded as values.
> (Furedi, 2005)

Without clear conceptual or geopolitical framing, investigations such as CELS become self-referential and thereby part of the problem.

The most resounding lack of clarity is around the envisaged geopolitical framework. The nationalistic, universalising citizenship education paradigm has for so long circumscribed both citizenship discourses themselves, as well as the scope for imagining an education project that can see beyond the national, that simply bringing together 'global education' and 'citizenship education' in recognition of today's necessarily wider frame of reference as some have urged (Davies et al., 2005b) does nothing to address the challenge of building a distinctive and coherent corpus of teachable-learnable knowledge. The status of equality, economic or political participation and the place of 'national' and other place-linked identities remain unresolved, as was clear in the 2001 Denham Report on Public Order and Community Cohesion that was criticised for defining cultural citizenship on the basis of 'Englishness' (Herbrechter and Higgins, 2006). It is hardly surprising that the CELS found young people identified citizenship as having little to do with political literacy or active political participation; the absence of intelligent discussion of citizenship and political participation in relation to place means that all they hear are examples of the *mis*use of such terms.

The second major conceptual obfuscation is around whether 'citizenship' is a *subject*, an *approach* to education or the *goal* of education. A study of a decade ago found both tutors and students uncomfortable with "the balance . . . between education about and for citizenship" (Smith and Ottewill, 2007:7). The Citizenship Foundation website describes citizenship as "this subject" before fairly swiftly contradicting itself by quoting Sir Bernard Crick's explanation that "Citizenship is more than a subject. If taught well and tailored to local needs, its skills and values will enhance democratic life for all of us, both rights and responsibilities, beginning in school and radiating out" (Citizenship Foundation', 2015b cited in Crick, 1999). And it goes on to describe citizenship education as "about enabling people to make their own decisions and to take responsibility for their own lives and their communities. That means we want young people leaving education with an understanding of the political, legal and economic functions of adult society; and with the social and moral awareness to thrive in it". ACT's catch-all approach to defending the place of citizenship in the National Curriculum is similar:

> Over the past ten years Citizenship education has become an established curriculum subject giving our young people an understanding of what it means to be an active citizen in a democratic society. Citizenship education prepares young people to be able to play an active role in democratic life. As Citizenship teachers we are imparting the **knowledge** and **skills** our young people need in order to be able to participate in local, national and international society. Not only are we teaching about the institutions where **democracy is** practiced at **national and international** level; but we're also giving pupils empirical experience of democracy by demonstrating these **values and practices** through our own teaching and through the culture of the school. The government proposal to retain this subject underscores how important this work is in inspiring young people to become **active** citizens, willing, able and skilled to take a full part in the life of their **community** and the **nation** as a whole.
>
> (Waller, 2013)

But this series of fudges are a long way off the critically political visions of citizenship reflected in the Crick (Isin and Turner, 2003).

And finally, there is further contradiction on the issue of whether citizenship education should be promoting a pluralistic or culturally homogenous society. The Citizenship Foundation is ambivalent on this issue. In 2012 its website proclaimed that "[i]t is not about trying to fit everyone into the same mould, or creating 'model' or 'good' citizens" (Citizenship Foundation, 2012), whereas by 2015 the vision seemed to have shifted strikingly towards one of responsibilised, self-monitoring, model 'citizens': "Citizenship education is also crucial because it builds **character**, explores **British values** and develops the **soft skills** of communication, initiative, interacting appropriately and team working that employers are crying out for" (Citizenship Foundation, 2015b). As for ACT, recent announcements have headlined the DfE's decision to make the teaching of 'British values' part of the obligatory spiritual, moral, social and cultural education (SMSC) offered in schools, to subject this to quality assurance processes through OFSTED and to test this (DfE, 2014). Press releases suggest that ACT is wholly supportive of these developments. SMSC was added to the contradictory set of themes ranging from the Magna Carta, Foreign Affairs and Global Learning at ACT's 2015 National Conference. And ACT appears to have assumed the role of ensuring compliance through the provision of training courses such as the half-day Continued Professional Development course 'Making Sense of SMSC through Citizenship', offered in 2014, where the aim was to help teachers:

> Understand the revised Ofsted inspection framework and guidelines for SMSC
> Get up to date with new DFE guidance on British values as part of SMSC in schools
> Explore the role of Citizenship in teaching about values and SMSC
> Build practical strategies to teaching controversial and sensitive issues
> Assess how well your provision develops pupil resilience to extremism and skills to challenge racism and discrimination Use the ACT Quality Standard and Self Evaluation tool (SET) to benchmark high quality provision.
> (ACT, 2014)

There are some suggestions that the DfE are aware of contradictions:

> We [the DfE] want every school to promote fundamental British values, including mutual respect and tolerance of those of different faiths and beliefs. . . . Citizenship education, as part of the new national curriculum, should cover the diverse national, regional, religious and ethnic identities in the United Kingdom and the need for mutual respect and understanding. . . .
> (ACT, 2014)

It is also, of course, possible to explain apparent obfuscation as fear of non-compliance. For instance, the Citizenship Foundation's ostensible mission to promote political literacy is undercut by the health-and-safety flavour of some of the Foundation's educational resources. Advice published for schools in 2003 on 'Teaching about Controversial Issues', for instance, now billed as 'essential reading', asks such questions as, 'To what extent is it legitimate for teachers to take part in protest?' and includes advice like, 'Where these provisos are met, however, there is no good reason why young people should not be allowed – or even encouraged – to participate in the political process themselves on the school premises?' (Citizenship Foundation, 2003).

The overall impression is not one of ambivalence over a concrete set of propositions, but one of uncertainty-driven vacuity and contradiction, especially when compared to the more straightforwardly nationalistic US civics project. Although the US is a federal system where each state has a high level of autonomy about what to teach and how to teach it, citizenship has long functioned as an ideological frame for education and citizenship *education* is mandatory across the country. The National Assessment of Educational Progress (NAEP) 'Civics Project' is unapologetically nationalistic at the levels of content and rhetoric. Un-ironic use of the phrase 'the people': "NAEP Civics: Of the people. By the people. For the people" (U.S. Department of Education, 2010), headlines content framed emphatically around the American constitution, history and civic institutions:

> In approving this Assessment Framework in civics for the National Assessment of Educational Progress (NAEP), the National Assessment Governing

Board was guided by the conviction that the continued success of the world's oldest constitutional democracy depends, in large measure, on the education of our young citizens. In each succeeding generation it is necessary to develop a firm understanding of the core documents of American liberty – the Declaration of Independence and the U.S. Constitution, including the Bill of Rights – and a reasoned commitment to their values and principles. It is also necessary, the Board believes, for students to show an understanding not only of American government but also of the workings of civil society – the voluntary associations and nongovernmental institutions through which a free people express their civic concerns.

(U.S. Department of Education, 2010:v)

Even in terms of method, the US project was more straightforward, "led by this Board and conducted under contract by the Council of Chief State School Officers in conjunction with the Center for Civic Education and the American Institutes for Research" (U.S. Department of Education, 2010:v). Although comments from committees of "scholars, state and local educators, civic leaders, and interested members of the public" fed into the process, the board appears to have been relatively untroubled by the English need to be *seen* to be conducting repeated rounds of multi-stakeholder consultation, which have not been genuinely consultative at a grass-roots level but stumbling, compromising and contradictory.

Counter-intuitively then, US civics represent a form of 'nationalistic' education that in many ways both invokes the critical perspective to understanding the world and one's place in it that was envisaged in the Ajegbo Report while also sharing a common ethos with the UK's recently introduced system of educating and testing new immigrants. In terms of the content and curriculum fit of US civics, while its *aim* – to impart 'knowledge, skills and dispositions' – is alarmingly reminiscent of the English citizenship curriculum's holistic ambitions, this is consolidated in the US case to items of knowledge or learning outcomes that can be tested. Thus, commitment *to* the nation is assessed by knowledge *about* the nation, including inter alia the life and works of Martin Luther King. This knowledge is in turn evidenced in a commendably aligned way by "identifying and describing important information, explaining and analyzing it, and evaluating information and defending positions with appropriate evidence and careful reasoning" (p.vi). And as a final point of contrast, US civics is intended to be threaded throughout the curriculum rather than bolted on as an extra timetabled class.

## Citizenship and universities

Links between education, citizenship and political literacy have not been the sole preserve of formal and compulsory education in the UK. Post-compulsory education has been brought more centrally into policy thinking about 'education', in large part due to increased student numbers and accompanying changes to funding arrangements, which have been the most visible manifestation of a radical reimagining of the social role of universities, even though part of this process of reimagining is a widely documented loss of purpose. Thus, "[h]igher education is pumping out people with degrees into a jobs market that doesn't need them" (Chakrabortty, 2013). The language used is 'experiment', 'gamble' (Collini, 2013), and the sector is criticised for 'infantilising' and 'cheating' students with excessive intervention, direction treating them as 'consumers' (*THES* 2011:13).

In 2006, the Higher Education Funding Council for England (HEFCE) declared that more attention was needed to fostering civic values (HEFCE, 2006:120–121). And although they neither defined these values nor said *how* they proposed fostering them, the Council has collaborated with the PSA in funding projects designed to promote the teaching of citizenship at university level, such as the 2005 Politics Online Learning and Citizenship Skills (POLiS) project that sought to encourage students to evaluate their own roles as politically engaged citizens (Smith and Ottewill, 2007). Meanwhile, the PSA itself has extended its scope to launch a 'Charter for Citizenship for Higher and Further Education', drawing particular inspiration from both the US civics model, the Campus Compact's 'Presidents' Declaration on the Civic Responsibility of Higher Education' (Campus Compact, 2012) as well as changes to higher education governance that have made it *possible* to attempt sector-wide interventions. This charter seeks to promote student political engagement, through critical and grass-roots campaigning as much as voting, by encouraging universities to work as 'sites of democracy' (https://www.psa.ac.uk/charter; Tonge and Mycock, 2009).

These allied strands of the politically engaged post-compulsory education policy agenda challenge the prevailing one of neo-liberal commodification. In fact, the tension between political and economic higher education visions has reached its apogee in a series of contemporary paradoxes. That is, the free-market business orientation has been accompanied by tighter central regulatory frameworks, which along with increasing global transparency have made a critical resistance movement possible. So, on one hand, the transformation of universities into non-distinctive players in 'for-profit' markets has produced forms of investment commodity trading – by students, governments, private investors and universities themselves, all equally preoccupied with risk avoidance, production–consumption and efficiency. We learn that students are governed by the sort of consumer mindset in which "[t]he value of a university education is the income it enables you to earn minus the cost of acquiring that education" (Collini, 2013). While the state view of higher education as a catalyst for economic development, which saw the Labour Party secretary of state for education dismiss the non-economic benefits of a higher education system that in his view exists entirely "to enable the British economy and society to deal with the challenges posed by the increasingly rapid process of global change" (Woodward and Smithers, 2003), is virtually indistinguishable from the business view of university as a first-line response to changing workforce needs, "[a]ll students should leave university with the employability skills they need for work" (CBI, 2009:43–44). On the other hand, the same mix of conditions has also galvanised scholarly and grass-roots resistance to this reductive market vision.

At the level of ideas, mounting academic outrage centres on both the marginalisation of higher education's role as what many including Giroux have called a "center of critique" (Giroux, 2014), which is linked here and there to the loss of emphasis on traditional 'disciplines', as well as the reduction of structural possibilities for the sector to help shape a more inclusive society. Thus, academic debate over the purpose of higher education has joined long-standing social science concern with 'the public good' and has centred on rival versions of this. Is it for job preparation, political engagement or wisdom? To better the lives of individuals or to improve society? Both workforce creation and the promotion of wisdom can be seen as routes to a better society, in the sense that increased levels of wisdom and life skills increase individual and societal well-being (Bynner, 2003). Pedagogically, should universities be making sure testable items are learned thoroughly or providing space and resources for young people to learn about their place in the world, to encounter new ideas, and to challenge prejudices and assumptions? Finally, who are higher education policy-makers, leaders and teachers accountable to and in what ways? But the most persuasive conception of 'public good' gives universities a critical role in shaping not only their own function but also the public policy space within which this role exists: "not only because it is a public good in itself, but because it exists to ask what constitutes the public good" (Nixon, 2011:1). Alongside persistent laments that the university sector is not up to this challenge any more (Blake, Smith and Standish, 1998; D'Souza, 1991; Evans, 2004; Furedi, 2005; Brown and Carasso, 2013Collini, 2013), some argue that the rot goes further, that the self-referential form of competition itself undermines equality and social justice. "It is the latest stage of predatory capitalism", argued Giroux in a 2013 interview, aimed at "restoring class power and consolidating the rapid concentration of capital" among the privileged (Polychroniou, 2013) – in essence, the classic Marxist argument that shoring up the vested interests of those with capital is not in the public interest.

While universities' own repeated rhetorical commitment to aims such as changing society may be regarded cynically ('student voice' rhetoric, for instance, is easily peeled back to reveal a much bigger interest in student's consumer power), a tranche of semi-grass-roots movements have emerged to promote critical and equality-focused conceptions of 'public good' universities. UK-based campaigns to recast higher education as a constructive channel for the development of citizenship-as-political-consciousness include the Campaign for Social Science, the Council for the Defence of British Universities, the Campaign for the Public University, and Society Counts (all cited as inspirations to the PSA's Charter for Citizenship for Higher and Further Education. Further afield, the US-based World Universities Forum (WUF) was founded in the early 2000s by a group of disenchanted academics who felt "that there is an urgent need for academe to connect more directly and boldly with the large questions of our time . . . as they consider the broader context within which they are located (and their) role to play in solving the global problems . . ." (WUF, 2009). Aligning its interests with those of the World Economic Forum (WEF), the WUF seeks to challenge hegemony, inequality and injustice by simultaneously harnessing the intellectual capital of universities and engaging with a range of and community (non-'academic') "sites and modes of knowledge production". Such attempts to reshape the university from the ground up reclaim the authority to shape policy

16  *The policy problem*

and ideology rather than simply responding to the market or government diktat. But elsewhere, disquiet at the forces of global marketisation have driven calls to "bring the state back in" in China to combat "the negative consequences of privatisation" have (Mok, 2012).

Thus, hooking higher education to citizenship means one problematic concept meeting another in four key ways. To start with, ownership of the citizenship education project is clearly contested: there's a tension between state, institutional and individual or cultural ownership. Also, the marketisation of higher education makes it unlikely that consumer and career-oriented students, especially international students who provide much needed income for universities, will choose a university or a course on the basis of its citizenship provision? Third, the modularisation of university curricula and emphasis on continuous transparent testing make it hard to teach holistically or creatively and especially things that are not easily testable. Fourth, there is the conceptual muddle in which higher education's use of the 'citizenship' tag is conflated in myriad ad hoc ways with other themes.

This conceptual muddle can be seen behind a range of policy–academic initiatives. The POLiS project's lack of impact, for instance, is hardly surprising considering its elusive 'civics'-tinged headline view of citizenship: "knowledge of public affairs, . . . attitudes of civic virtue, and . . . skills to participate in the political arena" (Smith and Ottewill, 2007, cited in Heater, 2004:343). The public-funded UK standards watchdog the Higher Education Academy (HEA) rhetorically links 'citizenship and employability', without explanation and contradicting the more sector-typical contrast between these. Terms are applied so arbitrarily in the Academy's literature that they become vacuous: "employability and global citizenship . . . enterprise and entrepreneurship . . . cultural and ethical competence" (HEA, 2013). Agenda-driven talks tag 'citizenship' onto whatever the actual focus is, as in "citizenship and international awareness . . . global and sustainability perspectives" (Shiels, 2009). While conference calls conflate terms like "moral and citizenship education" for no better reason than there might be people who would like to present papers attached to one or more of these themes (Institute of Education–Beijing Normal University, 2012), it is hard to think of something that would not fit under such framings of global citizenship.

The muddle is not limited to the UK. A Council of Europe on Education for Democratic Citizenship investigation into how universities in both America and Europe embed, apply and encourage citizenship is framed in terms that do not make at all clear what is understood by citizenship – particularly, it is noted (Bleiklie, 2000), in terms of the balance between educating for employability, transferable skills or a cosmopolitan view of citizenship stressing understanding of global relations and fluid identities. While in North America, credibility is undermined by contradictions. The schizophrenic attempts of the Canadian system to placate advocates of both traditional and liberal education were being lamented in 1997 for its "strange jargon", which included "multiculturalism" and "the canon", "political correctness" and "affirmative action" (Cahn, 1997:544). And in the US, a disconnect has been identified between the "civically engage" and "citizens of the world" themed rhetoric of liberal arts mission statements and what actually happens in classrooms (Langran, Langran and Ozment, 2009:5).

Back in the UK there are tentative signs of progress. The new ACT and DfE focus on global and controversial political issues in the Global Learning Project, for instance, hints at creeping convergence across the policy frameworks around the idea that the most productive 'citizenship' focus may indeed be membership of a community – conceptualised in terms of relationships between self and other, local and global. The revised core content of the UK's National Curriculum for Citizenship at Key Stage 4 is hopeful. State secondary pupils are taught about the following:

- the different electoral systems used in and beyond the United Kingdom and the actions citizens can take in democratic and electoral processes to influence decisions locally, nationally and beyond
    - other systems and forms of government, both democratic and non-democratic, beyond the United Kingdom
    - local, regional and international governance and the United Kingdom's relations with the rest of Europe, the Commonwealth, the United Nations and the wider world
    - human rights and international law
    - diverse national, regional, religious and ethnic identities in the United Kingdom and the need for mutual respect and understanding (KS4)(DfE, 2013)

ACT's 2014 contribution to the Global Learning Project (in the form of 'Global Learning and Citizenship') also points in the direction of critical engagement with global citizenship, human rights and social justice, conflict resolution, diversity and values, sustainable living, interdependence through a programme that explores "the interconnections between people and places around the world, (and) links . . . between local and global issues". The more political emphasis of this new ACT framework also commendably acknowledges the danger that "global learning can often lose its edge and drift towards reinforcing a charity mentality in pupils, as opposed to one that critically examines issues and tries to hold those with power or responsibility to account" . . . (ACT, 2014). Critical engagement, by contrast, in ACT's new position, involves

> . . . **knowing about** human rights legislation, including the UN Convention on the Rights of the Child, the European Declaration on Human Rights and the Human Rights Act in UK law. It also means that pupils **understand** the universality and indivisibility of human rights and that there are competing rights and responsibilities in different situations. This will ensure that teaching about human rights is always a **controversial** topic. Pupils will explore **case studies** and know some ways in which human rights are being denied and claimed locally and globally.
> 
> (ACT, 2014)

And yet, while *most* of the learning aims are educationally and critically sound, these are mixed with the more dubious ones about underlying values and behaviours. Children are expected to

- critically examine their own values and attitudes
- appreciate the similarities between people everywhere, and learn to value diversity
- understand the global context of their local lives
- develop skills that will enable them to combat injustice, prejudice and discrimination
- develop informed decision-making and the ability to take thoughtful and responsible action, locally and globally
- engage with aspects relating to human rights, sustainable development, peace and conflict resolution, social equality and the appreciation of diversity
- move from a charity mentality to a social-action mentality
- understand their role in a globally interdependent world and to explore strategies by which they can make it more just and sustainable
- promoting awareness of poverty, sustainability and ethical challenges, and enable schools to explore alternative models of development
- social and community values
- promote inclusive attitudes and behaviours

So once more the question of whether a 'citizenship' curriculum should teach students *about* citizenship (presupposing a distinctive corpus of knowledge), or how to *be* citizens, is avoided. Emphasis on aims rather than content perpetuates this ambivalence; the Programme of Study, for instance, begins by stating the obligation of schools to ensure that pupils across Key Stages 3 and 4 are equipped with the skills and knowledge to explore political and social issues critically, to weigh evidence, debate and make reasoned argument" (DfE, 2013). The holistic inventory of 'knowledge, attitudes and skills', repeatedly invoked, is not applied to other academic *subjects*. It is reminiscent of professional training programmes, or simply 'education'. Education and citizenship have long been intertwined; the skills, knowledge, understanding and opportunity that education *can* provide are essential components of citizenship. There are further circumventions. Even in terms of content, the ACT project like the rest of the National Curriculum avoids committing on the relationship between rights and responsibilities, or between action, knowledge, skills or values and entirely sidesteps the central issues of exclusion and marginalisation – not set out in the rationalised that a curriculum requires. Nor does it offer analytical frameworks for examining links between global and local. In sum, despite being an improvement on what went before, it is hardly a clear and distinctive corpus of knowledge.

The un-resolved questions over function, themes/content and geopolitical framework continue to hamper UK efforts to provide education either for *or* about citizenship, especially within the English National Curriculum. Attempting to create something called 'citizenship education' as compensation for the sector's otherwise increased performative orientation makes confusion and lack of engagement inevitable, not least on the part of teachers inadequately equipped to teach such a poorly defined curriculum area.

## Educating about cosmopolitan stakeholder citizenship

Educating citizens and teaching about citizenship, connected as they are, both require a clear framing concept of citizenship, uniting its identity, ideological, political, economic, legal, ethical, social and geopolitical dimensions. Political and historical understanding, social equality, political voice and community belonging can be summed up as in having a full *stake* in society.

Central to this concept of 'stakeholder citizenship' is the connection between self and mutual interest: "To have a stake is to have a right to representation and to vote in decision making which may affect one's other interests" (Blake, Smith and Standish, 1998:22). The idea is not new; long used as an organising concept in business and management where the stakes are predominantly economic, stakeholder theory has begun to be applied more widely. At the same time, businesses have been urged to think of stakeholders as citizens, in recognition of the similarities between the two concepts – participation, consultation and communication (Crane et al., 2004).

In citizenship terms, stakeholding has been applied most notably from a legal birthright perspective. For instance, in Bauböck's discussions of political participation and "shared core identity" that extends beyond borders (Bauböck, 2005 & 2007), where 'stakeholders' are "those who have a stake in the polity's future because of the circumstances of their lives" (Bauböck, 2008). Others, however, have written about the rise prominence of stakeholder citizenship as a side product of "increased interest in localised and community-based responses to, for example, environmental issues and social dislocation" (Scerri, 2009:390). 'Stake' as inseparable from the well-being of the whole (in contrast with commodity-focused, reductive 'interest') centres Scerri's interrogations of the voluntarist and cultural dimensions of individuals' levels of commitment to sustainability (Scerri, 2012). And in a third sense, the concept is used to make sociological sense of grass-roots citizenship movements, overlapping with 'cosmopolitan' citizenship understood as the ability and inclination to engage with difference – with the local and the global, the particular and the universal (Stevenson, 2012a & 2012b).

That said, the stakeholding concept is not a panacea; as a framing idea for citizenship it requires caution. There is the danger of connotative slippage into the area of *consumer* rights. Scerri has cautioned against capitalist *subversion*, with stakeholder citizenship becoming just another synonym for transactional individualism, with individuals like nations, institutions and communities seen as "self-orienting competitors in an irresistible, juggernaut-like globalising 'stakeholder capitalism'" (Scerri, 2009:473). In another context, it has been argued that the fundamental inequalities between different *kinds* of stakes limit the concept's usefulness (Blake, Smith and Standish, 1998:23–24). Still, in a world of global flows of ideas and people, it is arguably the *im*permanence of birthplace ties that, contrary to Bauböck's thesis, gives stakeholdership real currency.

## 20   The policy problem

So, while 'educating for citizenship' is not a new idea, 'global citizenship' is a relatively new framing concept for policy. But it is not easily operationalised.

It does not help young people to engage constructively with the localised issues and contexts that actually frame their lives. As a strand of educational policy and curriculum, unresolved conflict about what the term citizen means, particularly relative to the uncertain place of 'nation', is further compromised by new uncertainty over the relationship between citizenship and education as revealed over a series of faltering pieces of official consultation, policy-making and legislation. Attempts to yoke 'citizenship education' clumsily into the curriculum as a solution to shifting and short-term political agendas are bound to be ineffective. A poorly defined subject consigned to poorly funded classes achieves little. Certainly, relegating 'citizenship' to an extra hour in the week for PSHE classes that deal with things as diverse as litter, sex and finances does little but undermine the long-standing intrinsic connection between education and citizenship.

Stakeholdership may be a helpful way of thinking about citizenship educationally, in terms of either the many citizenship-related *functions* of education or citizenship as a curriculum subject, based on the ways that citizenship has been shaped and experienced through the interplay of policy, education and culture in specific societies. Increasingly reductive and commodified educational structures and the ratcheting up of results pressures make the chances of this look fairly remote. On the other hand, current uncertainties around identity as this relates to global geopolitical change make it very important.

## 2 Locating citizenship
### From the modernist education project, through regionalism to border crossing

From the modernist education project, through regionalism to border crossing
The difficulties in constructing a meaningful citizenship framework around both the one nation and global citizenship ideas multiply when imported into educational ideologies and policies. The origins and contours of citizenship education's current lack of direction and relevance can be traced to the sorts of huge shifts in ideas about education, citizenship, nation and community and the relationship between these that we have seen over the past century. A historico-spatial perspective helps us to appreciate the importance of place (as site, resource, territory and positionality) to the identity and action aspects of citizenship. It reveals how citizenship ideas are connected to particular sets of circumstances and geo-political or ideological change. It underscores the truth that while "computer networks and capital are global, the people are local", and thus, also, arguments in favour of "localization (. . . as) a radical alternative to neoliberal globalization" (Stevenson, 2011:68). And finally, it sheds light on the way that action and identity frameworks are shaped by the new *mechanisms* by which they are drawn and redrawn.

The 'spacial turn' refers to the "revival of interest in a social theory that takes place and space seriously" brings together "what can be called the geographical and sociological imaginations" (Agnew and Duncan, 1989:1). Anthropologists and ethnographers have long studied the debilitating effects of physical displacement, dislocation, on community identity and wellbeing. However, in the early 20th century modernist sociology focused on the *differentiation* between hierarchical, nationalist 'society' and 'community' (Wirth, 1938; Parsons, 1951). In the late 20th century, community was thought to be on the decline, and scholarly interest was in globally 'dis-embedded' networks and 'communities'. This was accompanied by a fragmentation of spatial elements (location, locale, sense of space) across disciplines including urban studies, economics and human geography, a fragmentation attributed to the analytically unhelpful term "national scale", which cast the business of some disciplines firmly either within or outside this scale (Agnew and Duncan, 1989:2). However, the late 20th century saw the work of people like Agnew and Duncan, as well as Doreen Massey's influence in explaining the centrality of place to social relations and social science – in belated reaction, she suggests, to the historical privileging of Einstein's 'fundamental laws' version of science over Kepler's observational, experienced and local one

(Massey, 2005:74). Since when the interdisciplinary turn has continued to focus attention on the lived connections between community, identity and locale, as witnessed in the increasing crossovers between micro-sociology and community engagement, and associated rises in research funding.

## The modernist education project

Accustomed as we are today to juxtaposing the 'national' with the 'global' or 'international', it is easy to forget that the term *nation* itself is contested, largely around the extent to which it is fixed, a matter of territory, 'country', legal rights and travel documents or a fluid and mutable manifestation of the exercise of collective will and imaginary. In fact, the two are closely linked. Across the world, what appears a simplistic conception of citizenship still has currency where there are categories of inhabitants who are 'refused citizenship', or distinctions between people who have 'citizenship' and who do not. However, in these cases it is fairly clear to those involved that it is not just about passports and legal status – it is also about those classic revolutionary ideals of *liberte, egalite, fraternite* – both concrete and imaginary dimensions. While legal status encompasses or symbolizes these distinct but interlinked dimensions, education develops them.

This complexity began long ago. Words equivalent to *citizen* have long been used to refer simply to the people who lived in a certain place, *cite* (Old French). However, the Roman Empire's political approach captures the essence of what has recently been understood as citizenship. When peoples were conquered by the Roman army, they became either members (citizens) of the Empire or servants (slaves). Imperial expansion made the concept of citizenship meaningful; citizenship bestowed share and rights that were not enjoyed by non-citizens. Belonging to a political entity powerful enough to bestow rights and share was a good thing when there were people who did not belong, and when there was a need for state protection and state provision. It was not until the 14th century that the term began to describe inhabitants of a country or a nation. Importantly, in none of these cases did citizenship correlate directly to ethnicity (as race – in indigenous/tribal terms), nor did it carry the expectation of particular sets of skills or dispositions. On the contrary, *where* you lived and who you lived *with* were sufficient to confer rights, status and identity, and the boundaries of both place and community were fluid and relative. A slightly more recent example of multilayered place-based identity illustrates this relativity, as well as the novelty of the idea that nations are fundamental, and fixed, building blocks. Thus, it is pointed out that in the early 20th century, the relatively newly constructed American 'nation' shared key characteristics with equally constructed 'communities':

> The relation of province to nation was parallel to that of individual to community. Both the nation and the community derived strength and unity through diversity. The community was held together by the loyalty of independent individuals to a common purpose, rather than through a fusion of many minds into a single way of thinking. . . . This same unity through diversity was also an essential quality for a strong nation state.
> 
> (Entrekin, 1989:35)

Variously bounded and defined, it was place (in the sense of shared space) that integrated diverse identities, ideas and backgrounds and anchored common purpose.

It is paradoxically a facet of globalisation that saw the 'national' become the dominant unit of political trading. In the modern age, after the decline of empire, the boundaries of community, identity and 'nations' were seen as coterminous with those of sovereign states. From the 19th century these were known as 'nation states', forged out of conquest and negotiated alliances that provided the critical mass needed to protect those interests. In this modern age of nation states, citizenship was seen in terms of responsibilities to the state in contrast with earlier provincial loyalties and importance was placed on what people shared, such as ethnicity, language and religion as the basis for whatever rights ensued. The state, as Durkheim explained, functioned as the bestower of territorial *identity* and guarantor of individuals' rights against the threats posed by other parties such as the church and employers (Durkheim, 1957).

Once citizenship was tied to the nation-state, schooling was, according to Hobsbawm (1977:120) "the most powerful weapon for forming nations". National education systems developed across Europe, North America and Japan during the 19th century, and so began what is often called 'the modernist education project' (Green, 1997:30; Gellner, 1983). This happened both economically through the creation of national workforces as well as culturally and politically. Economically, widespread literacy and technical competence were seen as central to the workings of a state that has 'citizens' rather than 'subjects' (Gellner, 1983). In a nationalist structure, the workforce was a national capital (a 'located' capital), and widespread schooling enabled citizens to participate in the socio-economic fabric of their country. But education also promoted national development through imparting 'official knowledge' and promoting collective identity. Supposed national 'traditions' were 'invented' to unify diverse populations. Contrary to widespread assumption, the advent of political unity under nation statehood had not automatically brought, much less did it reflect, cultural or ethnic unity. The new nation states actually comprised a diversity of peoples in terms of language, culture and race. Migration is not entirely a postmodern phenomenon, and immigrant cultures were assimilated through shared, *taught* ideologies of nationhood – as embodied in folk stories, what passes for 'history' and religion. Ricoeur is among the many that have written persuasively about the fundamental human need for narrative as a way of humanising and making sense of time and change (Ricouer, 1984). Thus education systems were charged with constructing the national imaginary (Hobsbawm, 1977:120), 'official nationalism' (Anderson, 1991), and what Durkheim called the 'conscience collective' – a shared value system.

In a classic example of the ways that policy – not least educational policy – can shape culture, this universalising process was enabled through a mixture of ideology (nation-state capitalism), infrastructure building (education systems) and technology (the printing press). The symbolic and instrumental aspects of each were intertwined and equally important in different ways, as we can see in the complex ways that language was used. A shared language served three related functions; as well as being a marker of ethnic identity, it also served as a resource for constructing that identity by facilitating understanding and conversation with fellow speakers of that language, and symbolically performing that identity. The role of language in *determining* ethnic identity is complicated and much debated. But particularly in a world of mass migration and shifting boundaries, the relationship is likely to be dynamic and dialectical rather than fixed or essentialist (Tabouret-Keller, 1998). However, it is partly this complexity that makes its performative and historical roles so strong. An official/shared language exposed citizens to officially sanctioned narratives about 'their country' and enabled them to participate in the workforce. In addition, though, speaking the same language helped citizens to *see* things in the same way as each other, of course, facilitated communication with their countrymen and more generally made them feel they had a relationship with them. These nations were being created not only in competition with other nations – first in war and then in commerce – but also through national symbols such as this shared language, as well as royalty and national flags. This process, the *creation* of nations, disrupted what had been in tribal times the symbolic link between the spirit of the language, and therefore culture, of the tribe – which was relatively fixed and which tribes fought to defend. Now linguistically embodied identity could, if needed for political reasons, be fluid and mutable. National education systems, through both message and means, provided the mechanisms for transmitting to students what or how the state wanted them to learn, know, think and behave.

## Counter-narratives

This nationalistic, universalising citizenship education paradigm has long circumscribed citizenship discourses themselves, as well as the scope for imagining an education project that can see beyond the national. In 1949, the British sociologist T.E. Marshall outlined a paradigm for understanding the development of citizenship, famous for his declaration that "[s]ociety is unequal but citizenship is equal." In this book, he outlined what he saw as the three-stage development of citizenship seen in terms of rights, from 'civil citizenship' (legal and personal freedoms) in the 18th century, through 'political citizenship' (the right to political participation) in the 19th century to 'social citizenship' (welfare, sharing and equality) and in the 20th century (Marshall, 1949). Marshall's paradigm is still a shared point of reference. But there is now wide acknowledgement of its limitations. In addition to the flimsiness of the nation state as evidenced by its supposed decline today, criticisms of Marshall's paradigm range from ideological, counter-hegemonic critiques to observations that it has never actually been quite as straightforward as that.

Marshall's universalist claims are challenged on two main grounds. First, the implicit association between citizenship and parliamentary democracy is widely seen as overly Eurocentric, while others have pointed out that it is actually *Anglo*-centric, since even other European countries had very different evolutions, with Germany, for instance, setting up the beginnings of a welfare system earlier in the late 19th century. Second, as Anderson has influentially argued, Marshall's focus on the imaginative and effortful process of national creation through the role of culture and its media – religion, capitalism, education, languages and print – reveals, that there was nothing natural about nations or nation states (Anderson, 1991). But the dismantling of universalist paradigms does not stop there. Anderson's portrayal of a smooth evolution of dynasties into sovereign nations through print capitalism has also been criticised as simply too linear and Eurocentric. According to anti-imperialists such as Edward Said and Partha Chatterjee, European colonialism meant that this nationalist model was *imposed* elsewhere; it is only properly conceptualised within this context, and thus, its significance is that it was constructed in a particular time and place through these means and then imposed for reasons of control on other societies (Said, 1993:5; Chatterjee, 1993).

Ideological critiques of the modernising project have focused on the inequalities and hypocrisies in the ways that education has been used to help construct subjectivities and inculcate an acceptance among pupils of education's hegemonic function – in both less regulated, non-state forms of schooling and in state systems shaped around national curricula. Thus, not only was political education in this project limited to *just enough* political literacy for democracies, where these existed, to function in formal terms (the state's aim being to get people to the ballot box and no more), but it is further argued that far from promoting equality, education as a tool of state has mainly just reproduced, entrenched and legitimised social inequalities. As Unterhalter explains, "subordinated groups like girls or children of particularly racialize or ethnicised groups 'learn their place' of unfreedom" (Unterhalter, 2003:11).

Thus, Durkheim saw the hegemonic function of schooling in terms of how extensively schooling is rooted in society: regardless of aims, curriculum and pedagogies what is learnt is not necessarily the same as what is taught and what norms and principles pupils are exposed to and socialised in (Durkheim, 1961). Feminist critiques point to both the extent to which women and girls were rarely included as equals in the modernist education project (Green, 1997:35; Lister, 1997), while Bernstein described the many ways that social class inequalities have been consolidated through schooling. On one level, the well-off were sent to (sometimes cruel) boarding schools, and the poor have been subjected to social experimentation and control. But Bernstein also showed how the social engineering was more pervasive than this, with hegemonic aims and practices embedded in class-driven 'codes' and mediated through the 'hidden curriculum' (Bernstein, 1975 & 1977). The process has been referred to as 'symbolic violence', the 'symbolic' element referring to the sometimes invisible exercise of power relations through educational codes, structures and practices (Bourdieu, 1990, 1991). Drawing on these tenets, Apple has written prolifically about the ways that both the construction and shape of educational curricula, even at the level of which textbooks to use, privileges what he calls 'high status' or 'official' knowledge (Apple, 2000).

Most significant is that these ideologically flawed, hegemonic processes themselves fatally undercut attempts such as Marshall's to construct smooth narratives about educationally mediated citizenship. In other words, if we appreciate the negotiated ways that texts and curricula emerge as products of "often intense conflicts, negotiations and attempts at rebuilding hegemonic control by actively incorporating the knowledge and perspectives of the less powerful under the umbrella discourse of dominant groups" (Apple, 2003:53), we see that there is nothing universal or inevitable about the ways that education and citizenship have shaped each other.

It is this realisation that has led to postmodern attempts to re-harness education in specific agenda-driven ways to promoting imaginary forms of citizenship fit for today's world. In using the term *global citizenship*, exponents are primarily revising the unit of belonging and frame of cultural reference; but the discourse is also often an intrinsically educational one in its emphasis on the role of education in preparing students for life and problem-solving in a borderless world. Oxley and Morris (2013) have described this balance in terms of contrasting models of global citizenship – cosmopolitan or advocacy ones – while others have identified more strands. Myers and Zaman (2009), for instance, subdivide global citizenship into membership of a global community (the moral aspect), belief in human rights and global institutions (the institutional aspect) and commitment to collaboration in solving global problems (the political aspect). Across the variant interpretations, the underlying constant is the link between shifts in moral and political scope. The moral aspect focuses on, "prepar(ing) students to include and engage others on their shared common humanity" (Bates, 2012:268), to "(understand) the politics of difference" (Rimmerman, 1998:100), or to promote peace and inclusion (Noddings, date; May, 1999). But what Schattle (2008 & 2009) calls the four ideologies of global citizenship, moral cosmopolitanism, liberal multiculturalism, neo-liberalism, and environmentalism can all be captured by the term cosmopolitan citizenship, referring to the will and capacity to engage with difference and be comfortable with the local and the global, the particular and the universal, and to move between these (Rosaldo, 1999).

In the case of citizenship *education*, however, 'global citizenship' is largely uninterrogated, and moreover has to compete with other badges for status as the ideological replacement of national citizenship: 'active citizenship', 'new citizenship', 'alternative citizenship', and 'feminist citizenship'. The first of these, 'active citizenship' is the most familiar policy slogan, extensively used in the ACT literature and largely uncontested as an aim we should all be aspiring to. One strand of the agenda, especially as used in America, conflates with 'service learning', which can be good in helping young people understand experiences they might not otherwise encounter (Langran, Langran and Ozment, 2009). A second relatively uncontentious strand of 'active citizenship' policy is that which focuses on education for employability as key to a just and inclusive society. The premise in this strand is that only by partaking fully in the socio-economic fabric of a country can people to pursue their rights and duties as citizens (Turner, 1993). However, in its weakest articulations 'being an active citizen' can be hard to distinguish from simply 'being good': "In other words, in the guise of studying an academic subject, school children have to adopt a particular form of behaviour demanded by the prevailing political code of conduct" (Furedi, 2005) and is therefore easily tagged onto anything that policy makers want to happen, from 'lifelong learning' to 'community action-service', which in both the UK and the US is its most frequent application. It is this politically passive strand of citizenship education that Leighton noted (almost a decade before publication of his 2012 'radical' approach to solving the problem) is most guilty of working "within a framework of established order, to encourage more participation in the system than to question it" (Leighton, 2004). And as Furedi noted, characteristically a bit more directly,

> [t]he significance that the curriculum attaches to the value of participation is symptomatic of the subject's [Citizenship's] lack of moral and substantive content. . . The exhortation to participate is not founded on any vision of what constitutes a good society or what it means to be a responsible citizen. Nor is it clear what kind of community-based activity pupils should engage in. Foxhunting? Going to the pub?
>
> (Furedi, 2005)

But the label 'active citizenship' is also subjected to the fairly widespread charge that it is a bit too closely linked (especially in the US) to unquestioning nationalism and social and political conservatism, and is the kind of *passivity* ('active' citizenship indeed!) that inspired the BTYCC counter-narrative – especially when exploited by the government, as a continuation of modernist hegemonic practice: "an institutional means by which the State uses political discourse and ideology to reproduce a postindustrialist economy in the name of good citizenship" (Gorham, 1992:1). Together, these slightly different positions represent fairly widespread acceptance that, as the then chief Inspector of Schools in England David Bell said in a 2005 speech, "[T] is a significant difference between a form of citizenship education that simply encourages decency and good behaviour and one that is rooted in political awareness and a commitment to social justice and equal opportunity" (Bell, 2005, citing Potter, 2002).

In their turn, then, 'new citizenship', 'alternative citizenship' and 'feminist citizenship' can be best understood as discursive responses to the limitations of active citizenship. 'New citizenship' and 'alternative citizenship' are badges for citizenship-themed movements distinguished by grass-roots mobilisation and participation but also defined merely by the extent to which they are simply calls to think differently (Rimmerman, 1998). Yet oppositional definitions like this are hard to conceptualise. Moreover, many of the central principles of these two slogans are actually very familiar from the various more discursively established stains of 'feminist citizenship'. On one level, we can think of feminist citizenship historically, as a reaction to the historically unequal roles given to women and girls in the modernist project:

> Typically, schools were entrusted with making boys into useful citizens and girls into wives and mothers who would rear the next generation of male citizens.
>
> (Green, 1997:35)

28  *Locating citizenship*

and to the ways that citizenship discourses themselves have been gendered: "[C]itizenship appears as a discourse of masculinism, as the universal notion of citizenship applies to an abstract, disembodied individual who is male" (Gouws, 2004). On another level, however, feminist citizenship has a broader remit than gender as sex. In the work of many feminist advocates for change, a feminist approach to both *being* a citizen and *teaching about* it would prioritise "internationalist and multi-layered . . . thinking" (Lister, 1997:196), inclusiveness (Skhlar, 1991) and be framed emphatically around what has been called "the new politics of the common good" (Sandel, 2009) at the expense of the short-term and vested interests. In contrast with a 'masculinist' model of citizenship, a 'feminist' approach to citizenship would be instinctively 'global', on the premise that being a citizen means being responsible for not only your own needs but also everyone's and not just now but in the future as well (Salleh, 1997). The connection has been borne out in the ideological merging of gender-focused feminism with a variety of environmental and radical causes, from the Greenham Common anti-nuclear protests in the 1980s to a host of environmental, anti-capitalist, anti-exploitation and anti-discrimination campaigns in the 21st century.

Belying their differences of emphasis, these non-nationalistic citizenship discourses are more or less united by an attempt to combine postmodern geopolitical realities and 21st-century ways of thinking ethically about rights, democracy, equality and social cohesion. The movements and agendas that emerge can be seen in various ways as ideational and identity replacements for the security that nation-state membership may once have carried. All of these new discourses reject the idea of citizenship as status and duty, in favour of citizenship as a more negotiated set of ideas about practice and values. That is, they are grounded in critiques of the unequal and hegemonic nature of 'the modernist education project' and have a concomitant emphasis on enlightenment, benign community spirit and inclusion – rather than obedience, status and exclusion. Yet it is hard to deny that, as a frame for education, they also each capture only a narrow slice of what it means to be a citizen. Under the surface each is a rather distinct and partial political agenda. Furthermore, while attempting to dispense with the nation state, no primary frame of reference is provided.

## But what of 'the right to name ourselves'?

Far from being anachronistic, Bates's and Stevenson's objections to the easy assumption of global citizenship rhetoric invoke the residual pull of statism, despite the multidimensional disruption of established nation-state structures and policies. Monarchies no longer have the same symbolic unifying function, the spread of global English is a result of increasingly individualistic and *pragmatic* choices, and the rapid strides in information and communication technology mean that communication is not restricted to those who speak the same language as us and live nearby. Surveys finding that today's youth today are 'less patriotic' than previous generations seem to confirm that nations are any longer capable of bestowing identity and attracting allegiance. Yet the picture is not clear-cut. Modernist notions of nationalism as coterminous and defining of ethnicity, society, language and 'the state' have given way to alternative ways of understanding interaction, policy, governance, identity, allegiance, rights and responsibilities. These range from pre-millennium announcements of the end of the nation state (Ohmae, 1996; Usher and Edwards, 1994) through a vision of nation-state governments becoming anti-progressive obstacles in the workings of global systems made up of regional, supranational units of governance and strategic alliance, to more measured analyses of a continuing role for nation states as important localising influences on global processes and flows. Overall, the residual hold of the national as an *imagined* unit at least in this process of re-scoping has focused attention on the relationship between the national and other collectives on cultural, policy and superstructural levels.

A growing body of work around inclusion and cultural citizenship focuses on making the nation-state framework fit for 21st-century purpose on the grounds that the national imaginary is not always, or not intrinsically, all bad, and moreover, it is incredibly resilient. While Anderson acknowledged that communities have never been coterminous with nation states, he also argued that the imaginative construction of the nation state was more intrinsically populist and actually fairly universal as an ideal. It is also easily overlooked that "the power of the state was never created only by coercion from the top down. Rather, the power of the state rested on thousands of "bits" of minute or local consensus" (Agnew and Duncan, 1989:3). Thus, "even when trying to resist nationalism", policies "often reproduce key aspects of a nationalist imaginary" (Closs Stephens, 2013: blurb). Thus, in 2000 the Parekh Report urged those responsible for making and implementing policy to "re-think . . . the national story" (Runnymeade, 2000: page 2, Summary). A quick look at shared themes in recent academic citizenship-related debates and conferences reveals a preoccupation with defining 'Britishness', while others such as Meer and Modood have taken up this challenge, calling for instance for an urgent "affirmation of a renegotiated and inclusive national identity" that properly accommodates and exploits postmodern national diversities (Meer and Modood, 2012:190). Even terms like *patriotism* and media discussions about the need for a more fitting national anthem have edged towards liberal rehabilitation, in a way that does not necessarily reek of cultural essentialism and ethnonationalism but feeds a growing discourse about unity built on difference as a resource. Yet there is un-silenced disquiet about precisely what this 'renegotiated and inclusive national identity' might be based on, with 'fundamental British values' rhetoric immediately raising shadows of intolerance.

This reclaiming of the national can be at least partly attributed to the way that globalism has produced an equal and opposite need for the local and concrete. The geopolitical grounding provided by nation states notwithstanding peripheral shifts is a fairly fundamental form of this. On one level, global citizenship in the sense of legal status and rights is really possible only metaphorically, as Bates and Stevenson have pointed out in balanced discussions of the emptiness of anything about governance of the supposed 'global society' (Bates, 2012:262; Stevenson, 2012b:114). And while the point is essentially legalistic, legal status and rights have continued currency and impact on feelings of belonging and social relations. Furthermore, the idea of 'local knowledge' (Geertz,' 1983) that has been so influential in cultural studies and anthropology provides another way of seeing the inadequacy of supposed 'global' frameworks, on several levels – political-ideological, cultural and theoretical. Policy, governance and framing discourses, despite 'globalisation' fanfare, are "realized and struggled over in local settings" (Ball, 1994:10). We can see this instinct for the local invoked equally in both 'one nation' political jingoism when the UK is set in the wider context of Europe, and in the various mechanisms of UK political devolution such as, most recently, the 'Northern Powerhouse' agenda aimed at returning to UK provincial cities the identities and status they once enjoyed.

The education perspective on the issue is fairly straightforward. Teachers know that it is the lived experience dimension of learning that makes it meaningful. Students struggle to find meaning in abstract concepts, and the only way that 'global citizenship' resonates for most students who have been educated to compete is in terms of preparation for life in a relatively borderless world – getting ahead, competitively, on an international scale. These considerations have long fed resistance to the kind of internationalisation that imposes values, standards and structures that are not always appropriate and where indigenous systems are cast as deficient and whose values are judged according to how receptive they are to the vested interests of the exporter (Steiner-Khamsi and Popkewitz, 2004; D'Alessio and Watkins, 2009).

Global citizenship as an educational framework is further undermined by competitive structures, tight regulatory frameworks and national curricula. It has been pointed out that while nation states may be losing autonomy, there is much less loss of sovereignty (Held, 1989). For a start, sources of investment in education are still largely national governments, so what are largely still state educational projects are driven by the need for short-term return to state investment. And as Keating et al. point out, "[e]ven in nation-states where curriculum construction is a sub-state power, citizenship education has still sought to instil nation-state allegiances as well as sub-state affiliations" (Keating et al., 2009:146). We have clear examples of such state control in the links between the state and organisations such as the Crick Commission, the Youth Citizenship Commission, ACT and the Citizenship Foundation – either started as government commissions or have been co-opted at some point. Thus, despite rhetoric about community, co-construction of knowledge, voice and empowerment, a subjectivity-constructing view of citizenship remains embedded in education policies and is reinforced at times of social or politically crisis. This fear-driven form of 'official knowledge' policy-making can also be seen in a range of major interventions including the Education Act of 1988 which, in producing the National Curriculum, limited teachers' autonomy to decide both how and what to teach, while the Education Act of 2011 limited students'/pupils' political freedoms and freedoms of speech in the wake of youth riots and political fears about extremism among the youth and led to the contentious Prevent Strategy. And outside the classroom, examples of hegemonic discourses are seen in higher education's 'employability' agenda and secondary school 'parental choice'.

The inadequacy of dis-embedded global frameworks meaning is also underscored by the resilient mix of protest culture and localism that has taken various forms – from political leaders being urged to 'go local' to 'cities of culture', local community action projects, examples of resurgent nationalism including but not limited to the recent UK referendum-fest, and a general surge in subculture awareness. Movements such as the Transition and Occupy movements, both place–locality based but with global reach, have been cited as evidence of "the politicization of location" (Agnew, 1989:25), with distinctive approaches to exploiting the liberating educational potential of space, connecting with people in and making meaning around the actual places and spaces where they live. In spatial terms, "the moment when so many of us who have been silenced begin to demand the right no name ourselves" (Harstock, 1987:196) is the ironic culmination of a technologically enabled means of communicating across old boundaries that has made more people aware of their right to protest in the pursuit of other rights. These autonomous movements have contributed to what is appearing a fairly chaotic political landscape in which the role of the state is far from clear. Boundaries are being not only redrawn but are also being redrawn increasingly rapidly and unpredictably, with narratives, sagas and traditions jettisoned before being reclaimed in different forms.

Resurgent 'nationalist' movements and their apparent contradictions underscore the novel shape-shifting nature of this phenomenon. What two decades ago was called "the recrudescence of exclusivist claims to places" (Massey, 1994) has since exploded into a series of protracted, place-specific conflicts – military and political – in Cyprus, Palestine and Israel, Iraq and Syria, Northern Ireland and beyond. Despite the undeniable existence of racisms and 'ethno-religious' tensions within and around these conflicts, there are some very clear differences between this new landscape and modernist nationalisms, with battles over autonomy, equal share of land and the resources that flow from this providing a context for interethnic bonding over shared histories and resources.

There are also rival ways of understanding this landscape. The Scottish independence referendum and campaign of 2014 illuminates some of its parts. Generally far less xenophobic than English nationalism, this campaign was all about championing the right of self-governance for communities (however diverse) small enough for everyone to feel his or her voice could be heard. Those eligible to vote for or against independence on 18 September 2014 were not ethnic Scots but those people who happened to be living in Scotland at the time of the referendum. The 'Yes' campaign led by the Scottish National Party (SNP) was portrayed as an expression not of ethnic separatism but of the need for communities small enough to make people feel that their 'citizenship' counts, including local autonomy and self-governance (owning the means and ends of production and investment). Rather than seeking xenophobic justification *through* arguments about community, self-governance and autonomy, the movement was actually *grounded in* those aims. Its persuasiveness was attributed to a groundswell not of nationalist pride in indigenous culture but of democratic disillusion with centralised power in the hands of people who live too far away and who neither understand nor are accountable to local communities. An unprecedented turnout resulted in a narrow victory for the 'No' campaign, which was attributed to the UK government's promising Scotland increased autonomy if the Scots voted 'No'. Since that time, however, a perception that the UK government reneged on its referendum promises has seen the SNP's popularity has surged with an unprecedented increase in membership. Its distinctive narrative about democracy and autonomy from a government too far away to be in touch with local concerns appears to have taken root, if belatedly for the Scottish referendum. The UK General Election of 2015 saw the SNP gain 56 out of a possible total of 59 House of Commons seats in stark contrast to its previous 6. The events also injected fresh life into arguments for independence or at least devolved self-governance for other UK regions and cities, for instance but not limited to regions such as Wales and Cornwall, and culminated recently in the UK's vote to leave the European Union for the same sorts of reasons – the desire for autonomy from remote governments.

In fact, European Union (EU) efforts at boundary redrawing have captured the complexity, difficulty and unpredictability of postmodern re-scoping and education's role in this process, in the an attempt to impose regionalism against the tide of structural and cultural pluralism. By the end of the Century20th century, nation-state policy-making seemed to be giving way to supranational frameworks of governance and stakeholder networks (Breslin, Higgot and Rosamund, 2002), and the EU was formed in 1992 via a treaty signed by member states in Maastricht. The EU was actually a latecomer to regionalism, and there were many other models available, mostly instrumental alliances: The Gulf Cooperation Council (GCC) and the Association of South East Asian Nations and the Americas, as well as older military unions and allegiances such as the North American Treaty Organization (NATO), had existed some time before. However, the Maastricht treaty had also introduced the rhetoric of EU 'citizenship' status, which the subsequent Lisbon Strategy of 2000 to 2010 built on in the attempt to create an EU policy space that would lead to a collective European *identity* – that could, in turn, facilitate collective EU economic goals. It was hoped that agreeing on a framework, shared mechanisms and spaces for drawing together existing systems, policies and traditions would lead to shared values, rhetoric and actual collective weight (S. Robertson, 2008).

Education was seen as key to both operationalising EU 'citizenship' and, in the process, revealing what this might actually mean. The Council of Europe had actually been busy producing materials about Europe, tagged 'civics' like the US, since the 1957 Treaty of Rome. But integrating the European dimension into the school curricula of member states was met with limited success in the early days until the collapse of the Soviet Union meant that Eastern European states were looking around for a new framework for political education at the same time as Maastricht and Lisbon offered solutions. It was with the aim of strengthening this European dimension to identity that the European Commission also set up systems of student exchange at school and university level (for instance, through the *Comenius* and *Erasmus* schemes) in the 1990s (Keating, 2009:148). In fact, by the turn of the millennium, educational policy regions were emerging as a cornerstone of educational *globalisation* – in the sense of freeing up movement across borders and challenging nation-state autonomy. This process was most apparent at the level of higher education, less central at the time to state education-work policy and as the PSA had discovered in its attempts to promote 'political engagement' more open-minded to external ideas about purpose and direction. The trumpeted 'new regionalism of higher education' (Yepes, 2006) seemed set to influence both national and international policy around the time, in 1999, of the Bologna declaration of plans for a European Higher Education Area (EHEA). With internal policy-sharing mechanisms (Alexiadou, 2007), standardised systems of governance, degree structures and exchange, the EHEA was to be both a regional standardising tool, helping to draw together existing systems and traditions, and key to interregional relations along with other regional consortia on the global stage.

The success of this complex project was always, even before the UK's vote to leave, mixed at best. To some extent, these new mechanisms and structures have indeed created new European policy spaces in the sense of venues and opportunities for a representatively 'European' variety of stakeholders influence policy, to different degrees and in different ways. And *some* cultural integration has been evident – in the emergence of forums such as the 2002 European Social Forum, designed as a European space for networks and individuals concerned about issues of social justice. But it is harder to see any evidence of European citizenship and identity, and the deep reservations about the possibility or desirability of cultural and economic integration – or even of the lesser ambition to work together on issues of common concern such as security – are what gave the UK's 'Leave' campaign the edge. European citizenship and identity remain an ideal at most, but a mere idea to many. Compounding the many structural impediments such as the incomprehensibly overlooked competing claims to sovereignty, the challenge to integration also derives from the difficulty establishing "what might count as a proper region" (S.Robertson, 2007:4). In some studies, for instance, supposedly interregional comparisons revert to comparisons between 'regions' such as the EU or the GCC, on one hand, and individual countries such as the US, China and India, on the other. And then there are persistent questions about the strategic 'point' of it all, as EU standardising frameworks are subject to being fatally undermined by others such as NATO's that appear to offer greater strategic interest. As far as education is concerned, a pessimistic midterm review of the Lisbon strategy was accompanied by an acknowledgement of the failure of early efforts to integrate the 'European dimension' into European school curricula (Lewicka-Grisdale and McLaughlin, 2002). Although the European Commission has maintained its rhetorical commitment to, if anything, intensify work on the link between EU economic success and higher education (EC, 2005), efforts to incorporate a European citizenship element into education policy or school curricula has been ad hoc and sporadic, attributed to the fact that there is no legal obligation to do so (Keating, 2009).

Underlying cultural differences in an area divided by different languages, cultures can account a lot for difficulties integrating meaningfully on other levels. Residual ethnonationalism can be seen as both local resistance to oppressive or merely non-representative rule, but it still manifests as fear of otherness. Studies of how young Europeans see their citizenship in national, regional or global terms are simultaneously pessimistic about imaginative European regionalism and dubious about the resilience of *fixed* 'national' identities. One such study, aimed at challenging nationalistically tinged patriotic citizenship education in favour of "a global imaginary", found unexpectedly that the geopolitical frameworks of affiliation drawn on by the respondents were either national or subnational (Myers and Zaman, 2009). And in another, an ongoing series of interviews with young Europeans found that while most felt 'Europe' was somewhere outside their country, they were also concerned to distinguish their feelings of patriotism from ethnonationalism on the basis that it was their *values* (not biology) that made them Swedish, Finnish or Danish. Even more interesting, this study also found that these identities were "performed" in the sense that these young people "shifted their identities over the course of the conversation" (Ross, 2015). This kind of shifting is not a new phenomenon. It has been labelled both 'multi-dimensional citizenship' (Cogan and Derricott, 1998) and 'flexible citizenship' (Ong, 1999). While Myers points out that the apparent prevalence of flexible citizenship is based largely on, "the experience of immigrant students who hold dual or transnational civic affiliations to both their countries of origin and their host country." (Myers, 2010:487), he has also done work (based on work among North American students) which he uses to argue that such flexibility is a feature of the 'citizenship' *beliefs* among indigenous well-educated youth (Myers and Zaman, 2009).

## Re-scoping and glocalisation

These are some of the ways that each neat way of analysing geopolitical identification crumbles, inadequate to capture complex and shifting patterns. The most persuasive analyses of regionalism 'soft' ones, where regionalism is seen as "a process of integration that arises from a combination of markets" (S.Robertson, 2007:4), where these frameworks for governance balanced by smaller, autonomous units that bestow community and identity (Breslin, Higgot and Rosamund, 2002:22).

Theoretically, if these re-scoping mechanisms are symptoms of a globalising world, it is a form of globalisation that far from meaning the end of community, in fact, reflects growing awareness that we are actually busily engaged in both crossing and reshaping borders and reclaiming our community rights. It is a process that underscores the importance of borders in the preservation of community. As Giroux has argued, far from borders collapsing, the rapid changes we have seen in the last few decades to the geopolitical landscape have been a process of frenzied rebuilding of borders, even though these are now much more complex and overlapping (Giroux, 1992a).

Another important theoretical question applied to this murky terrain concerns the relationships among policy~governance, contexts and trading or ownership of capital. With neo-liberal policy and governance increasingly aimed at facilitating competitive capital trading, the proposition that the loosening of state control might be producing globally shared, or at least 'flowing', capital has been considered (Robinson, 2004; Marginson, 2007). Some have argued that as far as corporate or state interests are concerned, globalisation means no more than "a trading environment" (Marginson, 2007:307), while others have focused on the distinct if interrelated spheres of custody – global or national. Castells, for instance, separates national governments' (contested) custody of the legal, economic and political spheres of public life from 'global civil society', understood as "the organized expression of the values and interests of society", which he argues has produced "ad hoc forms of global governance . . . increasingly constructed around global communication networks" (Castells, 2008:78). This reading casts postmodern nation states as small-time economic players in the international market.

Some have argued that the best way of understanding the role of nation-state governments in this environment is as continued localising influences, fine-tuning global policy and capital fields to local or national needs, and especially providing the local voice in the determination of purpose and values (Taylor and Henry, 2007:110). Others have pointed to evidence that actual interstate rivalry is thriving to argue that *internationalisation* is a fitter term than *globalisation*; flows of information may indeed be global, but interests seem still to be international or interstate (S.Robertson, 2009:66; Naidoo, 2011). However, what both analyses have in common is that national policy is seen as reactive to the sort of global–local interface that has "global pressures and local effects" (Ozga and Lingard, 2007b65), within which the scope for national or local *input i*s increasingly limited. And it is this aspect of the relationship that I think may be most in need of revision.

For one, there is the way that grass-roots expressions of citizenship continue to undermine universalist, structural attempts to capture the nature of sociopolitical relations across shifting boundaries. As we have seen, there are ways in which some forms of neo-nationalism are closer to 'localism'. The Scottish referendum fallout and European resistance to integration, for instance, point to a wave of pressure for autonomy that is less to do with ethnic ties and more an inevitable outcome of realisation that large units of governance are not conducive to genuine democracy. With successive 'happiness surveys' finding that small nations are happiest, commentators on the Scottish independence campaign pointed to high levels of social cohesion in similarly small countries as evidence that regrouping into smaller units is what is required by an otherwise globalised world, in which possibilities for strategic alliance are not so geographically limited as they were. In this light, the Scottish independence vision was closer to the premodern geopolitical landscape of communities united around daily life and autonomous city states shaped by shared political and economic interest. In the situational contingency of such regrouping, ethnic, cultural and emotional nationalisms may be increasingly irrelevant. Few of today's neo-nationalistic or separatist movements are coterminous with the boundaries of 'old' nations or nationalisms, and while the past is remembered and invoked when useful, this is done strategically and selectively. It may be that in retracting the social basis of the state has given way to a post-nationalist landscape of citizenship and community defined and claimed by various pressure and identity groups, existing in real places but with fluid boundaries, against which supra-regional policy frameworks are overlaid and compatible rather than competing.

It has been suggested that, far from having an all-out homogenising effect, what global processes and structures actually do through contact with local cultures is create a greater range of possibilities for reaction and regeneration. It has been influentially argued that the refraction of globalising influences through local lenses in this way underscores the interdependence of homogenisation and heterogenisation as part of the process of 'glocalisation', (R. Robertson, 1995). While the sociopolitical construction of "jurisdiction"-bound individual citizenship regimes includes the "setting of its boundaries" (Jenson, 2000:232–233), 'glocalisation' refers to the process of appropriating and repurposing (rather than just ameliorating) structures and priorities. Stevenson refers to a similar process when he uses the term 'cosmopolitan localism' (Stevenson, 2011:33) to refer to attempts to reverse the process of nation-state buy-in to global economies. The term cosmopolitan citizenship captures a similar spirit of negotiation: "Cosmopolitan citizenship allows us to make the links between the everyday experiences which individuals have within their communities and developments which are taking place at national and global levels" (Osler, 2005:4).

In much the same way as localism is actually compatible with globalism, counterpointing globalisation and the state is equally debate going nowhere since, as has been pointed out, they are not the same sorts of concepts or entities (Shaw, 1997:497). Yet the emerging *relationships* between state-driven, or structural, and cultural change are interesting. Grass-roots movements selectively draw on global concepts, networks and capital as a way of bypassing national constraints, and these twin concepts, glocalisation and cosmopolitanism, have been drawn on to point to structural possibilities for emancipatory action that bypasses the control of national governments and in doing so offers new, non-combative, ways of managing conflict (Kaldor, 2003). However, the resurgence of protest politics and grass-roots movements have combined with the disruption of old certainties to also *influence* policy and official narratives, suggesting an interesting form of state~grass roots collusion.

This new interplay of grass roots, dis-embedded, local, national and global seems to be at the centre of how we should understand place, scope and boundaries in the 21st century. Jameson argued in a seminal essay that postmodern culture was defined by what he called 'hyperspace' (Jameson, 1984), an open, free space, "a vision of totally unfettered mobility; of unbounded space" (Massey, 2005:81). It was "an imagination of the world's geography . . . which contrasts radically with the modernists' one. In place of an imagination of a world of bounded places we are now presented with a world of flows" (Massey, 2005:81). On one level, this reading would seem to echo Marx's prediction over a century ago of the "annihilation of space by time" (Marx, 1857). Yet far from being annihilated, it is clear that place~space is the bedrock of the flows that run within and between. The recent re-scoping exercises at policy and grass-roots levels actively deploy place and boundaries. Place is clearly *not* abstract but still central to life;

culture, history, identity, politics – the one thing that unites these is cartographical specificity. The conversation opener 'Where are you from?' has not lost meaning.

But it is also not 'either–or'. In some ways, the dynamic and fluid role of place's relationship with identity and community is dualistic, and paradoxical – as explored in Edward Said's seminal and extensive writings about imperialism. Said was concerned with the nature of place as positionality, site and cultural resource but in an emphatically anti-essentialist way, rejecting the de facto linkage of place and identity: "[T]he group is not a natural or god-given entity but is a constructed, manufactured, even, in some cases, invented object, with a history of struggle and conquest behind it . . ." (Said, 1993a). This view of place as nothing and everything is quite different from the postmodern (more reductive) *separation* of space from place and far closer to the work of anthropologists such as Anderson and human geographers such as Massey. Drawing on post-structural emphasis of the abstract in relation to the concrete, Massey criticises the incorporation of spatial difference into modernist narratives of location and community, on the basis that while it "instates a geography . . . of the production of knowledge" (Massey, 2005:74), it also represents an act of distancing from the differentiated and diverse sources of knowledge, which can result in "repressing the actuality of those differences". It is an anti-essentialist reading of the world of social relations, that sees them as series of dynamic and shifting in "the unutterable contingency of space-time" (Massey, 1994:5).

So there are several theoretical models for the ways that 'globalisation' both interrogates the assumptions we have made about the local and reclaims locality. Far from being synonymous with deterritorialisation, what this postmodern perspective does is reject modernist narratives of fixedness even applied to the past, revealing instead a fluid special perspective and a complex diversity that takes due account of the experiences of those excluded from dominant narratives – to create a global, undifferentiated dimension that Stuart Hall labelled 'post-colonial' (Hall, 1996:250). In this perspective, the scope and boundaries of communities are best represented by a complex structure of overlaps:

> [W]here localities can in a sense be present in one another, both inside and outside at the same time, which stresses the construction of specificity through interrelations rather than through the imposition of and the counterposition of one identity against another.

(Massey, 1994:7)These fluidly constructed spaces, subject to a multiplicity of influences and with shifting and intersecting boundaries, can be seen as sites for construction and deconstruction, for human relations, for struggles to exert power, exercise diverse voices and campaign for change. The identities forged within these fluid spaces are, in turn, as cultural theorists such as Hall have pointed out, not as fixed as even constructivist expositions suggest but also infinitely malleable and changing, partly as a result of these changing surroundings.

One thing this realisation does is underline the inadequacy of labels such as 'globalisation' and 'global citizenship' – yet we cling to them. We are rightly sceptical about the modernist certainties that attempted to "institute horizons, to establish boundaries, to secure the identity of places . . . to stabilize the meaning of particular envelopes of space-time" (Massey, 1994:5). We can see that links among global, international, national and local are not easily mapped. We can see that the increased pace and scope of shifts and changes produces increased cultural and epistemological hybridity. Even retrospectively, we can see the error in contrasting the 'flexible and multiple' identities of today's supposedly global citizens with modernist 'fixed' 'civic identity' (Myers and Zaman, 2009:9) since we know that national citizenries were as 'imagined' as many dis-embedded communities are today. There is nothing novel about so-called 'flexible citizenship'.

Yet efforts continue to do precisely such mapping, which Said portrayed through political eyes as "an act of geographical violence through which virtually every space in the world is explored, charted and finally brought under control" (Said, 1993b:271), making the scholarly task one of understanding the "overpowering materiality" of the "struggle for control over territory" (Said, 1995:331–332). And we continue to use labels whose meaning is overstated. Understanding communities as malleable, fluid and overlapping should direct our analytical gaze instead towards the ways communities of citizens are constructed and imagined and how those citizens imagine, cross, reshape and conduct relationships across borders.

If place and space are central but resist attempts to 'bound' them, does this mean that these processes of re-scoping evade structural analysis for the purpose of understanding citizenship? Well, the disruption of long taken-for-granted spatial, cultural and political boundaries certainly means that nothing is uncontested. It seems that place is both nothing and everything – a porous container, resource or perspective. While links among place, language, identity and belonging are not fixed, they exist. Anderson's imagined communities had physical territories just as today's 'virtual' communities are constructed to compensate for, or as precursors to, face-to-face meeting while the language around 'virtual spaces' focus our attention on the importance of space. And boundaries are what (even temporarily) define the places and spaces that shape the various aspects of citizenship and identity. 'Globalisation', far from meaning the end of either community or nation, reflects increasing border crossing and reshaping in which those borders and communities are extremely important if fluid, for example in the ways that have been described as 'glocalisation'. While the nation as a relatively recent construct is not the only container for social and political relations, it is clearly one and still meaningful. Yet like region, the state and the local, it is inadequate alone to capture today's geopolitical landscape. So appreciating the need for cartographical specificity while also acknowledging the limitations of traditional geopolitical frameworks may be the key to a postmodern model of citizenship. What we need is a framework holistic and fluid enough to recognise structures but not be tied to them, to capture something of the complex 'glocalised' processes of re-scoping, crossing and reshaping borders, of policy and identity, rights and responsibilities that is citizenship: a cosmopolitan, community-based, stakeholding form of citizenship framed by attention to local issues that have well-developed global dimensions, with a focus on the imagining, crossing and reshaping of borders.

Globalism as imported into the 'global~active citizenship education' project is clearly inadequate to capture these complex relations with place. Overlooking the importance of place, nation and community to the construction of group identity and personal meaning that is education leaves a narrative and identity vacuum. Instead, this way of understanding citizenship requires an approach to citizenship education that both reflects and shapes these fluid spaces and porous boundaries and the ways that people relate to them. Either across the curriculum or as a subject for 'citizenship *studies*', it needs to help young people recognise and understand these boundaries, communities and histories, the potential they offer and the right to 'name themselves' while at the same time providing the knowledge, confidence and skills to constructively transcend, cross or redraw them.

# 3 Educating for citizenship as radical democracy

While boundary or border crossing is making communities more diverse, this process appears to be accompanied by heightened fear of difference and curbs on free speech, which can be seen as responses. Meanwhile, prevailing rhetoric of 'youth disaffection' asks deep and complex questions about the role of education in promoting a form of political participation that does not contravene the growing range of rules and prohibitions. And yet the appearance of grass-roots, protest and subculture movements challenging the establishment from both the left and the right may represent a genuine democratisation of politics. This contradictory set of circumstances provides another level on which the relationship between democracy, political participation, political literacy, enlightenment and protest politics is key to understanding citizenship and education. The surprising EU Referendum result in the UK can be seen as a culmination of grass-roots democracy combined with lack of political engagement or understanding.

A conception of 21st-century citizenship as awareness, crossing and reshaping of boundaries gives education institutions an important job to do promoting a form of political in which the point is to challenge existing structures and *doxa*, among which might usefully be current, thus disapproving usage of the terms *radical* and *radicalisation*. The twin principles of enlightened political participation and deliberative democracy have long provided the ideological bedrock of both citizenship and educational thought as well as education's role in 'conscientisation'. In practice, however, while there are moves towards seeing political literacy and participation as important in education, lip service only goes so far. The challenge, in vision and practice, is to subvert short-term educational expediency guided by competition and risk avoidance in order to shape new realities appropriate to the way that the geopolitical landscape is being redrawn, and to avoid social marginalization, unrest and xenophobia.

## The democratic ideal

The UK government has long been aware of the need for politically literate citizens whose influence on the political decision-making process is not restricted to elections but who are rational and informed participators in public debate. The Reform Act of 1867 extended voting rights to many more people than had previously been the case. But this change required a larger number of educated citizens who could exercise their votes in an informed way, hence the 1870 Education Act that so radically brought schooling under government (rather than church) control and expanded schooling opportunities for the poor. And yet political education in the modernist project went only so far – only enough to make democracy (seem to) function and not enough to promote political equality. In the late 20th century, however, the central declared aim of the Crick Commission was "no less than a change in the political culture of the country both nationally and locally: for people to think of themselves as active citizens, willing able and equipped to have an influence in public life" (QCA, 1998:1.5, 7–8). Today the spread of democratic structures and discourses across the world combined with global access to these makes it harder for governments to sell any form of equality that is less than *full* political participation. One result of globalisation is, as Osler has argued across her work on global education and (in)equalities, is that 'global or international education' has to address democracy as well as competition. And while Stevenson's use of the term *cultural citizenship* is intended to capture its local, grass-roots dimension, it also refers to political empowerment at this level (Stevenson, 2011; 2012).

But precisely what democracy and full political participation are today, and their relationship with both citizenship and education, continues to be contested. If democracy means government by and accountability to the people, then a democratic and political form of citizenship implies that it is both the right and the responsibility of citizens to challenge the role of those with power to bestow and define this. The Citizenship Programme of Study for schools in England starts out well, declaring its aim to help pupils "become informed, critical, active citizens who have the confidence and conviction to work collaboratively, take action and try to make a difference in their communities and the wider world" (QCA, 2007:28). However, there is a lot of slippage. Although Crick himself interpreted the commission's purpose to be the politicisation of young people on the basis that learning starts not with "good citizenship" but with "politics itself" (Crick, 2000:14), key phrases in the report itself draw a distinction between political education and 'citizenship education': "So what some once argued for, 'political education and political literacy' (the title of the influential Hansard Society Report of 1978), might now seem too narrow a term to catch our meaning compared to 'citizenship education'", settling instead the holistic but ambiguous, "social and moral responsibility, community involvement and political literacy . . ." (QCA, 1998:11). From a political perspective, such a distinction is invalid: [T]he distinction between the social and the political makes no sense in the modern world . . . because the struggle to make something public is a struggle for justice" (Benhabib, 1992).

John Dewey's 'deliberative democracy', providing the political and philosophical template for much subsequent discussion, was a vision of the world where widespread political literacy could enable public involvement in decision-making and the questioning of previously 'fixed' ideas. Dewey saw this ability as the essential distinction between the status of 'citizens' and mere 'subjects' who might be permitted to air their views only for these to be ignored (Dewey, 1916). In Dewey's view, citizens should be provided with opportunities for exerting political influence through debate, criticism and cooperative effort in what he called 'the democratic ideal'. That is, shared interests of the governing and governed, free and equitable discourse, "the participation of every mature human being in formation of the values that regulate the living of men together" and "the democratic faith that (intelligence) is sufficiently general so that each individual has something to contribute" (Dewey, 1937). The alternative, he argued, was a dead-end: "Absence of participation tends to produce lack of interest and concern on the part of those shut out. The result is a corresponding lack of effective responsibility" (Dewey, 1937:4).

For some time we have been told that declining voter turnout especially among young people means that the youth of today are cynical, alienated, disaffected and/or disengaged, leading in turn to what has been talked about in terms of a 'crisis in citizenship' (Wattenberg, 2003; Macedo et al., 2005; Fieldhouse et al., 2007; Sloam, 2013a). A series of projects such as the Citizenship Education Longitudinal Study and those run by the PSA and offshoots have been established to both investigate and address this perceived crisis (AHRC Networking Project: Subcultures, Popular Music and Social Change, date?). Yet most findings are ambiguous: "CELS tells us that over 80% of these young adults have little or no trust in politicians, yet 50% still see it as their duty to vote" (NFER, 2010). And some have argued that what has happened is a shift from traditional forms of participation like voting, membership of political parties, churches and trades unions – that is, *class-based* forms of protest – to engaging with democracy in different, diverse and more individualistic ways that are often new media dependent (Banaji and Buckingham, 2013). Young people it is pointed out are actually more inclined than in past decades to take part in protest politics (Norris, 2002; Bennett, 2007; Marsh et al., 2007; Spannring et al., 2008; Sloam, 2013a, 2013b):

> Indeed, it is young people themselves who are diversifying political engagement: from consumer politics, to community campaigns, to international networks facilitated by online technology; from the ballot box, to the street, to the Internet; from political parties, to social movements and issue groups, to social networks. In established European democracies, young people are more likely to sign petitions, display a badge or sticker, participate in demonstrations, and express their political views in online forums (European Commission, 2007) than the population as a whole. They are also more likely than previous generations of young people to get involved in protest politics.
> (Inglehart and Welzel, 2005)

Even more recently, a series of new political behaviours have disrupted this analysis. The upsurge in voter turnout in the 2015 UK general election, the Scottish independence referendum and the UK's EU referendum points to a really interesting synthesis of conventional and protest political participation. The UK's radical left-wing Momentum movement, with its distinctively young membership seeking political power through formal democratic channels, along with the EU referendum use of votes, social media and marches appears as a new hybrid form of political engagement – voting to express disillusionment and marching to express positive engagement with political processes and structures.

## Education for enlightenment and participation

Education is at the core of this democratic ideal, for it is not *mere* participation in political processes but *enlightened* democratic participation that makes governments rational and accountable, politics less adversarial, and promotes inclusion, empowerment, health and the public good. This is because, as Puolimatka's exposition of education's role in democratic theory explains, "[o]nly an enlightened electorate can use its political power to promote policies that are in line with its real interest" (Puolimatka, 1996:272). Dewey's challenge to what he called 'authoritarian schemes', "[o]thers who are supposed to be wiser and who in any case have more power to decide . . . what is good for them" (Dewey, 1937), was based on two core articles of faith. First is that education is vital to the workings of a deliberative democracy: "[A] government resting upon popular suffrage cannot be successful unless those who elect and obey their governors are educated" (Dewey, 1916:87). The second is that everyone is capable of being sufficiently enlightened to contribute to this. It is recognised that "participatory skills in real life situations are the essence of any genuine education for democracy" (Crick, 2002:500–501). And not *just* skills; the UN Convention on the Rights of the Child obliges governments to guarantee young people the right to form views and "to have those views taken seriously in accordance (with) their age and maturity" (UNICEF, 1989: Article 12). The democratic ideal thus relies on a form of education that promotes wisdom through political knowledge and skills and an understanding of enlightened self-interest.

While the current prevailing focus on discrete *testable* skills in the service of competitive data production makes it hardly surprising to hear young people at university proclaim, 'We were taught nothing about politics at school!' there is pressure to change this. The Citizenship Foundation's emphasis on 'impact', for instance, is categorised into three areas – 'Shaping Schools', 'Inspiring Action' and 'Influencing Policy' – and is explained as a social imperative: "The world needs people who understand it and want to shape it for everyone's benefit. Our programmes give young people the motivation to do that. We open up opportunities for young people to take the lead and make positive and effective contributions to the world they live in. We give them a head-start for social action after school" (Citizenship Foundation, 2015a).

One thing current legal, market and curriculum emphasis on all taught content being definite, reliable and consistent does is compound teachers' caution around the teaching of politics, wary of their lack of knowledge or of being accused of indoctrination. Overcoming this requires rethinking at the levels of both approach and technique. A template approach is provided in Freirean thinking. 'Problem-posing education' is a form of critical pedagogy in which students debate freely without censor about issues that really concerned them. In this critical emancipation-focused pedagogy even Freire was reviving the much older dialectical, Socratic, method of posing critical (and real) problems to students and inviting them to question not merely answer questions as a counterpoint to the dominant Brazilian model of what he labelled 'banking education' – learning what you are told by those that have made the hegemonic decisions about official knowledge (Freire, 1970). The practical essence of critical-radical pedagogy is thus threefold: dialogue (instead of hierarchy), critique and real-life grounding.

Debate is widely endorsed as a way for young citizens to understand, voice opinion on and take part in big issues. As method and approach, debate can fulfil both the understanding and participatory aspects of education for enlightened political participation. Debate is not only fundamental to child/student-centred approaches to teaching and learning, as Rogers explained: "[T]he only learning which significantly influences behavior is self-discovered, self-appropriated learning" (Rogers, 1969:302), but it also aligns perfectly with the subject matter (politics, competing ideas). The work of an international group of researchers, educators and social activists in developing what they called 'open space for dialogue and enquiry' (OSDE), for instance, was commended in the Ajegbo Report (Ajegbo, 2007:47). OSDE is a five-step method "for engaging students with controversial issues in order to develop critical literacy and independent thinking . . . grounded in helping them to identify and utilise links between language, power, social practices, identities and inequalities" (Warwick, 2012:139), to appreciate diversity and to imagine alternatives. The steps are as follows: Step 1: Establishing ground rules/principles of participation (including attention to the facilitating nature of the space, and polite and respectful behaviour); Step 2: Critical engagement with different perspectives on a controversial global issues; Step 3: First thoughts and reflexive questioning (that includes prompting about how different perspectives may have been constructed); Step 4: Group Dialogue, which involves the children themselves proposing questions for dialogic discussion referring to the preceding steps. Step 5 of OSDE is Dilemma-based learning, in which students apply the lessons learned through dialogue to real-life situations:

> A dilemma-based scenario that is either real-world-based or a simulation exercise can . . . be presented to the students. This is in order to give them the opportunity to apply the skills and knowledge gained in the dialogue process to a situation of unpredictable change or mitigation that requires creative and collective decision-making. The aim here is to engage the participants in considering what they might now do in a real-life situation in the light of their critical engagement with this issue.
>
> (Warwick, 2012:141)

There is also a formal endorsement of the other important dimension of education for enlightened political participation – that it is not just 'practice' for real life but should engage students in real life issues and therefore not be restricted to classrooms and books. Schools' difficulties in facilitating real community engagement have been acknowledged for some time (Kerr et al., 2004), and the BYCC has been prominent among those urging MPs to visit schools to bring the two worlds a little closer together. ACT's pedagogic focus is increasingly on contentious political and ethical issues in the media, as a way of provoking and shaping pupil debate. As well as the more usual "local volunteering and charitable giving", ACT's Global Learning Project also stresses the importance of preparing young people debating controversial topics such as "controversy over intervention, military, political and social; . . . issues of religion, gender and sexual orientation as human rights matters; role of military trade between poor and richer nations; responding to international humanitarian crises; . . . strategic global challenges; terrorism, piracy, disease, climate change, pollution, resource depletion; . . . child soldiers; trafficking of humans and slavery; economic links between UK and other developing nations including child labour, slavery, corruption, workers safety and health; role of international human rights courts; . . . war crimes and international responses; . . . conflicting demands of human rights and the ambitions of nations politically and economically. . ." And it aligns well some recommended pedagogies and forms of assessment: "Assessment should reflect the extent to which pupils are able to apply their knowledge and understanding about global matters to real-life situations and in local, national and regional contexts, and to consider how this influences the actions they currently take and will take in their future lives." Suggested teaching approaches and strategies go beyond discussion and debate to include, "[r]eal life case studies on global topics and issues, . . . (and ideally) a research project into the world as a global community . . ." (ACT, 2015b).

Yet such political-professional interventions are undermined by the simultaneous pressures put on teachers and schools to do, in many cases, the opposite – with the result that the education system can feel by those working in it as much as those studying as little more than a system of constraints. Three kinds of risk in implementing critical pedagogies have been pointed out: first, the "larger time commitment"; second, the likelihood that there will be less social capital acquisition on the part of both students and institution; and, third, the likely negative feedback for students who "may not appreciate being asked to become active participants in their course" (Cappellano, 2013:3). Thus, teachers' understandable insecurities combine with unclear or self-contradictory policy frameworks to rule out risk taking as a reasonable option. And the tension goes deeper still.

## Token or real participation?

Factors both pragmatic (to do with markets) and hegemonic (in both geopolitical and institutional terms) undercut lip service paid to genuine participation. Studies of school community 'participation' have found this to be selective in the sense that only certain groups of students were involved (Kerr et al., 2004). Singled out as particularly hypocritical is the discrepancy between educating children about their rights and then failing to provide law ensuring they are routinely consulted on matters affecting them (Osler, 2005). Drawing on international examples of how principles of democratic learning have been enacted through school boards and school councils, Osler points out common inconsistencies, such as "[y]oung people are expected to learn 'how to reason, think logically and creatively and take responsibility for their own learning' (DfES, 2001:18, 3.2). For young people to take responsibility for their own learning implies that they will be consulted" (Osler, 2005:10). And finally, while ACT's Global Learning Project holds out the promise of genuine understanding of the relationships between individuals and local, national and international communities, the supposedly 'global' scope is still reduced to a developing world characterised largely by poverty.

Critically, however, 'participation' has also tended to be about taking part rather than effecting change (Kerr et al., 2004). Educators know that simply 'taking part' is not the same as real engagement, and critical literacy exponents will repeatedly caution us that 'literacy' skills are pointless without the scope to exercise those. It is easy, but pointless, to adopt the mechanistic aspects of Freire's 'problem-posing education' without the underlying aims: justice and freedom from oppression through the rejection of authoritarianism. "The banking concept of education, which serves the interests of oppression . . . transforms students into receiving objects." (Freire, 1970/93:58) "to avoid the threat of *conscientization*" (Freire, 1970/93:55), which he described as the process of developing an awareness of the possibilities of acting upon reality and changing it for the better through re-seeing one's own relationship with the world as key to the "democratisation of culture" understood not as dumbing down but enlightening the masses, and especially important for marginalised and oppressed societies (Freire, 1970 & 1973). It has been argued that adopting learner-centered critical pedagogic techniques based on a superficial understanding of the underlying principles is, moreover, harmful as it can "help to veil actually existing power structures" Cappellano, 2013:2). Far from liberating, then, without the possibility of structural change buzzwords such as 'active' and 'participation' used to persuade citizens it is in their interest to behave well become part of the arsenal of tools for hegemonic and responsibilising state control. Gorham (1992) is not alone in his condemnation of citizenship rhetoric that simply reproduce hegemonic practices (maintaining an unequal status quo with the active compliance of the underclass through convincing it is for their own good). ACT says nothing about citizenship as democratic risk taking and challenging power.

The hegemonic ways in which doxa, 'official' or 'legitimate' knowledge or 'truths' are legitimised or officialised, via the 'hidden curriculum' (Bernstein, 1975 & 1977), are what Hall was referring to when he described the 'limits' set on the range of ideas that we accept as "rational, reasonable, credible . . ." (Hall, 1988). We can see such attempts at political education only the appearance of freedom, and "[r]uling ideas may dominate other conceptions of the social world by setting the limit on what will appear as rational, reasonable, credible, indeed sayable or thinkable within given vocabularies . . . available to us" (Hall, 1988). These 'ruling ideas' may indeed be relatively uncontentious examples of Furedi's "unobjectionable and bland sentiments" but, notwithstanding their blandness, the powerful processes through which they are constructed and disseminated are a long way from democratic. For one, as Apple has pointed out, the state is intrinsically raced, classed and gendered and so 'truths' are the truths that happen to suit those interests while marginal realities and histories are expunged from the curriculum (Apple, 2003:10). This is why in education, "curriculum talk is power talk" (Apple, 2003:7). Furthermore, the 'capability approach' to evaluating education in developing contexts has pointed out the difficult balance between centring individuals' own values and goals as a framework and realising that these values, and perceptions of 'satisfactory', have been conditioned by their subordination. As Unterhalter reminds us, "to question the range of real educational choices . . . [w]e would need to ask whether people's educational aspirations . . . had become adapted to their circumstances . . ." (Unterhalter, 2007:2 of reprint). And perhaps even more insidiously these badges, or causes, can become a way of obliging citizens to work harder and to feel responsible for the failures of the state, that is, 'responsibilisation', or the imposition of artificial hoops for people to jump through instead of asking awkward questions about policy and social justice (Rose, 1996).

So, there are several reasons why true democratic participation requires more than just asking the oppressed what they want. The philosophical and political foundations of problem-posing education, where "the people subjected to domination must fight for their emancipation" (Freire, 1970:67), requires education to help people resist the 'symbolic violence' (Bourdieu, 1990, 1991) of 'official knowledge' (Apple, 2000) in its many forms. It is to disrupt *these* processes that a form of education that not merely a reflection of the status quo but a means to challenge it has been advocated by generations of critical pedagogues: education as the practice of freedom, a route to social change and a view of schools and universities as sites through which official ideals and policies are not only implemented but also resisted. Freire's ideas in particular have enjoyed periodical renaissance, with the basic idea of critically transformative education informing a range of influential educational discourses from Giroux's advocacy of teachers as agents of social change, or 'transformative intellectuals' (Giroux, 1988), through praxis, encouraging "the transition from critical thought to reflective intervention in the world" (Giroux, 1981:117), and institutional work on the social norming role of educational *institutions* (Meyer, 1977), to Stromquist's writing about adult literacy programmes as 'transformative education' "that raises awareness of social inequalities and enables individuals to organise for progressive social transformation . . ." (Stromquist, 2006:149).

If we accept this as the goal of education, we have to ask *how* education can liberate young people to think and act outside the preset range of ideas they are given, to help shape new realities appropriate to the way that our borders have been and are being drawn? After all, "[e]ducation, to be transformative, must not only provide knowledge about the conditions of one's subordination but also give the emotional support and political skills to visualise and implement social change. . . ." (Stromquist 2006:149). Or put another persuasive way, "[i]f citizenship education is to achieve more than merely encouraging functional participation and empower young people with the skills to challenge perceived injustices, it needs to confront a widespread fatalism about the fixity of politics and society" (Brett, 2007). But *how* to mobilise against a hegemonic system is a trickier question, and one with both ideational-cognitive and structural-spatial dimensions. The potential for teachers to be 'change agents', or 'transformative intellectuals' (Giroux, 1998), is undermined by the performative neo-liberal policy approach that has seen rapidly multiplying and changing rafts of regulations and targets and the incremental removal of teacher education from universities. From a citizenship education perspective, "what constitutes the public good" (Nixon, 2011) is *the* question student teachers should be asked to think about and why to prevent that happening and to consolidate the de-professionalisation of teachers, the UK government has moved teacher *training* out into schools. The resulting insecurity means increasing retreat behind what teachers *can* do, hence the 'citizenship education' emphasis on personal responsibility and character.

'Professional' as applied to teaching means very little without enabling structures. On an institutional structural level, democratic principles also imply that policies and discourses should be democratically constructed and governed. Institutionally, commitment to "the democratic ideal . . . makes stringent demands on those processes through which its members are educated" (Scheffler, 1985). "For young people to be able to take responsibility implies the democratisation of schools" (Osler, 2005:10). Thus, the structure of educational institutions should be consistent with the institutions' ideological and pedagogical values. That is, in addition to real possibilities for change in the outside world, there also needs to be an *institutional* structure that both encourages shared decision-making and allows the results of debates to be followed up – a school 'ethos' that takes students views seriously. Osler has written about this at some length: "For education in democracy to be effective, the institution of the school must be developed in a democratic way, guaranteeing the right of children and young people to form views and 'to express those views freely in all matters affecting (them)' and to have those views 'taken seriously in accordance with (their) age and maturity' . . ." (Osler, 2005:8). As for external structure, Unterhalter (2003) has argued that even if education holds out the possibility of liberation from social constraints it is nonetheless socially embedded therefore constrained by the same limitations as those in society at large. For instance, debate as a way to promote grass-roots involvement with issues that affect our lives, activism in other words, only works if girded by structural, policy and political frameworks that allow real possibilities to make a difference.

A widely cited example of what *can* be done structurally to directly challenge accepted ideas, practices and structures in order to bring about social or political change is the Citizen School Project in Porto Alegre, Brazil. This was a democratic schooling project set up in the 1990s by the 'Popular Administration' – a leftist coalition led by the Workers' Party to which Freire belonged – to democratise governance both within schools and in terms of the schools' relationships with society, in order to build "mechanisms of inclusion to struggle against a society that marginalises the impoverished students and denies them valuable knowledge" (Gandin, 2009:350). It had two distinct though importantly interwoven dimensions: pedagogic and democratic decision-making. Pedagogically, the project challenged what counts as knowledge through interdisciplinary 'thematic complexes', approaching curriculum areas "beginning with the . . . experiences of their families" (Gandin and Apple, 2003:207), promoted critical dialogue on the basis of this and removed the fear of 'failure'. In terms of governance, democratic school councils made up of from local community, teachers, parents and students had real monitoring and executive power in decisions including choice of curriculum, electing principals and budget distribution. Outcomes are widely reported to have been positive for both the people involved and the wider communities. Effective participation increased over time, the concept of 'citizen' became real as the participants were able to both interrupt the hegemonic marketisation of education and then share real economic and political power (Gandin and Apple, 2003; Gandin, 2007), neo-liberal marketisation and Brazil has since developed a very active civil society centred on novel ways of bringing alternative education and formal education together to make the most of people's life experiences in promoting conscientisation and sociopolitical change.

However, *why* the project worked is crucially important. First, its design was properly situated in local social, political, economic, cultural and ideological contexts. It was accompanied for instance by the Popular Administration's flagship 'participatory budgeting' approach to enabling the poorest citizens to resist hegemonic policy-making and participate in political and especially spending decisions. Furthermore, it was not voluntaristic but connected to an imaginative *and* policy vision of citizenship that is collective and spatial: 'the right to the city' (Gandin, 2009:359). And finally, it was built on a robust and coherent understanding of the relationship between sociopolitical change and knowledge, that is, decision-making procedures consistent with pedagogy, all *about* gaining knowledge that is useful locally and the acknowledgement that "participation was a process that had to be nurtured" (Gandin, 2009:351), with emphasis in the early years on transfer of knowledge as the basis for critical dialogue that would together develop the capacity to participate effectively (Gandin, 2009).

The Citizen Education project used "space (as) a form of power" (S.Robertson, 2009:18). In stark contrast, the English abandonment of Local Education Authorities (LEAs) and resulting muddle with school governance increasingly privatised while the central government attempts to impose a national model of Citizenship Education makes the slippage and lack of relevance unsurprising. Arguably then, truly accepting that politics both 'big' and 'small' is everybody's business fundamentally undermines the powerful attempt to even impose a citizenship framework.

## Disruption, disagreement, struggle and freedom

These examples remind us that structure is the expression of the power to define and in which therefore disrupting existing structures is political, difficult – and potentially dangerous. However, it may paradoxically be the hegemonic nature of this process that provides opportunity to disrupt these structures. It is well established that "reproduction is a complex phenomenon that not only serves the interest of domination but also contains the seeds of conflict and transformation" (Giroux, 1981:109). That is, its conflict-ridden processes mean that it requires constant rebuilding because, as Fiske explains, summarising Gramsci's struggle-replete version of hegemony: "Consent must be constantly won and re-won, for people's material social experience constantly reminds them of the disadvantages of subordination and thus poses a threat to the dominant class . . . Hegemony . . . posits a constant contradiction between ideology and the social experience of the subordinate that makes this interface into an inevitable site of ideological struggle" (Fiske, 1992:291). This dialectical nature of hegemony means, then, that "counterhegemonic groups and alliances are also crucial to any understanding of the relations of power" that produce such doxa (Apple, 2003:6). Even more promisingly therefore, as Apple announced over two decades ago, "[c]ulture . . . does not grow out of the pre-given unit of society. Rather, in many ways, it grows out of its divisions" (Apple, 1993/2000: 42–43). It is a view that has been extended by critical theorists such as Rancière, who has written about the necessity of conflict to politics in the sense that, "Politics exists when the natural order of domination is interrupted by the institution of a part of those who have no part." (Rancière, 1995:11).

Perhaps surprisingly, this dynamic reading of politics, democracy and equality has a parallel in the citizenship education rationale for dialogue, which tell us that "[d]isagreement is healthy and to be encouraged, both for the variety of experience it reflects and for its potential to change minds . . . Discussion around a common theme with . . . disagreement avoided is not dialogue but a monologue for several voices [sic])" (Leighton, 2012:65). That is, it is only in the cracks between different ideas and the divisions between people that truths and equalities can be found. The pedagogic and policy goal therefore must be "dialogue through disagreement" and "finding ways to reasonably disagree" (Smith et al., 2010:5/6), in the ways that have long been realised in conflict resolution circles (Morgan and Guillerme, 2014) and activism.

Over three decades ago, Giroux argued that simply accepting hegemonic reproduction was neither conducive to progress nor inevitable and that instead we should build on this dialectical understanding of hegemony to construct a working model of how unequal practices can be negotiated or resisted in institutions with the ultimate goal of transforming society itself (Giroux, 1981). Today the rise of spatial politics, the World Wide Web and the geopolitical re-scoping that has so disrupted traditional structures of power and reproduction have given us a heightened invitation to exploit these divisions to shape education and its relationship with society. Surely these are tools of democratic resistance, equipping citizens with the means for emancipatory action that bypasses the control of national governments and exploiting cracks between competing narratives to build new forms of cultural democracy.

Universities' residual grasp on their one-time status directs our expectant gaze to these supposed 'center(s) of critique' for some clue as to how we might do this educationally. Universities have always been political, tied to the state and state institutions in various ways, and in the landmark Robbins Report of 1963, the transmission of "common standards of citizenship" was accompanied by a commitment to the removal of authority and orthodoxy in the co-construction of knowledge (full ref). And indeed, evidence of political interest in government support for organisations like the PSA, the Society for Research into Higher Education (SRHE) has acknowledged links between "how student activity in politics influences institutional decision-making, policies and the curriculum" (SRHE seminars, 23/1/15), and there has been increased PhD funding for students seeking to study politics. But all of this comes up against the brick wall of how sector marketisation has shaped 'student participation'. A decade ago it was noted that "[u]niversities, under increased regulations and financial constraints, are not obliged to incorporate within the students' course anything that is not directly quantifiable" (Arthur, 2005:2). And in today's market, "[t]he value of a university education is the income it enables you to earn minus the cost of acquiring that education" (Collini, 2013). Thus even though students are far more included at all levels of university governance, and student *representation* in programme boards is normalised, this representation and inclusion has an emphatically 'consumer' flavour, topped this year by legal consolidation of students' 'consumer rights' in the form of the Competition and Marketing Authority (CMA) guidance: "Students have consumer rights. Universities and other higher education providers that don't meet their obligations to undergraduate students may be in breach of consumer protection law" (https://www.gov.uk/government/publications/higher-education-consumer-law-advice-for-providers). The costly and time-consuming contractual procedures that universities have had to adopt, and the increased difficulty they now face in unapologetically transmitting bodies of knowledge that may be 'difficult' or 'boring', do not promote enlightenment or genuine participation. Bleiklie warned 15 years ago that "rather than (having) a direct say in how the products they consume are produced and managed" (Bleiklie, 2000:1). Governing according to what students say they want does not help these students understand enlightened self-interest or how oppression works. As well as short-changing students, this turn undermines universities' public good roles and has largely overturned Robbins's vision of academic freedom.

The increasingly complicated nature of 'freedom', in turn, provides a further constraint on enlightened political participation. Freedom can be conceived in terms of either safety and seclusion or freedom to challenge and encounter new ideas and experiences. As societies have become more complex, the educational tension between these has been compounded by removing or curtailing the right to free speech, banning 'radical' views, and requiring people to report increasingly on their neighbours and colleagues. The introduction of, its various revisions and reaction to the UK government's contentious Prevent Strategy (changed in 2015 to 'Prevent Duty') capture some of these tensions.

Aimed at stopping people "becoming or supporting terrorists and to do this by challenging ideologies, protecting vulnerable individuals and supporting institutions, such as schools" (May, 2011:1), Prevent was set up following terrorist bombings in London in 2005 as part of the National Counter Terrorism Strategy known as CONTEST, and it has been subject to wide-ranging criticism for curtailing freedoms of various sorts. Its rationale was that

> [i]ntelligence indicates that a terrorist attack in our country is 'highly likely'. Experience tells us that the threat comes not just from foreign nationals but also from terrorists born and bred in Britain. . . . It is therefore vital that our counter-terrorism strategy contains a plan to prevent radicalisation and stop would-be terrorists from committing mass murder. Osama bin Laden may be dead, but the threat from Al Qa'ida inspired terrorism is not.
>
> (May, 2011:1)

Reactive in its inception and successively updated with more contradictory rationales and guidelines, the 2011 review saw the publication of resource packs for primary, secondary and higher education, accompanied by the declaration that

> [t]his resource pack has been created to work under the Prevent dimension of the strategy, to reduce the likelihood of young people becoming **radicalised** and then engaging in any form of violent **extremism**.
>
> (https://www.gov.uk/government/publications/prevent-strategy-2011)

And in July 2015, a further review both lowered the threshold for suspecting someone of harbouring extremist thoughts and made the reporting of suspicions a legal obligation for teachers.

The terms radicalised and radicalisation appear heavily in Prevent's literature in a condemnatory way. This misuse of the term is central to the strategy's shortcomings and contradicts the view of education as all *about* radicalisation in the sense of being encouraged to think outside the box. It also contradicts its own advice:

> In Primary Education we believe that children should be given the opportunity to explore the issue of diversity and understand Britain as a multicultural society. Providing a safe learning environment in which children can raise controversial questions and concerns without fear of reprimand or ridicule and explore boundaries of what's acceptable will engender an open attitude to multicultural and race issues. . . . promoting a positive attitude to others . . . building self-esteem . . . enable children to think for themselves by providing many opportunities for discussing debating, researching, questioning.
>
> (2011 Primary pack, preamble)

Throughout its revisions, the strategy has been fairly consistently criticised by student unions, the National Union of Teachers, critical commentators and academics as racist, 'toxic' (Halliday and Dodd, 2015), difficult for teachers to understand and implement and self-contradictorily anti-intellectual, and both ACT and the Citizenship Foundation have been enlisted to attempt to persuade the public of its virtues. An "expert subject advisory group in association with ACT" has provided guidance on "The Prevent Duty and Controversial Issues", "so as to develop resilience and critical thinking that is appropriate in the school's context, mindful of pupils' diverse needs and backgrounds". Yet these democratic shoots are quickly obliterated by the rapid return to blind antiterrorism rhetoric in the next aim, that teachers "be informed about what to do if they find a pupil is at risk of being drawn into terrorism or extremist behaviour" and "help(ing) teachers know where to draw the line between what is acceptable and unacceptable when sensitive and controversial issues are discussed" (ACT, 2015c). The Citizenship Foundation's attempts at balance are even more disingenuous: "Some teachers are worried that the Prevent Duty will scare schools into stifling debate, while others fear that anti-radicalisation strategies will nurture docile and uninquisitive citizens without the capacity to weigh ideas", it writes before continuing stating, "However, the Government's guidance takes pains to reassure us that this new duty 'is not intended to stop pupils debating controversial issues' ", before finishing with the revelation that "[t]his morning, the BBC reported that schools are being offered new software that 'helps teachers spy on pupils' potentially extremist online activity'. Are such developments scaring teachers into avoiding tricky subjects?" (Citizenship Foundation, 2015c).

In fact, the Foundation has compared Prevent's potential impact on teachers' fear of Clause 28, which banned the 'promotion' of homosexual relationships in schools and left children "with little practical support or help with understanding their world simply because teachers were too afraid of the consequences of discussing thorny issues". Furthermore, as the foundation acknowledges, the report about new detecting software came "hot on the heels of the now notorious extremism questionnaires for primary school children" (Citizenship Foundation, 2015c), which asked children as young as nine such questions as "I believe my religion is the only correct one", and "God has a purpose for me", with the purpose of identifying "the initial seeds of radicalisation" (Ward, 2015). As we know, where there is insecurity and ambiguity, people interpret in the safest way for them as individuals (Douglas, 1992), avoiding controversial issues and reporting suspicions. Presenting these measures to already insecure teachers under the guise of 'safeguarding' hijacks their vocational ethics.

It is a matter of public record that plenty of problems have been caused. For instance, "[t]he (NUT National) Conference heard of one student who was too scared of admitting that he found the Charlie Hebdo cartoon offensive" (Citizenship Foundation, 2015c). And stories are piling up about counter-terrorism measures being misapplied in schools. A 14-year-old Muslim boy in a French class was apprehended for using the word *eco-terrorism* in a discussion about the environment (Morris, 2015), while another 14-year-old Muslim boy was arrested in the US for taking a homemade clock into school (Teague, 2015). The same difficulties in trying to understand and apply Prevent measures have been experienced in universities, where the ivory tower meaning of 'safe spaces' has traditionally been as a site for the cloistered negotiation of challenging ideas. Yet a Muslim PhD student studying counterterrorism in Staffordshire, "spotted . . . reading a textbook entitled Terrorism Studies in the college library" (Ramesh and Halliday, 2015), was questioned by the university complaints officer over his views on Islam, al-Qaida and ISIS.

One of the most obvious ways that Prevent has compromised education's potential to promote enlightened political participation is in relation to visiting speakers. It has long been the norm for universities to invite controversial speakers to generate intellectual interest in topical matters. But Prevent now has guidance about this. In 2007, it advised against inviting external speakers for Islamic societies, because their 'radical' ideas could alienate young Muslims from both their parents' and wider society's values (DIUS, 2007). And the 2015 review set out to imposed yet stricter rules, requiring for instance that universities get advance notice of the content of all visiting speaker talks. The draft measures were diluted slightly in the face of opposition by senior academics, whose public letter urged a rethink:

> One of the purposes of post-compulsory education is to foster critical thinking in staff, students and society more widely. Our universities and colleges are centres for debate and open discussion, where received wisdom can be challenged and controversial ideas put forward in the spirit of academic endeavour. . . . This principle of academic freedom is enshrined in the Education (No 2) Act 1986, which places a duty on universities and colleges to 'ensure that freedom of speech within the law is secured for members, students and employees of the establishment and for visiting speakers.' . . . The best response to acts of terror against UK civilians is to maintain and defend an open, democratic society. Ensuring colleges and universities can continue to debate difficult and unpopular issues is a vital part of this.
>
> (UCU, 2015)

But universities have since warned staff that they need to get advance administrative approval for external speakers, and let these same administrators know if they suspect their speaker may raise "controversial issues". The contradictions between such panic-inducing legislation and continued public endorsement of education for critical consciousness lay policy-makers open to the charge of hypocrisy. Critical commentators were pointing out a quarter of a century ago that reactive political diktat equally undermines academic freedom and critical thinking (D'Souza, 1991). You can have education for change and real (radical!) political participation – or not. The raft of reactive, fear-driven, risk-averse policy measures that have been imposed on schools and universities over the past decade has incrementally co-opted academics and teachers, despite piecemeal backtracking when pushed, in a project of counter-insurgency that is reminiscent of the anti-Communist campaigns of the 1950s – vigilance, suspicion and fear of any view that may be slightly challenging. It is a climate of fear, as many have realised, that is both self-fulfilling and socially fragmenting.

As for the Prevent Strategy (or Duty) itself, it both *continues* to "confuse the delivery of Government policy to promote integration with Government policy to prevent terrorism", in the words of the present government's criticisms of its Labour predecessors (May, 2011) and, in linking it so firmly to the Citizenship curriculum, to actually say a lot about the *real* government conception of Citizenship. The Prevent recipe for "building pupils' resilience to radicalisation" is through knowledge, critical argument, understanding of laws and values of mutual respect, and "[i]n secondary schools, the Department for Education recommends using the citizenship curriculum for this" (Citizenship Foundation, 2015d).

In the midst of this confused scenario, words have become worryingly dislocated from their range of (sometimes apparently contradictory) meanings. While students are arrested for suspected 'radicalism' and political leaders and commentators across the world are soul-searching to identify the 'causes of radicalisation', the political climate that accompanied the election of 'radical' left-wing veteran politician Jeremy Corbin to the leadership of the British Labour Party has also seen the word used again, along with 'conviction politics', as a political badge of honour. So we can see that prevailing political understandings of the terms radicalism and radicalisation are temporary and contextually situated. Inconsistency in media use of the term should be no surprise then. However, this linguistic uncertainty is worrying because it both signposts and compounds the prevailing climate of risk and fear. For instance, in response to the Staffordshire student arrested for reading about terrorism, "[t]he university . . . warned that making a distinction between 'the intellectual pursuit of radical ideas and radicalisation itself' was a significant challenge" (Ramesh and Halliday, 2015). The response captures not only many people's inadequate grasp of what academic study is but also the apparent 'success' of the official line that 'radicalisation' is intrinsically bad. Radicalisation in the sense of learning to see beyond "the given vocabularies . . . available to us" (Hall, 1988) *can* be socially threatening and potentially unlawful. Nonetheless, if real participation involves the right to challenge the status quo, it is the business of education to provide both awareness of that right and the means to exercise it. Condemning radicalisation helps neither to understand youth disaffection nor to provide a constructive framework for engagement with politics. Hence, the belated realisation in some media~policy quarters that one answer to combatting dangerous antisocial behaviour is to encourage critical (thus potentially 'radical') thinking that helps young people really engage and challenge arguments – not only by those in power but also by those seeking to overthrow that power – and to have critical discussions in the open rather than forcing them underground (BBC, 2013). Yet governments everywhere are more inclined to respond with fear, heavy hands attempting to silence discussion and in the process sowing more fear. While the problematic nature of this critical~security conflict is acknowledged, the ability to resolve it appears beyond reach.

## Education and sub-politics: Citizenship as resistance and cultural learning

Clearly, state politics that silence discussion are both anti-educational and anti-democratic. Their counterpoint lies in ongoing projects of resistance, a rejection of authoritarianism through debate and democratic structures, which leads to the kind of activism that in turn opens up policy and political spaces for further democracy. Today, the desire for a 'say' traditionally seen in separatist movements and violent revolution, has been accompanied by a wider ballot-box rejection of the political establishment, from the Middle East through Europe, the UK and the US. The resurgence of the left wing in Greece, along with the rise across Europe and America of Far-Right anti-migration parties, and non-traditional voting patterns are symptoms of the desire for a voice, of protest politics rather than extreme politics. We have also seen this in the large referendum turnouts in the UK; non-habitual voters using the ballot box as an expression of their *rejection* of, rather than engagement with, politics.

At a sub-political level, anger against unjust central systems has produced not only grass-roots political movements such as the civil disobedience Occupy movement but also a return to the people power of old-fashioned unions. In the

US, Soja used the late 1990s work of the Los Angeles Bus Riders Union in taking on in 1996 the city's Metropolitan Transit Authority to overturn top-down governance as the basis for his 'spacial justice' manifesto (Soja, 2010). Another union moment of more immediate relevance is when, on 28 March 2016, the National Union of Teachers annual conference in Brighton agreed that Prevent was making it harder, not easier, to protect young people. While considering the argument that the problem was at the level of implementation, not the legislation itself, the conference nonetheless voted to reject Prevent.

These two instances of union clout, while clearly distinct, are both collective attempts at claiming cultural citizenship rights, which Stevenson sees as the essence of 'sub-politics', the reclaiming of political space and the right to make political decisions, or "interrupt[ion] from below" in which "collective forms of understanding are mobilized in order to criticize dominant hegemonies and practices of exclusion" (Stevenson, 2011:66 & 73; also 2003 and 2010). It is this aim, that of unpicking official knowledge, that Stevenson argues distinguishes sub-politics from 'social movements', although both use and produce 'subculture' through "carving out alternative spaces" (Stevenson, 2011:67). They can also both be seen as manifestations of glocalisation leading to awareness of the right to not only name ourselves but also define our strategic ideologies and agendas. The shaking up of political structures has been enabled by new ways of deploying space; local resistance and dis-embedded networking are not contradictory but rather two aspects of the new porosity of boundaries and fluidity of space and their exploitation. That is, far from dispensing with place and space, the critical consciousness that has led to these forms of sub-politics has done so only by utilising spaces created by fluid and porous boundaries are important, facilitating rather than reducing the ideational traffic across those.

It is a boundary crossing phenomenon that Soja has also looked at through an educational lens, characterising educational institutions as 'thirdspaces', that is rejecting the binary opposition of physical and mental spatial imaginations in favour of a unification that sees strong links between these dimensions (Soja, 1996 & 1999), with porous boundaries on both counts creating spaces of "radical openness" (Soja, 1996). Examples of radical education as cultural learning, drawing consciously on the resource that space provides through its expansion and constriction are actually numerous and diverse, including the rise in popularity of alternative and progressive schooling, religious schools, homeschooling, free schools and the continued popularity of independent schools despite the recession, as well as radical approaches to higher education. The classic Progressive schools movement, committed to students learning in a non-compartmentalised way about the world and their place in it, railing against the competitiveness and controlling emphasis of mainstream schooling, and grounded in democratic principles of anti-authoritarianism and respect for others that also dictate systems of governance. Summerhill, founded in 1921, is the English exemplar of the movement that saw the early-20th-century establishment of a number of radical utopian institutions, some of which are still going. Two principles distinguish Summerhill's democratic approach to schooling: first, that teaching and learning happens everywhere and that children can choose to go or not to where formal teaching is happening and, second, a conflict resolution system grounded in the community and dialogic principles of governance expounded by Freire and others and developed in the Citizen School Project. On one level, *this* is citizenship education: learning through belonging to a defined community and taking part in debate and decision-making about how that community will run, and it is recognition of Summerhill's role in making its students aware of the importance of thinking through issues themselves (rather than simply following others) that alumni have praised the school.

This 'progressive' space~voice pedagogy can also be seen at the level of sub-politics, in the cultural learning basis of several new grass-roots protest movements, both local and national. The Transition movement, aimed at preparing the world to make social choices for life without oil, has been analysed as a form of 'cultural citizenship' as it seeks to change relations between individuals and communities, challenging dominant hegemonic frameworks that fail to address the issue of what Stevenson calls 'cultural meaning' (Stevenson, 2011:66). Transition's distinctive approaches to exploiting the liberating educational potential of space are grounded in questioning, learning, "cultural respect and cultural democracy" (Stevenson, 2011:66). Unlike Life Friends of the Earth or Greenpeace, Transition groups have no formal system of membership or centralised structure, no actual 'start date', and instead of either market considerations or the views of experts, they rely on their own local, grass-roots, education and research groups. Meanwhile, Occupy London, an offshoot of the global Occupy movement, set up a camp in the centre of London in 2011, with a message grounded in what it called 'democratic pedagogy' – people, anyone, could simply wander in and learn from those in the camp. Similar to the Summerhill practice of physically wandering in and out of places where learning was taking place, the movement sought to appropriate "the social space and time of education" (Neary and Amsler, 2012:114), in a way that made learning and information~ideational transfer a democratic event of sharing rather than a process of control and symbolic violence.

In spite of the recent reductive commodification of higher education, it is also possible to see residues of a similar radical orientation in the form of a range of higher education movements, each in their own way seeking to transcend physical as well as ideational borders. Critical movements such as the Campaign for Social Science, the Council for the Defence of British Universities, the Campaign for the Public University, Society Counts, the World Universities Forum (WUF) and the Really Open University are central to the claim that while the higher education sector is "dominated by neoliberal globalization (it) is not reduced to it" (Santos, 2010:280). For instance, like the Occupy movement to which it is related, the Really Open University, founded in 2010 as response to the supposed de-politicisation of universities, is based on both space and the porosity of physical~ideational boundaries. One of its most high-profile projects, for instance, is the 'Space Project' – a temporary autonomous education space for meetings, talk and courses, self-managed by Leeds students and lecturers aimed at reimagining and restructuring the connections between university and community:

> We want the Space to be a meeting space; meetings of thought, of practice, of people, of ideas. We see it as a place of critical engagement with ideas and practices of transforming the world and ourselves within it. We are

trying, awkwardly, imperfectly, to create a space where everything overlaps and influences each other. So instead of separate groups putting on events in isolation we want to encourage collaboration, cross-contamination. This isn't to grow a singular project but to hopefully move us all a little bit, in personal and political transformation.

(Pudsey, 2015; www.spaceproject.org.uk)

But this cultural moment is not limited to grass-roots or protest movements. The current rush across UK universities to bring back the liberal arts can be seen as both a counterpoint to reductive and narrowly instrumental curricula and an establishment attempt to capitalise on a trend. A number of UK universities (Birmingham, Cambridge, Durham, Edinburgh, Exeter, Kent, Kings College London, Oxford, UCL) have, since 2010, introduced liberal arts undergraduate programmes and limited cross-disciplinary study in the form of degrees that allow students to take a wide range of subsidiary subjects. These developments were presaged by persuasive arguments in defence of America's liberal arts tradition, on the basis that far from being "a luxury that most families can no longer afford" (Ungar, 2010:190), a sluggish economy requires bright young people capable of 'thinking outside the box'. Yet the 'aspirational' by-lines attached to liberal arts degrees offered at Russell Group universities suggest that the move is a more competitive response to a market hungry for distinctive positioning than an ideological shift. And the UK has also seen the neo-liberalisation of education policy result in official approval in the UK of a swathe of alternative forms of schooling as well as Academies, united in paying lip service to the rising demand for local autonomy.

However, there has been the occasional less ambivalent space~voice~education scheme. Creative Partnerships was a flagship New Labour creative learning program between 2002 and 2011 and a policy-led creative educational use of space, exploiting links between schooling, social intervention and participation, creativity, structure and enlightenment. Through more than 8,000 projects with schools in England, mostly in what were deemed 'disadvantaged' communities, the programme sought to foster collaborations with artists and people in the creative industries. One such project stands out for its commitment to exploring and developing porous spatial imaginaries. A multicultural primary school, taking issue with the boundaried 'school as citadel' ethos, used creative and dialogic pedagogies, as well as links with external politics including connections in the countries of the pupils' origins in order to promote "a more 'capacious' understanding of children's home cultures and backgrounds (and build) . . . links and connectivity between the school and its community in relevant and meaningful ways . . ." (Manchester and Bragg, 2013). The aim was also to support students to explore and disagree about issues that felt risky, and the children are described as instinctively embracing a spirit of social protest, "spontaneously and enthusiastically" taking to the streets following a community project-based curriculum, inventing their own protest chants, "determined that others should know what they thought, and demonstrating they understood forms of protest that the adults had not formally 'taught' them about during the project" (Manchester and Bragg, 2013:824–825). These porous boundaries that both "let the outside in" and "the inside out" (Manchester and Bragg, 2013) had indeed created a space of "radical openness" (Soja, 1996). And the staff involved saw the emergence of "active, responsible citizens who are agents of change within our local and global community" (Manchester and Bragg, 2013:822).

There are also *institutional* narratives in which more holistic, socially and critically transformative visions of higher education have (at least in part) slipped the education-as-commodity net. In North Staffordshire, Keele University was created during in the mid-20th century in order to promote a form of enlightened participation that in the process challenged and sought to redraw territorial, social and epistemological boundaries. Keele's identity was grounded in a commitment to forging enlightening links among labour movements, politics and 'higher' learning and to making higher learning socially relevant in the sense of promoting understanding as widely as possible. Founded in the same climate of social revolution and democratisation of knowledge that saw a great expansion of higher education in England, the 1944 Butler Act and then the Robbins Report of 1963 and saw big shifts in ideas about the purpose of university and learning, Keele was in many ways a product of its time. Yet the strength of its anti-competitive vision, of universities as inherently political venues for righting wrongs, also marked it out and sealed its identity as a radical institution.

Keele University was built on long-standing proposals for a university in North Staffordshire combined with the ideas of R.H. Tawney, a socialist educational campaigner and vocal critic of individualism as capital acquisition without responsibility who practised these ideas through teaching tutorial classes to miners at the Workers Educational Association (WEA) in nearby Stoke-on-Trent (Tawney and Cartwright, 1907; Tawney, 1922). Tawney saw the WEA as a community of learning and actually a catalyst for the sort of democratisation of learning that provided the ideological foundations for the Butler Act and then the Robbins Report:

> [Education's] main aim is not to impart the specialized technique of any particular trade or profession, but to develop the faculties which, because they are the attribute of man, are not peculiar to any particular class or profession of men, . . . because they are the condition of a rational and responsible life in society.
>
> (Tawney, 1922)

After the Second World War, Tawney was joined by his former Oxford and WEA colleague Lord Alexander Dunlop Lindsay, who was also committed to bringing to this socio-economically deprived area what he felt it needed – a combination of global and local forms of higher learning. Lindsay's most revolutionary idea was that technical expertise should always be accompanied by social and ethical understanding of the use and impact of such technology. During his time as master of Balliol College Oxford during the Second World War, he had been horrified to hear news of former students from different countries killed on the battlefront – indirectly by each other. He attributed this to a political and cultural climate that polarised world views and to a narrow education system that led to mutual incomprehension through the use of language that was too 'specialised' (Kolbert, 2000).

Despite ongoing vocal opposition from contemporary guardians of higher learning as the preserve of the elite, permission was eventually granted for a new kind of college, and it opened in 1950. Instead of the normal process of becoming a satellite of London University, this new college would set its own syllabus. This syllabus would serve the community not just by way of imparting technical 'skills'; it would take from the Oxford model a commitment to free, wide-ranging discussion. Yet unlike most universities at the time the aim was not simply preparation for specialised professions; rather, it was to promote education is a fundamental human activity addressing *all* aspects of being human, of balancing "democracy" and "social security" and "goodness and cleverness" (Lindsay, 1957). In short, its aim (before Freire coined this term) was to 'conscientize', a vital component to which was interdisciplinarity. A revolutionary 'integrated curriculum' thus required all students to study two main subjects and subsidiary subjects from the 'other side' of the arts~science divide, while its Foundation Year (a course that covered a bit of everything) marked it out as a route to university that did not demand expert prior knowledge in one particular subject or pigeonhole you into a narrow route (Iliffe, 1968:69; Kolbert, 2000). The new college was also going to be democratic, with staff and students living together to make a 'learning community' ('Aims of the College'). It is a political conception of higher learning that the university has endeavoured with varying success to hold on to ever since.

## Cultural citizenship, the state and education: Ongoing struggles in the production of knowledge and shaping of policy

So what light do the persistence of education as ideology and enlightenment, the apparent re-popularisation of non-utilitarian forms of education and the apparently ambivalent role of the state cast on the relationship between education and citizenship?

The sorts of enlightened political participation discussed here can be understood as the crossing, dismantling and reshaping of both physical and ideational borders in a postmodern world of 'hyperspace' and 'flows', of spaces, ideas and people. The postmodern landscape of widespread functional literacy, superfast mass communication and ease at many aspects of border crossing both physical and ideational has enabled a proliferation of grass-roots and sub-political movements, selectively drawing on global concepts, networks and capital to claim cultural citizenship rights. A succession of educational movements – Progressive schooling, Occupy, Transition, the Really Open University, Keele's radically democratic interdisciplinarity and the ideological rebirth of the NUT – have deployed space and place, in a range of 'thirdspace' and sub-political ways in order to promote understanding and the freedom and skills to exercise a political voice.

In some ways, this landscape represents a significant break from the days when the modernist education project was limited to imparting just enough political literacy to maintain the status quo in good working order and confrontation in the form of revolt was the only emancipatory option. By contrast, glocalisation provides structural possibilities for widespread emancipatory action that bypasses the control of national governments, shifting power through the radical act of rejecting what is on offer and claiming the citizenship right to a say in defining what is important.

In other ways, however, today's boundary challenging landscape is properly understood as the continuation of a historic process, not a radical break. We can see this in the relationships between state-driven (or structural) and grass-roots (or cultural) change, in examples of educationally mediated critical awareness of injustice and the mandate to act represent an interesting form of state~grass roots collusion, with the state both resisting and facilitating, and eventually even co-opting, boundary-challenging knowledge and agendas while there is also ambivalence on the grass-roots side. We have seen that state endorsement of sub-political agendas seems often limited to lip service, rhetoric undermined by increased social, political and educational censorship and efforts to clamp-down on dissent. We have also seen ways in which state ownership of education is limited to exploiting the capital it generates in rapidly changing political, cultural and economically driven terms. Neo-liberal attempts at ideological control, driven by both fear and the competitive preoccupation with accountability and performance data, contradict global rhetorical consensus on the desirability of democracy, emancipatory education and dialogic inquiry. Meanwhile, among sub-political actors we have seen both regrouping following state buy-in, as part of a perennial counter-hegemonic commitment, *and* fear-induced educational (especially at an institutional level) mirroring of neo-liberal public policy. Underneath this ambivalent bipartite process of resistance or endorsement, then co-opting or re-grouping, however, is a fairly consistent dynamic of opposition – the inevitable and ongoing struggle for power between politics and sub-politics – that seems fundamental to the nature of change. And in this light, while not a *radical* break, an increasingly glocalised landscape that is subject to more physical and ideational cracking, debates, disagreement, struggle would seem indeed to open up the possibility of *more*, and more rapid, shifting of the power to define values and knowledge.

This reading of 21st-century citizenship requires an approach to educating that provides understanding of the present and the past and the skills to act on those. We have seen that critical awareness of injustice and the mandate to act are the essence of social and political change, without which the alternative is a pointless cycle of transnational competitiveness. Furthermore, 'thirdspace' thinking involving learning from difference requires border crossing, and to do that effectively requires *understanding* of those borders. Understanding of those borders requires an understanding of history and politics along with genuine social and political participation – equally far from the safe topic of personal responsibility or the reactionary one of 'fundamental British values'.

# 4 Education for community citizenship

## Equality and critical multiculturalism

This chapter continues the idea of flows – of ideas, identity, relationships – and porous boundaries, with a focus on the changing nature of 'community' and communities. While the last chapter discussed ideological aspects of education's role in changing society for the better, there is also a structural aspect to this role. Recent media shifting from 'radicalisation' to 'nation within a nation' rhetoric (Channel 4 'What British Muslims Really Think') is an opportunistic case of Islamophobic othering, as has been pointed out (Nawaz, 2016)), similar to the deep-seated xenophobia validated, channelled and revealed by the EU referendum. However, the ways that recent political events have ruptured traditional sociopolitical fault lines demands that we scrutinise the evident sharp polarisations. In the long-term longer term, these challenges to identity, equality, community and the links between them may if interrogated and debated openly and responsibly lead to better communities.

Community was critically important to both the establishment of democracy and the development modern sociology that bridges the human and ecological, the empirical and theoretical, aspects of the social order (Entrekin, 1989:36), and little has changed to contradict Talcott Parsons's (1965) definition of citizenship as full membership of "the societal community". Clearly, however, in terms of definition the word *community* understood as "human participation in networks of primary, interpersonal relationships within a limited geographical context" (Hays, 1967:154) is shifting. We know really that they have both imaginary and concrete and practical and physical dimensions. And as Agnew acknowledges (1989:10 & 13) attempts to structurally differentiate between society, community and place just reduce the scope of community.

Yet while these communities may be shifting in terms of membership and their relations with specific places and traditional institutional structures, while they may be dis-embedded, 'imagined' or virtual, they are still grounded in a fundamental sense of located space, providing narrative, identity and belonging. Indeed, the continued instinct people have for community is evidenced counter-intuitively by the increased use of smartphones, the Internet and 'virtual communities', which have normalised the urge to 'share' and actually far from displacing physical connections have brought the nature of physical space into greater focus, as youngsters use digital networking to organise and add value to face-to-face socialising. The ability to work in dis-embedded ways has also seen a rise in cultural citizenship projects in which the grass-roots approach to knowledge exchange seems to be as important as the outcomes, hinting at a form of 'global citizenship' comprising a multitude of local rather than national communities united in their differences through local involvement partly mediated through educational institutions. Writing almost a century ago (1927), Dewey attributed cultural tensions to the lack of local community. And today we see that lack of community inclusion, lack of a stake in the place where you live, both alienates and leaves the door open for alternative concrete but destructive, ideas. Since communities are defined in terms that make them distinct from other communities, they bestow a much-needed identity. Reactions to loss of place-based security and disruption of identity have included urban youth riots, extreme right anti-migrant protests, the supposedly 'religious' extremism of al-Qaeda and the group known variously as the 'Islamic State' or 'Daesh' and, most recently, the shocking EU referendum result – inward-looking, and, at worst, destructive, ideologies to give meaning to the dispossessed.

This chapter considers the nature of these new communities and how they connect to citizenship, and interrogates both social and educational policy efforts to 'manage' communities, focusing on the complex tensions between facilitating "the right to name ourselves . . ." (Harstock, 1987:196), while promoting equality.

## Education and diverse communities

We are used to hearing about 'inclusion', but the existence of grass-roots movements does not necessarily mean that there is fair and equal distribution of voice, rights and responsibility, and in public policy discourses the label tends to be applied to the enlisting of more and more people into competitive capitalism – by definition neither 'inclusive' nor equal but instead promoting individualism, a system of vested interests and inevitable inequality. In a world where geographical boundaries are dissolving and identities are so fluid, 'equality' is thus very challenging for education. Thinking about how best to ensure that all members of a community are, and feel, equally valued switches regularly from emphasising diversity to legislating for equality. Often these two words are lumped together – 'diversity in unity'. And while there is little wrong with this much-invoked phrase and underlying ideology, it is often used as a superficial panacea and, in fact, produces the kind of vague and contradictory policy framing we saw in Chapter 1. Moreover, the two goals often pull policy in opposite ways. For instance, Leighton argues that "Britain is a country of multiple identities – as are many other countries to varying degrees – so that recognition of difference cannot sit comfortably with a desire for a single identity" (Leighton, 2012:63). Again, answering this charge with the ideal of 'cosmopolitan citizenship' (Rosaldo, 1999; Osler, 2005) is easy enough, but it still begs the question: As far as the relationship between education and citizenship is concerned, does inclusion mean valuing diversity, or is equality only really possible in uniformity?

In the current global geopolitical context, 'British' and 'Britishness' have become newly politicised terms, accompanied by a return to what some, taking

Cameron's cue, see as a return to assimilationist rhetoric and policy defined in opposition to more pluralist multiculturalism (Back et al., 2002). In most of this debate, 'migration' and 'integration' are imagined in the sense of 'them coming here' - recently approaching to the way people speak about actual invasion. In an attempt to provide a counter narrative to this perpetuation of Huntington's seminal 'clash of civilisations' thesis, his argument that cultural-religious incompatability will drive global conflict (Huntington, 1996), a raft of academic explorations over the past few years have explored the concept of 'Britishness' (e.g. Bournemouth, BSA, 3/11/15; Keele, 'Britishness in the 21st Century', 19/6/13). These have focused (some) attention on the fact that imposing a monolithic values set would rather arbitrary since there is "little consensus . . . once one scrapes only a little beneath the surface" on what these should be (Pring, 2002:85), and on hybridities, new ethnicities and diasporas as "the very embodiment of the problematisation of the . . . national" (Gholami, in press:2). There is less academic coverage of the impact on national identity of British people going abroad, learning and returning or staying put – but producing accounts that would shed useful light on the impact of shared experience and location on the feeling of belonging.

Belatedly, some sections of the media started to catch up with this limited conceptualisation of British identity: an exploration of 'Britishness' as defined by the multicultural and shifting cultural history "of these islands" (BBC, 2015), or a historico-political consideration of the benefits and inevitability of immigration (BBC, 2014). However, since the start of recent social unrest and heightened security fearfulness, other mainstream media and political rhetoric have slid inexorably into far-right ethnonationalism or xenophobia – especially Islamophobia. It is argued that this, especially targeted at Muslim students, has recently replaced anti–Afro-Caribbean social prejudice in the context of policies that pretend to be about 'integration' but actually shade into 'management' and even 'containment' – as if it were the individuals themselves, not society, that are the problem (Shain, 2013). While "[r]ace has not been mentioned overtly by the Coalition government, . . . the continuation of debates about forced marriages, 'extremism' and immigration have targeted racialised groups, namely Muslims and asylum-seekers . . ." (Shain, 2013:69).

This form of racist othering has been analysed as scapegoating (Hall et al., 1978) – a process with a long historical pedigree, of blaming economic decline, overcrowding and on those who are new or different. Indeed, the extent to which recent UK integration discourses have been framed around UK Muslim identity has resulted in the economic and political marginalisation of Muslim communities in what can be seen as both scapegoating and neo-imperialist responses to existential fear. The irrational and fear-driven nature of the process has been captured by surveys like that reported by *The Independent*: "[S]ome 31 per cent of the population is thought to consist of recent immigrants, when the figure is actually 13 per cent" (Paige, 2013), which cited an Ipsos Mori phone survey of 1,015 people, conducted for the Royal Statistical Society and Kings College. Yet the scapegoating continues.

UK Conservative MP (and at the time secretary of state for communities and local government) Eric Pickles's letter to imams in January 2015 asking them to do more to combat extremism among their congregations (Pickles, 16/1/15) was a flashpoint in what has since been criticised as a mounting 'us~and~them' narrative, singling out Muslims. This climate, which saw a Rochdale taxi firm providing 'white only drivers' as a unique selling point in 2014 (https://bnp.org.uk/news/national/white-taxi-driver-only-please) in a fairly horrific echo of post–World War II signs – 'No blacks, no dogs, no Irish' or the anti-Jewish fears in Germany that led to the Holocaust, has, according to Prevent statistics, increased exponentially since the November 2015 Paris terrorist attacks and included a rise in reported Islamophobic violence in the UK. As a result, 'hate crime' law was altered in 2015 to include 'Islamophobic' hate crime as a named category of crime. Yet the political and popular media narrative has continued largely unabated, with occasional clumsy attempts to disguise racism or Islamophobia as positive nation-building, as in the UKIP leader Nigel Farage's argument that employers should be able to distinguish in favour of UK-born applicants: "This is not about race; it's about nationality" (Today, Radio 4, 12/3/15, 8.05am). Nor could the change to UK law prevent the Nazi-like declaration on 12 July 2015 by the contender for the US Republican presidential nomination Donald Trump (at the time of writing riding a wave of popular support from people who are scared, ignorant and poor; fear difference; and need to blame others) that Muslims should not be allowed into the country.

The sorts of feelings that have fuelled such responses, especially as embodied in the ideology of the British National Party, European and US far-right rhetoric, the persuasiveness of UKIP and most recently 'Britain First', have further been explained in terms of whiteness as a pathology: "I do feel sometimes that there is no white history. There's either Black History Month or they do Muslims and Sikhs" (reported in Ajegbo, 2007:30). Some insights into this can be seen in the popular condemnation of Labour MP Emily Thornberry's March 2015 tweeting of a house in Rochester draped in England flags – widely understood as a positioning shorthand for 'look how fascist they are here'. The popular response can be understood as one of fear, of previously impervious positions of moral, political or economic superiority under threat, the understudied complexity of which has led to Hooks (and others since) calling for the study of 'whiteness' (Hooks, 1994).

Whatever the truth about competing claims of marginalisation, the Prevent Strategy can be seen as the educational culmination of these tensions in what has been described as the nationalistic "hijack(ing) and nationaliz(ing of) intrinsically human capacities such as feeling responsible" (Gholami, in press:5). Attempts to revise its clumsiest and most racist aspects have been undermined by repeated political interventions, reactive to each perceived 'threat' – from actual terrorism or public opinion. So as Shain argues (2013), instead of becoming less stigmatising each revision has increased the rhetorical polarisation of 'Britishness' and anything Muslim or Islamic. Shain notes that above all, the "militaristic language" that has accompanied the policy of concentrating Prevent funding in regions with high Muslim populations:

> 'Winning hearts and minds', the subtitle of the Prevent Action Plan (DCLG, 2007), was a key slogan of the British Army . . . The Prevent strategy has been a central tool in the construction of a 'war at home' with a 'new enemy within' through its underlying assumption that all Muslims may be susceptible to condoning terrorism.
>
> (Shain, 2013:76)

Shain argues that despite the key focus on teaching Imams about child protection, increased surveillance and associated lack of freedom has actually exposed Muslim children to harassment (Shain, 2013:77).

In an era when mass migration and multiculturalism are facts (inevitable and not all bad), time spent worrying about migration may seem better spent on what happens after migration has taken place. That is, how to include, around living in the same place. The compatibility of value sets that have underpinned a range of interfaith community responses to terrorist outrages over the past few decades undermine Huntington's thesis, which is primarily cultural. And as even Leighton points out, "despite stereotypes, it is not always the case that young British Asians adopt the values and practices of their parents" (Leighton, 2012:63). Instead, as Eisenstadt has explained, social change and continuously changing diversity results from the selective adoption by minority cultures of features of the dominant culture. This process results in not one but multiple 'modernities' in "a story of continual constitution and reconstitution of a multiplicity of cultural programmes" (Eisenstadt, 2003).

But it is also true that there are multidimensional tensions on both political and cultural levels. Relatively uncontentious aspirational rhetoric about inclusion, community and diversity, such as "developing a non-essentialist concept of cultural difference" (May, 1999:30), "creating space for recognition of and open discussion about difference" (Leighton, 2012:65) and "see(ing) conflict from multiple perspectives" (Smith and Fairman, cited in Noddings, 2005:4), misses the point. The locally embedded experience of tensions – cultural and subjective or economic and pragmatic, jobs and 'subjective' belonging alike are place-bound – requires local approaches to resolving them. This is a perspective that has received persuasive airing in recent urban centre-based on work on multiculturalism and national identity (Meer, 2010; Modood and Meer, 2013). The central intractable question of whether cultural pluralism or uniformity is 'better' dissolves when the focus shifts to real problems and projects in real places. The most productive attempts to balance and integrate subjective and objective citizenship are grass roots, about belonging and contributing to the community.

As communities, schools and universities can be, and have been, seen as sites for citizenship. This is, clearly, in a limited sense; schools and universities neither bestow economic share nor require political allegiance. But they do socialise, demanding a lot of time, critical engagement and participation and bestow rewards including identity and belonging. Dewey championed the ideal of schools not as places where youngsters practice for 'real life' but as real, intimately and daily experienced social systems themselves (Dewey, 1938), where most of the action elements of citizenship are played out and the ideational ones crystalised. Educational institutions as 'sites for citizenship' was also the title of a turn-of-millennium working party sponsored by the Council of Europe (CoE) on Education for Democratic Citizenship that set out to investigate how universities in America and Europe embedded, applied and encouraged (uncontested) citizenship principles such as 'democratic beliefs', structures, governance and decision-making (Bleiklie, 2012).

But the easy adoption of the phrase 'sites for citizenship' is clearly problematic, or at least begs some excavation, when we consider that not all students have the same form or experience of education, and likely a rift between diverse and unequal experiences and what educational institutions say about citizenship. One of the ways the challenge manifests itself is that education systems in newly multicultural communities are having to reconsider issues of cultural difference (*as well as* with equality) and move away from unquestioningly promoting shared cultural norms as part of a universalising project. Equality, different sets of rights and academic excellence have vied with each other as priorities for national education systems. But how schools and universities should respond is contested. Navigating the thin line between equality of experience, of outcome or of opportunity means, in practice, either treating everyone the same regardless of background or attempting to reflect through curriculum, pedagogies, value-laden discussions and even language of instruction the diverse backgrounds of young people. Although current political focus may be on Muslim citizens, there are many other people whose social marginalisation is consolidated through ignorance of their cultures in school. It was not long ago that black and Irish people were unapologetically excluded, while the often-forgotten 'traveller' community are still seen as outsiders and culturally deficient by teachers (Deuchar and Bhopal, 2013).

Across the higher education sector, conflicted though it may be, an increased international frame of reference has prompted universities to ask what it is that international students want and, therefore, what 'internationalisation' means in the sense of catering for diversity. This needs-must policy-making model may provide clues for a critically engaged form of social and educational policy that far from stigmatising inherited *different* traditions utilises these as capital in an educational 'contact zone': "social spaces where cultures meet, clash and grapple with each other" (Pratt, 1991:1). Thus, the effects (if not the cause) of the international student trade can be seen as providing a counter-discourse to the anti-marketisation, anti-league tables lobby. Granted, the 'rubbing-off' nature of this cross-cultural encounter may be limited by the "highly asymmetric relations of power" (Pratt, 1991:1) and thus one-directional flow of cross-cultural capital defined as. But the lack of defensiveness in this context is striking; migration contexts also provide contact zones, and this has led to arguments that we should be using what are called 'diasporic pedagogies' characterised by "mutual respect and recognition", where diverse cultural heritages are reclaimed and given educational recognition as valuable (Gholami, in-press:13).

## Understanding community and communities today

Despite attempts to analyse the nature of 'community' today and its relationship with citizenship, society, culture and place, a continued tendency to favour categorisation has allowed culturally essentialist political discourses to be under-challenged – which we saw not only in Eric Pickles's conflation of 'Muslim' with an essentialised 'Muslim *community*' but also in the repetition of this in the various outraged responses to his letter. Furthermore, the Crick Report's inclusion of phrases emphasising the value of uniformity over that of diversity:

> Minorities must learn to respect the laws, codes and conventions as much as the majority – not merely because it is useful to do so, but because the process helps foster common citizenship.
> (QCA, 1998:17–18)

This led to the charge that the commission had both ignored and, in "presenting certain ethnicities as 'other' ", colluded with racism (Osler and Starkey, 2001:292). And although these were among the shortcomings that the Ajegbo Commission was set up to address in its focus on 'Britishness', the Ajegbo Report's findings were limited mainly to noting that there was a huge amount of ignorance about cultural diversity, too much negative stereotyping of 'otherness', and insufficient resource, knowledge or training of teachers – very little, that is, that was concrete, illuminating or actionable. The fundamental assumption categorising people is worthwhile is contradicted by two main factors: first, evident diversity among people who share demographic characteristics (the UK media have been making concerted headway recently in trying to rectify Pickles's clumsiness in this regard) and, second, evidently strong community relations among people who share no demographic characteristics other than where they live.

Diversity within demographically identifiable groups and has tended to be ignored in the predilection for labels – in policy circles, and even in scholarly work, though there is ample ethnographic work on mixed communities that should caution against this. In Baumann's influential London-based study of 20 years ago, the unit of ethnographic analysis ('culture' or 'community') is the borough of Southall itself rather than each ethnic group. And the main finding was that the borough's physicality united ethnicities in a fluid, flexible way that was characterised by hybridity: "The people of Southall affirm ethnic distinctiveness in some contexts, but they are also engaged in rethinking their identities and in debating the meaning of their cultural heritage" (Baumann, 1996, Abstract). Yet a decade later a continued tendency towards "mapping cultures onto places" in perpetuation of the myth of "a single cultural identity" is simultaneously both noted and compounded (Vertovec, 2007:1042). Though, as Vertovec partly acknowledges, such cultures are increasingly spread across locations as too are the processes of blending and diversity among transnational practices, it seems that even in culturally sensitive writing it is hard to avoid categorical generalisation.

What local, socially constructive intersectional, action-focused, community relations and identities *might* look like is a succession of grass-roots organisations set up over the last decade or so to tackle the educational and social exclusion of marginalised groups including white working-class, black and Asian inhabitants. For instance, in multicultural Birmingham, local racisms have prompted local solutions – in the form of place-based educational and cultural projects such as the Pakistani Community Development Network and 'Asian People's Welfare Society', which have sought to balance the competing imperatives of respect for difference, and for different religions, with equality and integration. The APWS, for instance, is emphatically inter-religious rather than secular, actively embracing the religious basis of culture and the cultural basis of religion, proclaiming its inter-religious welcome, and meeting every week in a local church.

These examples of grass-roots mobilisation, reclaiming citizenship as place-based, community inclusion sit interestingly against the inadequacies of policy attempts, including the Crick and Ajegbo commissions, to do the same. Mohammed Ali, founder of the Arabic and Islamic-themed Hubb arts centre, run by Muslims but open to all: "I have travelled to a lot of places but I am very pro-Birmingham. This is my city: my father was buried here, my three kids were born here" (Adams, 2015). Moreover, it is argued that those formerly marginalised groups have become intrinsic to the city's well-being. Since Pakistanis are on course to become the city's largest single ethnic group, explains local activist Karamat Iqbal, "[t]he success of Pakistanis is, therefore, intertwined with the continued prosperity of the city", with a resulting collective identity that is definitely 'Brummie' but with a Pakistani accent (Iqbal, 2013).

So how *should* we think about community, citizenship and education today? What strategy, from the available models of transnationalism, liberalism, multiculturalism, pluralism, integration and separatism, is adequate to both capture present realities and point a way forward for educating about citizenship? It is an item of common knowledge that "[i]n France and the United States of America considerable emphasis is placed on similarities, on what makes pupils French or 'American' . . ." (Leighton, 2012:62). But the UK has engaged in what has been seen as a "linear progression . . . from assimilation in the 1950s to integration in the mid-1960s and multiculturalism since the 1970s" (Shain, 2013:63). Multiculturalism is such a well-used term now, but its familiarity can obscure what it means. It mixes many elements: individual and community, freedom and diversity, identity and cohesion. Furthermore, while it is important to distinguish in any given context between 'multi-cultural' as a demographic description and *active* 'multiculturalism', which Stuart Hall influentially explained as the "strategies and policies adopted to govern or manage" the societies it describes (Hall, 2000:209), the term actually represents both, as befits its subjective essence.

Hall's persuasive expositions of multiculturalism as a world view demanding action was premised on two important, connected, observations: first, identities are fluid, non-essentialist, and people have 'multiple identities'; second, this is partly because the social world including the ascription of identities is discursively and powerfully constructed. The policy implications are also two-fold. On one hand, the fluid, discursive nature of cultural identity means that there is nothing fixed or irresolvable in cultural conflict. On the other hand, the role of powerful

70  *Education for community citizenship*

actors in the problematic construction and delineation of so-called cultural identities also becomes clear. For instance, on an educational level, it is pointed out how multiculturalism was "born out of the resistance of parents and teachers to the racist assumptions embedded in education systems in the 1950s and 1960s and the unequal educational outcomes that followed" (Shain, 2013:66).

The Parekh Report, (Runnymede, 2000) outlines five distinct (peaceful) ways in which states have attempted to reconcile cohesion, equality and diversity:

- Procedural – the state is culturally neutral, and leaves individuals and communities to negotiate with each other as they wish providing they observe certain basic procedures
- Nationalist – the state promotes a single national culture and expects all to assimilate to it; people who cannot are second-class citizens
- Liberal – there is a single political culture in the public sphere, but substantial diversity in the private lives of individuals and communities
- Plural – there is both unity and diversity in public life; communities and identities overlap and are interdependent, and develop common features
- Separatist – the state permits and expects each community to remain separate from others, and to organise and regulate its own affairs, and largely confines itself to maintaining order and civility

A 'nationalist' approach is broadly assimilationist, that is promoting buy-in to the dominant culture and full economic participation enabled by skills and shared language. The dominant strand of this thinking is economic assimilationism, which is usually modelled on Marxian premise that "[i]deas of local culture emerge only as residual effects of this dynamic of capital . . ." (Nicholas Entrikin, Chapter 3 in Agnew and Duncan, 1989:33). This view is undermined by the ways in which these very dynamics are "part and parcel of how dominance and subordination are reproduced and altered in this society" (Apple, 1993:222), that is, inherently unequal and hegemonic.

Assimilationism is often contrasted with multiculturalism, of which there are several variants. Smith suggests three: liberal, pluralist and critical (Smith, 2003), of which the easiest contrast is between liberal and pluralist approaches. The classic exposition of political *liberalism* is that of Rawls (Rawls, 1993). This pragmatic vision sees society based on 'political' (not absolute) concepts of justice, with freedom and equality balanced by mutual respect in the pursuit of what binds people as members of the same society. Rawls advocated a political modus operandi based on a clear separation between the public and private realms, where government and justice by consensus would unproblematically overlay a plurality of private value sets and world views. In direct reply to Rawls, however, Habermas argued that such separation was a bit unrealistic as it was both impossible and undesirable to avoid the philosophical, value-imbued big questions about public good, purpose, truth and so on that guide public debate (Habermas, 1995).

However, that is not the only critique of liberal multiculturalism, in which it is often pointed out that "[t]here may be an implicit assumption that equal opportunities exist . . . The language of 'colour blindness' is sometimes used to denote the aspiration that inequalities based on social group have been overcome.... By contrast, *pluralist* multiculturalism places more emphasis on differences between groups" (Smith, 2003:29). Yet pluralist multiculturalism is nonetheless problematic on other counts. The vagueness of pluralism means that it is often used as a last resort, to fill a rhetorical gap or as a relative term along the lines of 'diversity is good and should be appreciated'. It is the detail, often missing, that makes it possible to operationalise. Most articulations obscure the extent to which integration is the aim, and whether this is at structural/policy or cultural levels. As a result, 'pluralist' policy can tend to be an admission of defeat, used as a coded rejection of separatism or integration, and drawing to mind Meer and Modood's (2012) distinction between 'interculturalism' and 'multiculturalism', where intercultural means communities living parallel not integrated lives. Moreover, the term can also be dangerous when used with a neo-nationalist undercurrent that essentializes, categorises and 'ritualizes' ethnicity (Grillo, 1998:195). In a context of hybridities, new ethnicities and diasporas and a world where people and cultures change, this can be less than helpful. As a result of these shortcomings, most states attempt to balance liberal and pluralist multiculturalism to some extent. The Parekh Report does likewise, in some ways invoking Rawls's classic *political* liberalism in which citizens with diverse backgrounds that include incompatibilities like conflicting truth claims nonetheless reach a point of 'overlapping consensus' around which policy is constructed (Rawls, 1993), except that Parekh's brand of pluralism puts communities higher, defining the goal for Britain to become a 'community of communities' (Runnymede, 2000:2, 1.4).

Each of these approaches, even though they overlap in practice, carries a distinct mandate for education. Liberalism requires children to understand what is needed to enable them to be free, capable and responsible citizens. The emphasis is on functionality – *enough* about their history and institutions, rights and freedoms and learn to work together. Integrative pluralism, on the other hand, dictates that all students be exposed to a wide range of religious, political and cultural ideas and artefacts, separatist pluralism would clearly educate people from different cultural backgrounds separately.

'*Critical* multiculturalism', on the other hand, is rather different and more obviously problematic as it demands genuine reflection and action. The term describes an approach that actively drills down into the diversity~equality site of tension by inscribing a careful line between counter-hegemonic and non-essentialist approaches. This version of multiculturalism has a lot in common with 'cosmopolitanism'. Critical, dialogic and reflexive, it is grounded in the same sorts of interconnectedness of self and other. Critical multiculturalism sets out to challenge norms, right wrongs, and to address histories and *all* feelings of marginalisation or disempowerment including the 'What about us?' feelings of majorities:

> The first step in developing a non-essentialist conception of cultural difference is to unmask, and deconstruct, the apparent neutrality of civism – that is, the supposedly universal, neutral set of cultural values and practices that underpin the public sphere of the nation-state.
>
> (May, 1999:30)

Educationally, critical multiculturalism "places a value on acknowledging, understanding and challenging inequality and social injustice and this obviously takes it into more controversial areas" (Smith, 2003:29). Indeed, there are also hints at a form of criticality in the approach Parekh recommends: "to build resilience in each child, so that every child can intervene if they see others being hurt or abused, and that all children have the emotional and verbal tools to defend themselves". Parekh talks about a Handbook that would "draw on the discussions about national identity, racism and cultural differences provided in the first part of this report; and would provide guidance on both the content and pedagogy of multicultural and anti-racist education. We recommend that education for citizenship include human rights principles; stress on skills of deliberation, advocacy and campaigning; understanding of equality legislation; and opposition to racist beliefs and behaviour". Moreover, points out Parekh, this approach is not actually new: "The importance of political literacy and an anti-racist perspective was stressed in the 1980s by the Swann Report, and also by *Murder in the Playground*, the Burnage Report" (Runnymede, 2000: 149)

In seeking to find a social policy and educational approach that ticks the important citizenship boxes we have found ourselves back then, circuitously, at 'participation' – essential as Dewey reminded us to belonging (Dewey, 1937), and in a global climate marked by mass migration seen by assimilationists as the key to reducing feelings of exclusion that can lead to tension. Some have dismissed the idea that socio-economic inclusion could persuade "marginalised cultural and ethnic groups (to) focus less on the specific concerns and more on national issues and priorities" (Banks, 2001:7). And the Crick Report spectacularly glossed over the possibility and implications of such a link in its summary acknowledgement of "the reasons why some people 'opt out' of the moral social set-up" (Crick, 1999:19). Yet no one has silenced the voices that continue to stress the importance of adequate and up-to-date knowledge and skills to take part socio-economically. The neat 'assimilationism-or-multiculturalism' alternative is also undermined by the acknowledged need, as in some of the Birmingham projects, for enabling structural responses such as council-led ethnic minority recruitment quotas and Youth Worker schemes to match the critical ones. It has been argued that government policies have in fact been fairly consistently 'assimilationist', if assimilated means fully included socially, politically and economically in the larger society (Grosvenor, 1997). Furthermore, it has also been argued that the failure of (benevolent) assimilationism, understood as equality of share and opportunity, was due to the emergence not of multiculturalism (valuing of sociocultural diversity) but of a political system that took a sharp turn to the open market in the 1980s – an unequal market controlled by those with existing local capital and therefore power (Shain, 2013). It is a reading that not only asks us to reconsider whether assimilation(ism) and multiculturalism are incompatible after all but also that underscores that perennial truth – that it is not the 'model' that matters, but values and a commitment to equality and sharing.

## Language, free speech and cultural~religious diversity

The language issue captures some core aspects of the diversity~equality problem. On one hand, freedom of language and freedom of speech are widely endorsed citizens' rights. On the other hand, a shared language is key both to the socio-economic functioning and to the culturally 'imagined' aspect of communities where the language ethnonationalistically embodies the culture of the community and gives people their collective identity. We saw in Chapter 2, for instance, how the universalising process of modern nation-state building relied on a shared educational language. A place- (and future-)centred approach to multiculturalism, however, means *letting go* of this struggle to preserve the spirit of the language of the tribe in favour of creating new knowledge, traditions and structures. This process, the linguistic equivalent of the struggle to disrupt ideological and political hegemony, is central to the way that languages have evolved to both reflect and shape culture over millennia.

A place-centred citizenship framework that embraces linguistic change adds to the difficult educational questions about policies to protect minority languages. In multicultural settings, it can be challenging to do justice to potentially conflicting priorities: indigenous cultures, students' ability in their native rather than a second language, and their socio-economic opportunities in the country of residence. Anglophone dominance including Anglo-centric processes that require students to learn *in* English when it is not their native language result in the loss of linguistic functionality and, because of the close relationship between language and culture, of indigenous culture and knowledge as well. Concerns about this process have been expressed using terms like *language death*, *language decay* and even *linguistic genocide* (Skutnabb-Kangas, 2000; Gogolin, 2002). As well as negatively impacting students' sense of self-worth, this can impose an unfair practical burden on non-native English speakers who are likely to do less well academically in a foreign language (McKinnon and Manathunga, 2003).

This 'equality of opportunity' problem has further implications for citizenship. For instance, what does the transferability imperative mean for the reproduction of particular, local, forms of knowledge? Is, as May has suggested, "the enforced loss of their own ethnic, cultural and linguistic habitus . . . the necessary price of entry to the civic realm" (May, 1999:31). Drawing on hidden curriculum theory, "[t]he manner in which a student's home language is valued or undermined, for example, can be read as a reflection of wider policy and political perspectives as to how (and whether) they should be integrated into society" (Curtis and Pettigrew, 2009:110). Levinson, writing about deliberative democracy in an American civics education context, captures the dilemma:

> [It is] troubling to teach citizens (or future citizens) that they are 'outsiders' of a civic community. . . . In order to teach them to function effectively as insiders in the deliberative process, however, the school must simultaneously teach minority students that they are 'outsiders' in the sense of having to learn and use a 'language of power' that is initially not their own.
> (Levinson, 2002:267–268)

Different language policies reflect different positions on the relationship between language, education and citizenship. The United States, Singapore and Wales provide interestingly contrasting approaches. The melting-pot nationalism of the US has been constructed around ethnic blocks in which other languages are lingua franca, reflecting a pluralist notion of citizenship in which flag-flying and an overwhelmingly secular education system brings together the cultural diversity of many different languages spoken at home. Yet recent educational policy suggests a move away from this multilingual heritage towards promoting English. The 2011–2014 Education Strategic Plan presented 'equality' in terms of "educational opportunities . . . for all students regardless of race, ethnicity, . . . language", whereas the 2014–2018 version gives English-language competence a much higher profile, with English-language competence seen as a main prerequisite to success, both in the career market and because "children with a primary home language of English scored higher in reading and math than those coming from homes with a primary home language other than English . . ." (p.26, U.S. Department of Education Strategic Plan: Fiscal Years 2014–18). Singapore's efforts at national identity building since the end of British rule has sought to both unite and cater separately for the three main distinct ethnic groupings. A two-sided 'global' awareness is reflected in educational language policies. Primary pupils are all required to learn English because it is the "lingua franca of international business, science and technology" while also learning their "Mother Tongue language" – Chinese, Malay or Tamil (MoE, 2014:5). The reasons cited for learning these various 'official languages' of Singapore are to do with cultural preservation. Yet these are actually *not* the mother tongues of large proportions of the population. Rather, in what appears a rather unique form of state-driven shaping of even 'indigenous', these people are simply slotted into the nearest of the three linguistic-cultural categories. Finally, education and language policy in the very small country of Wales showcases a political devolution-led approach to reclaim indigenous heritage that can be seen as either ethnonationalist, elitist or democratic. From the first protests against its neglect in 1962, support for Welsh has been an intellectual protest led by the Universities of Aberystwyth and Bangor in the form of the Welsh Language Society. While clearly about 'cultural' preservation, today Welsh-language medium education is largely the preserve of the elite who can afford the luxury of private tuition to learn it.

But freedom of language leads into hot waters, raising again the issue of free *speech* and its rather different impact on community. The problematic nature of heterotopias and the scope and contradictions within freedom of speech, both principles and practice, has been brought into focus by wide-ranging discussion over satire in multicultural societies where cracks are ever-present. While these cracks are potentially productive, they have certainly widened recently in response to events involving satirical comments on Islam, on religiosity in general and on violent extremist movements masquerading under assumed cloaks of religiosity. Satirists say it is their right to cause offence in the cause of bursting bubbles of pomposity and challenging assumptions. Recent media coverage of this issue following the extremist shooting of staff (7/1/15) at the headquarters of the French satirical magazine Charlie Hebdo has juxtaposed these rights, championed by the French state against (it was felt by many) those without such power – socio-economically or culturally marginalised Muslims living in France, who felt their identity and own freedoms were being mocked. Despite the dominant official rhetoric 'No conflict between French and Muslim!' that the satirists were allowed to reprint a picture they knew to be religiously offensive made this a very uncomfortable compromise for many Muslims who were forced to pick a side: 'Are you for us or against us?' was the largely unspoken ultimatum behind the mass declarations of 'Je suis Charlie!' As the dust settled, there was a slight shift in media rhetoric towards understanding that the most fitting response could not be captured or enabled by 'either/or' ultimata and that the choice between gratuitously insulting politically powerless people and murder is a false and unnecessary choice.

Yet the debate about the conflicting rights to offend or not be offended continued – and continues. On the BBC Radio 4 programme Any Questions, everyone agreed that "[n]o one has the right not to be offended" (Any Questions, 10/1/15). And indeed public opinion seemed to on the side of free speech against perceived political correctness (e.g. R4, 9pm, 6/11/15). Yet others responded along the lines that freedom should be balanced against a *wider* sense of equality, which in some cases involves righting past wrongs and making a show of giving greater respect to those who may have been denied any. A principle that is neatly captured by Harari's argument that the supposed "fundamental values" of freedom and equality in a capitalist, secular society are usually contradictory: "Equality can be ensured only by curtailing the freedoms of those who are better off. Guaranteeing that every individual will be free to do as he wishes inevitably short-changes equality" (Harari, 2014:164–165). These restorative justice principles truly set the cat among the pigeons. Columnists argued that widespread calls for 'free speech' by supposed champions of political correctness were hypocritical, in reflecting the rights of only *some* marginalised groups. Liberal eagerness to challenge Far Right bigotry but not extreme religious (namely Muslim) bigotry was highlighted as ethically problematic (Cohen, 2015:33), to which it was, in turn, pointed out that this particular form of free speech (satire) evolved *in order* to equalise, to challenge power and its abuse (e.g. Will Self, R4, 6/1/15). That is, the playing field is inherently uneven, and satire's role is to attempt to even it out.

While the Hebdo attack, other anti-state violence since, and the ensuing media discussions have forced prominent British Muslim people to go on public record denouncing the "brainwashing" of the group calling themselves Islamic State (Townsend, 2015), the Donald Trump affair illustrates this topical intersection of freedom of speech, national values and offensiveness in an entirely different way. Public protest in the UK following Trump's call for Muslims to be barred from entry to the US resulted in the required number of petition signatories to mandate a Parliamentary debate (Hansard, 2016), giving the lie as the House acknowledged to the 'apathetic public' narrative. In this debate, British "shared values" were cited and responded to as if they were implicitly understood. The debate measured freedom against responsibility in a well-balanced way, paying attention to impact, weighing individual against public good and citing Martin Luther King on freedom of speech. While this reference missed the point in some cases (for instance, missing the point that such freedom is not absolute), Naz Shah drew on the principles of enlightened democracy to do a much better job: "Our lives begin to end the day we become silent about things that matter".

## 76  Education for community citizenship

The most significant contributions expanded on the *divisive* nature of Trump's comments and on the extent to which it is the acceptability of such irresponsible comments depends largely on their *impact*. The point was made repeatedly that running for US president, so far from meaning you are above the law, means that airing views contravening Home Office guidance and fanning flames of discord demand an official response:

> We are not talking about just any man. This is a man with an extremely high profile who has been involved in the American show-business industry for years – a man who is now interviewing for the most important job in the world. His words are not comical. His words are not funny. His words are poisonous and risk inflaming tensions between vulnerable communities.
> (Hansard, 2016; Siddiq, Column 444WH)

The potential for danger was underlined by Tasmina Sheikh:

> Trump's statements have bolstered the twisted narrative promoted by the terrorist cult Daesh and others, which pits the west against the Muslim faith. He has fuelled racial tensions across the world, while undermining the national security of the US and the UK. Indeed, in the words of Pentagon spokesman Peter Cook at the time Mr Trump made his statement: 'anything that bolsters ISIL's narrative and pits the United States against the Muslim faith is certainly not only contrary to our values but contrary to our national security.'
> (Column 455WH)

Sheikh also made a heartfelt and personal point about cultural inclusion:

> [I]t is important for Members here to understand what it is like for Muslims in this country when people take comments made by those such as Mr Trump as expressing genuine concerns about those of us who practise the Muslim faith. That is a very uncomfortable place to be in, . . . Mr Trump condemns my family.
> (Column 455WH)

But there was one comment that captured the need for a genuinely critically multicultural education in promoting understanding:

> What has Donald Trump actually said? . . . "51% of those polled, 'agreed that Muslims in America should have the choice of being governed according to Shariah'." He said: "Shariah authorizes such atrocities as murder against non-believers who won't convert, beheadings and more unthinkable acts that pose great harm to Americans, especially women." It is little wonder that after those remarks a rise in attacks against Muslims in America was recorded.
> (Jack Dromey, Column 459WH)

Media incitement to 'other', associated with Trump's presidential campaign or the UK's EU referendum, is both morally wrong given the contexts of unequal power and irresponsible in a climate of heightened militarism, tension and fear.

## Education and cosmopolitanism

The parliamentary Trump debate in Dromey's example of gross misunderstanding and misrepresentation of *Shari'ah* law and the uncomprehending protest voting we saw in the EU referendum both underline the need for exposure to other ideas, and to content, as the basis for rational and open debate about these differences. Instead of 'othering' in a fear-inducing way, critically multicultural, cosmopolitan education both celebrates and explores differences, intelligently and truthfully, from a position of common/shared ground. State-controlled, competitive schooling has been limited in its ability or inclination to do this. A decade ago, in the US context, "[m]ost high school . . . classes do not teach students to analyse multiple sources of conflict or to see conflict from multiple perspectives" (Smith and Fairman, in Noddings, 2005:41). While in the UK, the Ajegbo Commission found that history teaching was "too Eurocentric", with 'other' viewpoints not addressed, despite the availability of Runnymede's "practical guide for use by teachers, to promote 'race' equality in schools" (Ajegbo:110, Appendix 2, citing Runnymede, 2003).

However, there are signs of progress. Recent ACT advice (2014) on 'Diversity and Values' ticks several critical multiculturalism boxes:

> This concept also links to human rights. In the Citizenship curriculum of 2007/8 this concept was more explicit and linked strongly to living in the UK. It also related to policies and issues about cohesive communities and resilience, to prevention of extremism and inclination towards terrorism. However, exploring diversity must not become trite and focused on difference as a negative or folkloric tradition. It must be deep and meaningful, and enable pupils to ask critical and reflective questions about rights and respect, about difference, tradition, culture, custom, religion, ethnicity, and the values and ethical perspectives people have. Pupils should engage with learning that helps in appreciating diverse perspectives on global issues and how identities affect opinions and perspectives, understanding the nature of prejudice and discrimination and how they can be challenged and combated. Interdependence links to how people, places, economies and environments are all inextricably interrelated, and that choices and events have repercussions on a global scale. In a way it brings together all the above concepts back to the first, that of global Citizenship.

Three main ways of promoting understanding and appreciation of difference are identified run as themes across the critical multiculturalism literature and policy advice: first, content across the curriculum that enlightens about locatedness and interconnectedness; second, full use of schools and universities as heterotopic spaces; and, third, engagement with society outside the classroom in recognition of the socially embedded nature of schools and educational institutions. When breaking down these themes, it is argued that curriculum content should provide understanding through clear narrative of the ways that identities and cultures have always shifted and combined, which we have forgotten in our fear-driven prioritisation of competing. Since we know that state-sanctioned, official counter-narratives are "unappealing and unsuccessful" (Atran, 2015), this narrative needs to be diversely sourced and to combine historical, geographical and legal understandings of the relationships between the local, national and international. It needs to teach about diversity locally *and* globally; the teaching of British history should incorporate links with other histories as well as reflecting the demographic diversity of British history. And finally, this approach to teaching from diverse perspectives also needs, as Ajegbo cautioned, "to be woven through a subject and a school curriculum rather than bolted on" (2007:39).

The spatial element of such a project has several layers. For a start, it is clear that critical discourse, to be effective and meaningful, needs to take place equally inside and outside the classroom. Implicitly, it also involves crossing boundaries in terms of encouraging 'dialogue through disagreement', "not through some vacuous notion of avoiding offence at all costs but through the informed and reasoned exchange of views" (Leighton, 2012:65) and "making the classroom a democratic setting where everybody feels a responsibility to contribute" (Hooks, 1994:39). Reconceiving schools and classrooms as heterotopic 'thirdspaces' and 'contact zones' is not only good classic pedagogy (Piaget, Vygotsky, Bruner, Montessori), but also addresses the difficulties around *teaching* what we have discussed as arbitrary 'values' without indoctrinating.

Models for what such a heterotopic approach to education might look like in practice are also various. On the level of pedagogy, an international network of activists has ensured that OSDE methodology, requiring structured 'Critical engagement' with "alternative worldviews, knowledge bases and values systems" (Warwick:140), has been taken up by and in schools, grass-roots educational movements and universities (http://www.osdemethodology.org.uk/partners.html). A place-oriented approach to educating for citizenship would also use the 'larger spaces' outside the classroom, like the 'capacious school ethos' of the Creative Partnerships project discussed in the previous chapter. Exposing students to lives other than their own, through community involvement and international exchange, while reflexively drawing on their own experiences in relation to big global as well as local issues can help students to learn through direct experience what it is like to live the circumstantially framed lives of people that they would not normally encounter (Davies et al., 2005a). In this spirit, combatting both racism and sexism were core targets in the world-renowned and formalised Porto Alegre Citizen School Project (Gandin, 2007), while the Muslim Council of Britain recently announced a scheme to encourage more than 80 mosques across the country to invite non-Muslims to take "tours, talks and tea" on an annual Visit My Day (Sherwood, 2016). Langran has argued that these kinds of activities are ways for students to "become temporary citizens of another community" (Langran et al., 2009). But this misses the critical multicultural point; it is not about being in or out, an honorary or temporary 'citizen'. Rather, the 'citizenship' value of educational engagement with geographically and culturally diverse lives is that it promotes awareness of intersecting communities, boundaries and the multiple ways these can be crossed and enrich.

So why are such structured boundary-crossing approaches not happening automatically? As ever, ignorance and fear are powerful constraining forces, structurally and culturally, each feeding the other. Official advice and rhetoric notwithstanding, helping youngsters to appreciate difference and to build identities, skills and social roles that look both inwards and outwards relies in large part on teachers. Teachers' 'ignorance' has been a persistent theme in policy literature, and is suggested in the unhelpful reply cited by Ajegbo:

> We did about the Civil Rights movement. I asked her (teacher) if there were any Indian people there and she said it wasn't what we were studying – so I said when will we study it and she didn't answer me.
>
> (Ajegbo, year 9 pupil:39)

But given its close relationship, fear may be the cause for much of what passes as 'ignorance'. The Ajegbo Report acknowledges that teachers were *afraid* of teaching about what they did not know about, and it can be hard for teachers to navigate the difficulties and contradictions inherent to ethnic and language issues, especially when you are supposed to be encouraging open debate in such an ethical, political and cultural minefield. Official exhortation and now legal obligation to 'apply' Prevent guidelines, for instance, both draws on and feeds heightened fear – of insecurity, surveillance and difference. Neither is misapplication of Prevent guidelines limited to teachers, to wit the clumsy (and "now notorious", CF, 2015) tool used by Prevent to help identify problem children: "Local council accused of racism after quizzing young children on race and religion with survey critics claim is clearly aimed at Muslims" (Ward, 2015).

Notwithstanding these constraints, education *has* been put to the service of community cohesion in a range of diverse settings in projects that have simply got on with the business of renegotiating old and new nationalisms, narratives, identities and communities in different ways, some grass roots, some with official endorsement and some even outlawed. The Middle East has been the site of much sectarian fighting. It is also, however, the site, and focus, of various attempts to promote peace and shared place-based, future-oriented, citizenship through education. The media have commended political power-sharing, such as March 2013 elections making 'The Joint List' Arab and Arab–Jewish alliance the third-largest party in the Knesset, cross-cultural awareness-raising projects. They have also charted the evolution of Edward Said's and Daniel Barenboim's East–West Divan, and even sporadically reported the conflicts between the Turkish state and the Gulen Movement, whose declared commitment to education stresses dialogue, peace and multiculturalism in place of competitive advantage has inspired international schools on the lookout for a modern, tolerant and commercially savvy Islamic-inspired educational model. But slipping under the wire of media attention is low-profile cultural–educational *linking* work, such as that conducted under the Creative Partnerships scheme in the form of a UK–Lebanon school partnership – an example of creating cross-cultural competence and capital through intercultural exchange, instilling awareness in children of both cultural differences and similarities and allowing these children to discuss these freely (Manchester and Bragg, 2013).

However, it is Northern Ireland that provides a really insightful example of how the interaction between education and place can both reflect and shape citizenship in a context of political and cultural discord where the shifting approaches to balancing equality and diversity through educational pluralism shed light on the failure of underlying social pluralism. In Northern Ireland, where the concept of citizenship is complicated enough, education (through a frame of broadly 'pluralist' policy) has been both cause and solution to community disharmony. The need for exclusive ethnonationalist belonging against a background of economic and military insecurity has produced two 'nationalisms' (British and Irish) and a deep fault line. Smith captures the challenge: "As there is no consensus on nationality . . . or even the legitimacy of the state itself . . . Any civic or citizenship education curriculum must go beyond simple 'patriotic' models . . ." (Smith, 2003:24). By 2011, of a total recorded population of 105,650, 47,519 (45 per cent) were Catholic, 52,605 (50 per cent) Protestant or other Christian and only 893 (0.85 per cent) 'Other' (http://www.nisra.gov.uk/census/2011Census.html). But of Parekh's five models of managing equality and diversity, only two seem to have been in real contention in: pluralism and separatism.

But the polarisation is not entirely due to these demographics. Northern Irish politics, culture(s), religion(s) and place(s) are intertwined. British rule had been established through most of Ireland by the 17th century. There were many rebellions, with the Easter Rising of 1916 one of the most famous, for the apparently pointlessness of the bloodshed at a time when there were already well-developed negotiations towards independent sovereignty. In 1921, however, a compromise was agreed in the declaration of the Irish Free State, with a parliament in Dublin and a truce based on the establishment of the British province of Northern Ireland that included the six counties where there appeared to be a majority of unionist (mostly Protestant) inhabitants. Far from bringing peace, however, what the division succeeded in doing was sealing the link between culture, religion and political allegiance. Thus, not only have unionist (mostly Protestant) fears of assimilation and Catholic resentment at centuries of marginalisation continued to undergird often violent politics and impede social policy in the north, leading to the eruption of the 'Troubles' in the 1960s and 1970s, but the Irish (Free State) Constitution of 1939 also reacted by institutionalising and privileging Catholicism. Among the towns and cities in Northern Ireland, Derry/Londonderry more than Belfast has been a crucible of discord and dissent, and because of their different histories, roles and demographics, "[s]ectarianism in Derry Londonderry . . . is differentiated from sectarianism in Liverpool – or indeed Belfast . . ." (Smyth and Moore, 1996:2). It was no accident that Derry was the locus of the 1960s revolt; it had a long history of discrimination, unlike Belfast a majority Catholic population, and its proximity to the Irish Free State border included family cross-border ties.

Despite this deep-rooted sectarianism that has also drawn lines across the region, there are ways in which spatial awareness is also key to the complex process of post-Troubles *Northern* Irish identity building. Awareness of the potential of this small shared space has triggered a shift (albeit uneven) from what has seminally been called 'resistance identity' to 'project identity' building (Castells,

1997). Since the Good Friday Agreement (GFA), debates over values and politics, the prioritisation of tradition and now difficulty opening up and integrating new arrivals such as Chinese and Eastern European immigrants has mixed with a booming food culture and European connections, producing an iterative inwards and outwards process of both city- and province-based Northern Irish identity. Even in Derry, where signs of a new urban pride have been bolstered by EU money for rebuilding and also nomination as the UK's City of Culture in 2013, sharing stories of a shared conflict through the theatre and the People's Gallery testify to an emerging sense of shared ownership rather than preoccupation with internal differences and memories of resisting British imperialism appear to melt away, piece by piece, into a new identity, a redefined position in global society and a transformed social structure – the core elements of Castells's 'project identity'.

This project of place-based Northern Ireland identity construction has not only relied on political~military agreements and EU money, though. Education has been key (along with shared creative endeavour, language policy and legal and restorative justice measures) to an emerging sense of citizenship based on living together – just as it was key to sparking the Troubles in the 1960s. The beginning of the Troubles had a lot to do with the way that free education along with the availability of television brought awareness to young Catholics of the existence of injustice, the ways that inequality works, and to their rights as citizens. Higher education in Northern Ireland was like elsewhere deeply political, and its politics reflected the sectarian schism. Queen's Colleges at Belfast, Cork, and Galway were established in 1845, and in 1850 they were united as the Queen's University of Ireland. The *Catholic* University of Ireland was created as an independent university in 1854 for the education of Catholics but was not granted degree-awarding powers. In 1880, the Queens University of Ireland was replaced by the Royal University of Ireland as a degree-awarding body, on the model of the University of London. The Catholic University became the University College Dublin and separately, in 1882, St Patrick's College, Maynooth. Eventually, the Irish Universities Act of 1908 formed the National University of Ireland – a federal university system of the constituent institutions that included the Catholic University in Dublin, Maynooth College and the previous Queens Colleges of Galway and Cork (later to be universities). The secular Queen's University of Belfast remained separate. Growing sectarianism and economic injustices across Ireland meant that the student bodies at these institutions were largely self-selecting, with few Catholics attending secular, and royalist~unionist, Queens University, even if they had not been subjected to discrimination and had been able to afford it. The 1947 Education Act of NI was modelled on Britain's Butler Act, mandating the right to free schooling for all. This increased participation in secondary schooling and opened up the possibility of higher education on merit. Although Queens University does not publish data on the religious affiliation of its students, it is estimated that between 1958 and the 1990s, Catholic representation amongst undergraduates at Queens rose from about 22 per cent to 54 per cent (Taylor, 1988). The increased demand for education led to a recommendation in 1965 in the form of the Lockwood Report that second university be built in Northern Ireland. A campaign to have this second university established in mainly Catholic city of Derry (also known as Londonderry by Unionists) was unsuccessful. For what are widely seen to be political-religious reasons, 'Ulster University' was established in (reasonably) nearby Coleraine. Media reports suggest that the disappointment felt across Derry actually went some way to uniting the people of Derry (*Derry Journal*, Feb. 1965).

Prominent in this campaign and widely cited as the personification of this case of education for critical consciousness was John Hume, a Derry schoolteacher educated at St Patrick's College in Maynooth. Hume gave up his former commitment to separatist nationalism in order to become a leading figure in the late 1960s' civil rights movement with both the Northern Ireland Civil Rights Association (NICRA), which was challenging the unrepresentative government, and the Derry Citizen's Action Committee (DCAC), which was less confrontationally aimed specifically at a *local* campaign to improve the situation in Derry.

In spreading across the population, the civil rights movement foundered in the morass of protracted sectarian conflict, but many of its aspirations were to become embodied in the eventual Good Friday Agreement (GFA) that in 1998 set out an agreed (political and sub-political) commitment to equal rights and respect for diverse cultures and a 'culture of tolerance':

> The two Governments recognise the birthright of all the people of Northern Ireland to identify themselves and be accepted as Irish or British, or both, as they may choose, and accordingly confirm that their right to hold both British and Irish citizenship . . .
>
> (The Belfast [Good Friday] Agreement, 10 April 1998, Article 1 [vi])

The GFA was accompanied by a raft of confidence-building measures, to go alongside decommissioning and demilitarisation and prisoner release scheme. As befits a context where 'citizenship' was felt in the areas where it was most absent – in terms of legal and political rights. These included democratic political structures such as the new devolution-enabled legislative assembly. In this, political 'power sharing' was tightly structured in the form of proportional representation. 'Democratic' and representative systems of justice and policing sought to correct the under-representation of Catholics through a 50:50, positive discrimination recruitment policy. The justification in this case was also the immediate pragmatic need for a more representative force to help establish and maintain peace on the streets. The establishment of an Equality Commission in 2000 brought statutory responsibility to all public bodies to implement anti-discrimination legislation.

Given the deep-rooted sectarian divisions and mistrust, however, such government legislation for equality was inevitably going to be seen as tinkering – irrelevant and removed from the lived experiences and problems of those still in the grip of sectarianism. An extensive ethnographic and action research project among the sectarian enclaves of Derry aimed at promoting intra-community dialogue through sharing the data with those communities has located sectarianism in an axis of "systems of subordination" including sexism, racism and class (Smyth, 1994:1). The project found that the reasons why people chose to either stay in or leave enclaves were a mixture of practical and ideological. They left because of poor housing, anti-social behaviour and intimidation. But why they stay more interesting. The study participants cited commitment to the area, stability, a sense of the past and familiarity but also that it felt safer to engage in open dialogue within the enclave areas, seen as 'safe' environments: "Being seen to talk to the 'other side' is . . . seen as risky, and potentially disloyal" (Smyth,1994:22). As the levels of violence do not support such a feeling, Smyth hypothesises that fear is being used as a cover for collective identity taking the form of bigotry: "Precisely because these communities formed and consolidated around safety issues and gathered together against an outside threat, the collective identity and consciousness is very strong" (Smyth, 1994:25). These are communities formed in opposition to 'the other', with expressed religiously and politically.

This deep-rooted sociocultural sectarianism, which in 2002 saw 90 per cent of six-year-olds aware of the community divide and a third making sectarian comments (Connolly et al., 2002), was recognised in the anti-discrimination legislation. The GFA was also therefore accompanied in 1989 by Education Reform (NI) Order. Integrated schooling was seen as the key in a place where Catholics had long gone to Catholic schools and Protestants to Protestant schools to tackling the problem on a sociocultural level, despite reservations, circulated at the time, about the difference it would make (Smyth and Moore, 1996). However, in a context where identity narratives were and are really important, yet where "[n]either British nor Irish national identity provides the basis for a 'patriotic' model of citizenship that could be accepted in all schools" (Smith, 2003:15), the GFA adopted a strongly "pluralist approach" to integration, by which it meant structured equal respect accorded to both cultures, including religion, language and traditions. The reasons parents have given for choosing to send their children to integrated schools reflect pedagogic and ideological beliefs about the centrality of education to citizenship and social cohesion, in the sense of "[w]e'll send (our children) to an integrated school because education is where it all starts" (Gault, 2012). Yet progress has been slow. By 2003 there were fewer than 5 per cent of children in integrated schools (Smith, 2003). It is hard to find reliable, up-to-date statistics, even from the Northern Ireland Council for Integrated Education (NICIE). Though a piece of investigative journalism in 2012 using the Freedom of Information Act to obtain Department of Education data found that "[i]ntegrated school pupil numbers have increased from 8,154 to 21,170 between the two school years" (1997–1998 and 2011–2012). However, it also found that "493 schools in the 2011/12 year educated almost exclusively pupils of just one religion (95% or more) – compared to 827 schools in 1997/98" (Torney, 2012).

The slow take-up of integrated schooling is partly explained by the continued segregation of heavily relied-on public housing in Northern Ireland. However, progress is also impeded by complex attitudes to change, and the way attitudes to change themselves become cultural capital in such a divided society. A survey, for instance, found more Catholic support than Protestant for the idea that schools should engage with political issues (Gallagher and Smith, 2002). Differential buy-in between the two communities (to either embrace or resist change) itself becomes culturally defining, and part of this mistrust is due to cynicism about official use of the word *equality*. As Smith explains,

> [e]ven where considerable effort has gone into the creation of integrated schools with pupils enrolled from both communities, this is no guarantee that issues of equality and diversity will be reflected in the public spaces and communal discourses of such institutions.
>
> (Smith, 2003:29)

The mistrust is underscored by a similar fault line in the teaching profession, central as we have discussed to actually driving through policies, curricula and pedagogies that will create critical consciousness. Catholic and Protestant teacher training in Northern Ireland are still separate. Stranmillis University College and St Mary's University College are the two main teacher-training providers in Northern Ireland for primary teaching, while Queens and Ulster Universities train for the secondary sector. Recent proposals to integrate teacher training were quickly objected to by both sides, citing ongoing social injustices against which only they, from their partial positions, could provide the necessary bulwark (Meredith, 2015).

A more recent attempt to bridge the gap between full integration and none in Northern Ireland has its roots in 'critically multiculturalist' approaches. The 'Shared Education Programme' was introduced in 2007 with a view to acknowledging and addressing the issues of bitterness and mistrust that segregated schooling was felt to be ignoring (Hughes and Loader, 2015). The programme draws on earlier pre-GFA attempts to impose 'Education for Mutual Understanding' and 'Cultural Heritage' as statutory themes (NICC, 1990). Much like the frustration in English efforts to impose the statutory subject of Citizenship, teachers' reluctance to address difficult but potentially productive topics meant that the innovation had limited impact (Smith, 2003:22). The follow-up attempt, a Citizenship Foundation–supported pilot project to develop a 'citizenship education' curriculum, with 'Mutual understanding in the local and wider community' at Key Stages 1 and 2 and 'Local and Global C/ship' at Key Stages 3 and 4, was initially up to individual schools to decide when and if to join the programme. Writing about the curriculum in its early days, Smith notes its defining features as "less prescription about the programme of study to be followed or the time that must be devoted to citizenship education", its inquiry-based pedagogy (into such issues as volunteering and the police) and its reliance on materials developed by local voluntary organisations (Smith, 2003:26). In a climate of pervasive suspicion, such a recipe does not suggest overwhelming buy-in. In the Northern Ireland context then, the challenges posed by schools' competitive orientation, prescriptive curricula and performative teaching cultures are compounded, as Smith notes, by the overwhelming error of expecting pupils to engage freely in debating such issues as if all was fine outside (Smith, 2003:27).

But there are some distinctive approaches rooted in greater acknowledgement of the importance of grass-roots involvement in change, bonding over shared cultural heritage, some of which involves critically excavating the contested nature of this heritage. 'Prison to Peace' is a social and education innovation sponsored by the EU in 2009 (McGearty and Buchanan-Smith, 2012), aiming through organised personal contact with ex-political prisoners on different sides of the conflict to promote understanding in a discursive and direct way of the local history of discord and contested identities, through exploring why and how people became involved in conflict and to "demonstrate to young people alternative ways of dealing with conflict which do not necessarily require individuals to give up their political aspirations or cultural identity" (Emerson et al., 2014:4). The programme was also developed for use in the Key Stage 3 (KS3) History curriculum and the Key Stage 4 (KS4) Local and Global Citizenship curriculum in Northern Ireland. KS4 Citizenship focuses on promoting understanding of the challenges of diversity and inclusion, and teaches about the roles of grass-roots organisations, government, non-governmental organisations and other democratic institutions, while KS3 History asks pupils to explore "how history has affected their personal identity, culture and lifestyle and how history has been selectively interpreted to create stereotypical perceptions and to justify views and actions" (Emerson et al., 2014:19). By bridging these two curricula, the programme was intended to help young people explore how to contribute to the place where they live, by drawing positively on their understanding of links between the past and present, and between different cultures and traditions.

Evaluation of the educational impact of Prison to Peace notes that participation produced "a more nuanced understanding of the complexity of conflict, . . . increased . . . knowledge of the Troubles, as well as their support for non-violent means to deal with conflict. Additionally, the programme has increased young peoples' likeliness to participate positively in political activities, as measured by several indicators, i.e. their likeliness to participate in democratic activities in school, their tendency to talk to others about politics and their frequency of information seeking. Furthermore, although not considered as one of the main outcomes, the programme has reduced sectarian prejudice" (Emerson et al., 2014:45 & 48). However, it is emphasised that these positive results were best achieved when certain conditions were met, most notable among which are careful coordination institutional commitment, including commitment to building the relationships with the ex-political prisoners involved (Emerson et al., 2014:100).

Another form of shared, and contested, heritage is, of course, linguistic. The way language is being used in Northern Ireland is unique, with almost a struggle between state and citizens for control of this cultural resource. Yet while engagement with the Irish language appears to be pointing towards genuine recognition of shared place and heritage, it is not unproblematic. On one hand, GFA support for the Irish language has led to official bilingual policies that are similar to those in Wales. However, the widespread and long-standing use of English as lingua franca has mean that this has been very costly, disproportionately in relation to the numbers of people who value or use Irish. Other inhabitants see official bilingualism as divisive, drawing attention in the same way that positive discrimination and ratios do to difference. But a recent development has been the establishment in affluent areas of Irish-language schools for both Catholic and Protestant citizens (Whelan, 2013). Overall, the postmodern use of the Irish language in this way is one manifestation of how the more cosmopolitan and better-educated citizens are seeking to establish a romantic but *inclusive* Irish cultural identity.

The Northern Ireland citizenship project shows that 'identity' need not be ethno-religious-nationalist. It also, therefore, provides an interesting illustration of the limitations of broadly 'pluralist' policies to manage social divisions. Sociopolitically conditioned fear of submission to authority, of going outside tight sectarian community boundaries, makes self-imposed segregation the default position for many people, particularly those with least social and cultural capital. State policies that mix *imposed* attempts to integrate on one level, while undermining this on other levels with *categorical* pluralism that segregates, 'others' and alienates, continue to send mixed messages that consolidate mistrust.

Continued segregation~separatism is mostly seen as negative, "a symbolic labelling process" used "as an ideological justification for discrimination, community conflict and political violence" (Sugden and Bairner, 1993). Yet there is also an acknowledgement that segregation "as a strategy" (i.e. not a principle) can be useful, as both "a method of coping with violence and conflict" (Smyth, 1995:15), and preserving the integrity of subcommunities. Subcommunity events such as Orange Day bonfires (impoverished enclave Unionist communities continue to burn symbols of Catholicism as effigies every 12 July in Orange Day 'celebrations') are among the ways that the economically and politically marginalised, both Nationalist and Loyalist, cling to exclusionary and defensive traditions. These may be horrific to the outsider but in the context provide pride and identity important in this context, though the dividing line between pride and aggression is hot-wired. The immediate follow-up of the 1998 'Integrating Education' working group (DoE, 1998) with a second called 'Educating for Diversity' (DoE, 1999) can be seen as a hasty response to the power of subcommunity, and that educational integration needed to acknowledge this. Back in 1996, this ideal certainly had currency – Smyth and Moore, for instance, calling for "urgent and special support" to ensure that The Fountain (a Protestant enclave) was to "survive culturally and socially" (1996:18) and actually (again – this was 1996 – before the GFA) discussing the "desirability of segregation". The options considered in the run-up to the GFA were to either "allow" or "support" increased segregation (Smyth and Moore, 1996:18). The violence inherent to such sectarianism was taken for granted, as a reflection of the violent wider context, rather than being cited as responsible for its perpetuation.

So what Northern Ireland does most clearly, perhaps, is illustrate the complexity of pluralism as broad approach. In many ways, the particular forms of pluralist policies here have been coded admissions of defeat – continued acceptance of the post-1916 ethno-religious construction of citizenship. Northern Ireland's version of pluralism has been criticised for promoting "an ethno-national group-based understanding of politics that is inherently illiberal", an extension of criticisms of the 'coercive' power-sharing approach that has been called 'consociationalism' (Taylor, 2006:217). This strategic outcome-focused attempt to blend liberal integration with pluralism appears to have produced a cultural response in which internal boundaries in this small, shared space have continued to be used as tools

– for defence, protest and incursion – and education has been drawn into the fray. On the other hand, proportional representation can allow space to adjust and come to terms with past wrongs, including disproportionate power and the abuse of this power, and educationally, 'pluralist' strategies that are accompanied by critical excavation of a shared past can seem more realistic than a form of 'integration' that attempts to draw a veil over fractures but actually leaves them festering.

## Reconciling equality and diversity through critical multicultural education?

We have seen in this chapter changing contexts where mounting ideological cracks have caused communities to rupture into fighting over resources, the right to name themselves and input into wider policy but with slivers of light provided by an understanding of shared space, border-crossing and education working as a resource for social transformation. Economic instability combined with more structurally and technologically enabled ways of crossing borders has led to historically unprecedented levels and patterns of migration, shifting boundaries, less resource, more inequality and resurgent protest politics, which has led to some complex processes of renegotiating both collective identity and the relationships between policy-makers and grass roots.

In Northern Ireland, culturally and materially impoverished Loyalist communities burn symbols of Catholicism as effigies, while the worldwide cultural polarisation and increase in largely but not exclusively Islamophobic racism has according to Prevent statistics increased exponentially since the November 2015 terrorist attacks. Prevent have warned that the increase in xenophobic messages fuelled by fear and ignorance will further marginalise more young people of different backgrounds and cultures, leaving more people open to the sort of exploitation that forms the basis of totalitarian extremist ideological recruitment campaigns. The causal link between fear and violent xenophobia accompanied by wide-ranging risk aversion underline the need for an identity framework that is defined by place rather than social class or ethnonationalism.

Yet the same examples also reveal the irrepressibility of dissent, and the ways that grass-roots mobilisation has been key to creating new frameworks for belonging as community-based efforts to re-frame citizenship as inclusive shared decision-making and endeavour makes up for the inadequacies of policy attempts. The Northern Ireland story to date presents another case of 'global citizenship' that comprises a multitude of local communities united in their differences through local involvement. Human, cultural and economic capital have been somewhat freed from artificially delineated or powerfully imported *nation-state* shackles and traditional emphasis on competitive trading/transaction. Grounded instead in local cultures and we can see how capital can be fed into collective contributory systems for the good of the community you *find yourself in*. Acknowledging the complex and changing, rather than polarised, flow of experiences and imaginaries entails admitting different experiences of both community and marginalisation. Community identities can be both backward-looking and forward-looking, drawing on whatever traditions, narratives are available.

If this is what is meant by 'pluralistic', fine. But the limits of separatist pluralism, which categorises divisively and draws a line under problems that cannot be solved, are well illustrated by the persistence in Northern Ireland of parallel structures and communities that above all underline the need to work together. The theoretical difficulty of applying any one model (plural or separatist, assimilationist or multicultural), on either grass-roots or policy levels, as a solution or a description underlines the shortcomings of these models. None captures the complex, lived, local whole and none provides the policy solutions. We have seen that sectarianism is different in different contexts, and so, too, are the solutions. Like the Northern Irish language project – a merging of formal and grass-roots educational and cultural resources – grass-roots movements show what is possible, drawing as appropriate on both global and local cultural resources, recognising differences as positive attributes and bonding over what is shared as the way forward.

What is clear is that a sense of equal belonging, along with skills to challenge ignorance and hatred of difference, requires both equality-oriented political structures and an educational approach that is 'critically multicultural'. That is, to mediate such social transformation, education needs to provide skills and opportunities to influence policy, community engagement, inclusive narratives and an understanding of diversity as a resource.

Ideologically, this form of education would be grounded in a fluid shared narrative of belonging incorporating an inclusive 'national' identity, reaffirmed rather than dismissed as a relic, but one built rather than imposed, drawing on grass-roots understandings and movements. It would be equally grounded in a commitment to helping young people develop their *own* ideology through dialogue and exposure to people and ideas in order to understand both difference and what people have in common, to appreciate the importance of equality, to see through both hate speech and policy/structural inequalities and to develop the critical tools to do something about it. Such critical multiculturalism would reflect the fairly fundamental conceptual shift from tribal or ethnonationalistic identity to place-centred cosmopolitan identity. It would also involve learning the lessons of the past, addressing injustices, focusing on difference, freedom and (in)equality, on the ways that hegemony and conflict work and on political, ideological and epistemological conflict.

Structurally, a critically multicultural form of education that is going to make a positive difference needs to facilitate meaningful contact with communities outside the school or university, local and global, and provide opportunities for students to influence policy both inside and outside the school or university. When outside the classroom is conflicted, unequal and frightening, free classroom discussion can only work if those issues are addressed rather than smoothed over. The examples discussed here, particularly in conflicted Ireland, show structural and cultural approaches to both equipping students to play active roles in righting wrongs and to letting them talk productively about their feelings about these.

But the examples here also highlight the inevitable inconsistencies of seeking to shoehorn social policy into education policy or curriculum. In complex situations with injustices on many sides, clumsy attempts to right wrongs by decree (integrated schooling or bilingual education, for instance) appear to be relatively ineffective. Institutional buy-in and policy commitment to grass-roots knowledge, shaped through discussion to meet *shared* agendas, seem to hold out more promise. Above all, these examples underscore the impacts, good and bad, of education as a fluid space or interlocked network of spaces for disagreement that can lead to new understanding and shape more inclusive and cosmopolitan identities and narratives, with the state's role limited to *providing* that space rather than ideologically dictating what those identities and narratives should be.

# 5 Education and protest citizenship

The previous chapter discussed examples of democratic progress through education towards achieving societies based on equality and respect for diversity. And we have seen ways in which education is critical to both awareness of (in)justice and to providing the space and skills to do something about this, and that there are multiple stakeholders in this process. However, history has shown us that when freedom, inclusion and identity are in short supply and when the ideological and structural cracks that open up possibilities for change are not investigated *democratically*, social change is achieved instead through violent collision between powerful and grass-roots actors. In such scenarios, it is possible to see particular ways that *grass-roots* use of education is re-shaping society, for good and ill, opening up awareness of both the nature and possibility of social justice, and providing opportunities and skills to recognise, exploit and challenge the cracks in dominant narratives and structures.

Recent and growing academic interest in the radical function of higher education was recently brought into media focus by the reported (but perhaps not much noted) suicide of the Indian student Rohith Vemula. Vemula was a Dalit PhD student at the University of Hyderabad who was excluded, along with some of his peers, from campus rights including attending classes and using canteens and voting, as punishment for political activity highlighting caste inequalities. The story captures the double-edged nature of education for the marginalised, both oppressing and liberating, or *promising* liberation through ideas only for the weight of institutionalised education systems with their vested interests in maintaining inequalities to come crashing down. Interviewed following her son's death, Vemula's mother recounted the sacrifices she had made as a seamstress: "I earn 150 rupees (£1.50) a day. With that money, I brought my children to this level. We only had enough to eat one meal a day. Even in those conditions, he got this far" (Doshi, 2016). But without social and political justice, Vemula's learning and critical consciousness took him only into conflict where the odds were stacked against him. Among the many obstacles this student, like others from his background, encountered was a linguistic one. Doshi points out that while systems of positive discrimination make it possible for Dalits to enter top universities, their progress once there is compromised by having have been educated in the regional language of Telagu: "We have ideas," said a friend, "but we can't express them." Yet, said other friends, "You cannot kill an idea," and "He must be thinking, 'I couldn't do this in life, and now look at all this, after I'm gone.'"

How shall we understand this mixture of education, social injustice, knowledge, marginalisation, disaffection, protest? Even ACT is coming round to realising its importance, if not understanding its nature:

> Pupils must understand the nature of conflicts, their impact on development, and why there is a need for their resolution. They should know about different examples of conflict locally, nationally and internationally and different ways to resolve them, understanding that there are choices and consequences for others in conflict situations, and the importance of dialogue, tolerance, respect and empathy, negotiation, compromise and collaboration.
> (ACT, 2014)

Clearly it is not simply a matter of respect and empathy. And commendably, an article in ACT's magazine, *Teaching Citizenship*, acknowledges the media and political tendency to offer over-simplistic analyses of social unrest (Nicholson, 2012).

We have known for a long time that education can change one's sense of self in relation to the world through first critical transformation, and then 'conscientisation', which can lead to 'enlightened political participation', we should also be prepared for the inevitability that any attempt to shape consciousness will also have unintended consequences. Apple, for instance, reminds us of the ironies in the elite cultural politics of the Enlightenment, as captured by Voltaire: "One should take care to prevent the masses from learning to read" (Apple, 2000:50). Thus, widespread knowledge and understanding of inequality, combined with functional literacy, increased confidence and skills, also open the door to the possibility for power shifts and structural change as educated populations develop the confidence, skills and understanding to challenge hegemony and to shift the balance of power.

Notwithstanding overlaps, it is possible to identify three underlying models of the educational nature of this process: first, social injustice-driven disaffection; second, a more individualised search for meaning; and, third, subversive critical pedagogy. In the first, classic model, youth disaffection occurs when education promises but does not deliver, and dissent happens when people obtain the tools to question and evaluate political arguments but not the space or rewards in the form of empowering social policy or underlying social structures that would allow these educated people to determine their own lives. As well as revolt against a state felt as oppressive, including destruction of property that symbolises this oppression, anger combined with insecurity can also manifest in socially divisive 'othering' as a form of frustrated protest. The second model, by contrast, invokes the competition fetish thesis to argue that reductive, commodity-focused and performative neoliberalism has changed the relationship between education and dissent through fundamentally changing the nature of education. This explanation focuses on the risk-averse *removal* of critical outlets for students, which renders them ill equipped to deal constructively with difficult realities. Educational risk, particularly but not exclusively at the level of university, is increasingly only experienced in financial, not ideological, terms; increased *financial* stakeholder risk means that there is little willingness to engage critically with ideas in a way that carries the further risk of unknown outcomes. The large-scale removal of places to engage critically with real issues in an enlightened environment, to create, and to participate in shaping society has resulted in students feeling disenfranchised, disempowered and angry to find university no longer the opportunity that they thought they were getting. Although we tend to think this is a post-1990 phenomenon, it was documented presciently as long ago as 1970 (in relation to schools, at a time when there was not mass higher education). Freire argued that it was the imposition of official knowledge by those desperate to keep power via 'banking education' that produces cycles of oppression and violent uprising (1970), while Illich wrote about the contrast between this kind of disillusion and the older kind of 'alienation' felt by the socio-economically marginalised:

> Now young people are prealienated by schools that isolate them while they pretend to be both producers and consumers of their own knowledge, which is conceived of as a commodity put on the market in school.
>
> (Illich, 1970)

That is, if constructive and equal channels for the development and exercise of radical ideas are not available, destructive ones are found. Moreover, the widely supposed individualisation of politics has meant that such protests "more closely reflect life experiences than overarching class interests" (Sloam, 2013a). Finally, however, the third model returns to the critical pedagogic function of education and higher education, expounded by Freire, Giroux and Apple et al. This explanation focuses on the ways that critically engaged academics and teachers attempt to subvert powerful discourses and hegemonic structures through continuing to teach critical engagement despite the pressures to deliver measurable commodities.

## A century of student protest

The combination of economic injustice, youth, knowledge and freedom of voice (or its absence), therefore, have been critical in periodically rupturing and reshaping society throughout history. At the level of higher education especially, universities have been historically political in a variety of ways, providing students with the venue, symbolism, disposition and means to directly challenge the status quo. Four main social factors are threaded through the long history of student protest: highly educated populations; a largely youthful demographic; perceptions of government corruption or economic, social and political inequalities; and sociopolitical change that opens up cracks of opportunity.

From Nazi student fraternities in pre-Hitler Germany to the Arab Spring and the 2010 student protests in London, it is precisely the relationship among social (in)justice, youth, knowledge and freedom of voice that history has shown to be critical in rupturing and reshaping society. Germany welcomed Hitler in the 1930s because they were ready to. In a series of chilling parallels with the popularity today of extreme political candidates like Donald Trump, the Great Depression saw a period of introspection and ethnonationalistic 'identity' building. Nazi student fraternities were pivotal to the way this evolved, drawing equally on National Socialism and Fichtian German Romanticism as combined economic and cultural routes to overcoming adversity; outsiders including Jews and people who did not fit the mould were easy scapegoats. Shortly after the war, returning Japanese students started criticising university policies and then their government's economic policies before joining ideological forces with the Japanese Communist Party, which had opposed going to war (Kowalewski, 1982). In 1950s' Cuba, student anti-corruption protests broke out in against a government that permitted large-scale organised crime and prioritised international tourism at the expense of providing for the needs of locals, including an economy that provided jobs for graduates. Seeing all youth as potential revolutionaries, in 1956 the soon-to-be-overthrown dictator Batista closed Havana University. Many of the estimated 20,000 killed by Batista's secret police were students. In its wake, the Cuban Revolution paved the way for widespread student rebellion throughout the 1960s, including the overthrow in South Korea (1960) and Turkey (1971) of governments seen as oppressive, attempts to remove imperialist control in the Prague Spring of 1968, and widespread anti-capitalist, anti-authority protesting in the Paris Spring of the same year.

Different ingredients, resentment about the lack of economic share, government corruption, the experience of inequality and a dawning grasp of how things should (or could) be were spread unevenly across the rebellions of the 1960s. But they all came together in the various strands – the Free Speech Movement, 'Students for a Democratic Society', and the voting rights movement – of the 1960s' civil rights movement in America. The most well-known aspect of this movement was the three 'Selma to Montgomery Marches' of 1965. The previous year, the Voting Rights Act had ended legal segregation and permitted black people to vote. However, the ruling was not observed, and black people were still prevented in practice from actually registering to vote. Activists of the Dallas County Voters League protested against this violation of their rights, enlisting the cooperation of the Student Nonviolent Coordinating Committee, the Southern Christian Leadership Conference and the Reverend Martin Luther King. After local Methodist preacher Jimmie Lee Jackson was shot by a state trooper in Marion near Selma during a small, peaceful protest claiming the right to vote and later died, these groups united to vent the community's outrage at this illegal shooting by organising a large march on 7 March 1965 to the state capital, Montgomery. When the unarmed marchers were attacked, the event became known as the first 'Bloody Sunday'. The second march took place two days later. Although the police confronted the marchers, no physical blows were exchanged, and Martin Luther King persuaded the marchers to keep on the right side of the law by not provoking the police. That night, local white men beat to death another of the activists, James Reeb, a church minister from Boston. There was a national outcry at the televised breaches of both moral codes and the law by the police and this local mob in the face of the marchers' unblemished actions, and the president, Lyndon Johnson, was shamed into pushing through further legislation to guarantee that black citizens could exercise their legal right to vote.

Although there were many leaders in this movement, King's articulate leadership galvanised determination and wider support. And the ideas he drew on and embodied underscored a particular ideology, education and political activism relationship. King's belief that protest against injustice was both the duty and the right (as enshrined in many US state constitutions) of citizens became a major thread in many of his speeches, including those following the death of Jimmie Lee Jackson and the Bloody Sunday march. In fact, he had written much earlier about what he saw as the 'true' function of education, in which equality and citizenship were intrinsic, publicly decrying the view of education that equips the elite "with the proper instruments of exploitation so that they can forever trample over the masses." Rather, he expounded in true critical pedagogic manner, education should "train one for quick, resolute and effective thinking. To think incisively and to think for oneself . . . to save man from the morass of propaganda . . . to sift and weigh evidence, to discern the true from the false . . ." (Washington Post.com.blogs). Further echoing his near contemporaries Dewey, Lindsay and Freire, he explained the importance of what he called 'character', in the sense of "the accumulated experience of social living" as an essential accompaniment of intelligence. And in his acceptance speech on 14 March 1964 of the John Dewey Award from the United Federation of Teachers, for instance, he had spoken of the way that the fight for equal opportunity for education had been a central part of the fight for racial equality.

The 1960s' US civil rights movement prepared the ground in several ways for not only the more outward-looking anti–Vietnam War protests but also the Northern Ireland civil rights movement (NICRA), which shared many features – not only their own 'Bloody Sunday' but also long-standing segregation, social, political and economic marginalisation of a major demographic subgroup, and awareness among educated members of that subgroup of economic, political and cultural inequality. In both cases, education and TV had opened young people' minds up to not only the existence and nature of inequality, but also to the possibility of freedom and given them the understanding and skills to do something about claiming it. Moreover, the upwardly mobile and educated of Northern Ireland had seen the American civil rights marches and outcome on TV. Yet the way protest unfolded in the Northern Ireland civil rights movement was very different, becoming mired in decades of cyclical violence unlike the US case.

Leading protest at unfair distribution of public housing, John Hume had overseen several provincial marches, then a large march in Derry itself in October 1968, which led to the formal establishment of the DCAC. Police stopped this march and beat up MPs. The whole process was televised, and an inquiry ensued. A compromise allowed the Northern Irish government time to deliver on promises of more equitable distribution. However, over in Belfast, students responded differently. There, Catholics had just started to go to Queens University in numbers in order to experience the 'free' education brought about under the Butler Act. Seeing university as more than just getting a degree, they were eager to rebel. Bernadette Devlin, the other major civil rights figure whose image adorns walls in Derry today (and who was shortly to become Northern Ireland's first Catholic female MP in 1968), was a leader in the People's Democracy (PD), a Queens-based student group within the broad civil rights movement who opposed lack of economic equality and political representation. On 2 January 1969, the PD marched from Belfast to Derry proclaiming the state to be irreformable. The march was attacked en route, and as in America, images of students being hurt and police doing nothing to help were caught were by camera. The marchers arrived in Derry to great welcome and anti-state rioting in Bogside. The riot was stopped and police beat up people in their houses. In the wake of this, the DCAC was set up, so-called peace lines or security fences were built in Belfast and Derry, firmly delineating Catholic and Protestant areas, and those elements of NICRA who had elected not to join the student-led march of 1969, resumed their protests. In April of that year, following clashes between police and NICRA marchers, police attacked the Catholic Bogside estate, and a local man was severely beaten by police. He later died of his injuries, and his 'martyrdom' gave way to more anger, political opportunism and bombings. Orange marches in July provoked rioting in Belfast, and heavily armed police charged into Catholic areas, killing several people to widespread horror. In August, Apprentice Boys marches commemorating a historic Protestant victory at the Siege of Derry (1689) proved too provocative for Derry Catholics, who had been forbidden to march for civil rights. Several days' rioting erupted in Bogside (Bernadette Devlin among them) while civil rights protests were organised across the country to distract police. The strain on the police led to the involvement of the army and Westminster, as the Stormont government was unable to control the widespread political violence. The increased tensions associated specifically with NICRA culminated in Derry, in Northern Ireland's Bloody Sunday. On 30 January 1972, a NICRA-led anti-internment march in Derry ended when British paratroopers were called in to keep peace in the event of a Loyalist counter-demonstration, but they opened fire on the marchers, killing 14 and wounding more than a dozen others.

The different evolutions of the US and Northern Irish movements can be accounted for by the presence (or absence) of underlying shared ideological vision as distinct from mere anger. The Northern Irish movement's grounding in a more recent violent past and socio-economic marginalisation less mediated by ideological and humanitarian vision allowed it to be overtaken by uneducated militancy. In Northern Ireland, the revolutionary cause was taken over largely by paramilitary organisations such as but not limited to the Irish Republican Army (IRA) and large-scale violent unrest continued for the next three decades until the Good Friday Agreement in 1998. And since then, the province's complicated version of 'pluralist' (equal respect but largely separate) structures and relatively unsuccessful attempts to officially promote 'integration' continue to be accompanied by continued low-level sectarian violence and sectarian enclaves, walled in, with militaristic banners and murals depicting images of the 1960s riots.

In more recent times, 2010–2011 saw the eruption of a fresh wave of protest across a more networked world. Instability and unrest in the Arab Middle East are often assumed these days to have started with the now-failed Arab Spring, but actually long standing, as the region sits on various cultural, religious and political fault lines, and universities have been involved for a long time. Middle East student-led protest at foreign-led policy-making led first to Arab nationalism and then with the involvement of Iran to political Islamism. In 1908, Cairo University was established as a nationalistic, anti-imperialistic, secular 'Egyptian' university for 'the people' to compete with the religious imperialist Al-Azhar that trained young men to be administrators and clerics for the Ottoman regime. Lebanon's civil war was immediately preceded by a powerful student protest movement at the American University of Beirut, started by Christian missionaries and established on a religious fault line. Calling for social and political justice, recognition of the country's Arab roots and rejection of Western and Zionist imperialism in the Arab world, mainly Muslim student activists skirmished with conservative Christian students and led strikes and demonstrations against university policies and administrative actions. Even the anti-imperialist and anti-corruption impetus for the Iranian Revolution started in universities. In 1979, the Tehran University students' siege of the US Embassy, protesting US support for the shah (seen as corrupt, a US puppet, in the pocket of imperialists), was a tipping point in the early days of the Iranian revolution.

The Arab Spring of 2010–2011 erupted across several initial sites starting with Tunisia, then Egypt, Libya, Bahrain, Syria, Yemen, Morocco and Oman. These were all Arab states under tight central government control. They were also all countries with youthful (60 per cent under 30 was a widely cited statistic) and highly educated populations, and (rapidly, in some cases) rising demand for higher education, economic disenfranchisement and long-standing perceptions of government corruption. Although the rebellions were not portrayed as student-led, the student voice was far from silent as the youth rejected their elders' deference to the establishment and seized its chance to protest. In Bahrain, for instance, students both joined the collective protests and aired their own student-specific grievances in response to mooted plans for gender segregation at the country's main university. In spite of attempts in some quarters to portray the latest wave of revolt in Bahrain as a continuation of long-standing sectarian tension (Sunni–Shi'i), a range of causes were subsumed in the protest, which rejected religious extremism along with established political parties and economic injustices. Protesters in this wave as in earlier ones in Bahrain were campaigning for social and gender equality, and a political voice for minorities. Those protestors who represented their cause in the media present things as 'pro-change', nationalist and democratic (Abbas, 2011).

Elsewhere, the UK student riots of 2010–2011 against higher university fees were cited as evidence of the resurgence of protest politics against a recent context where we had been told that student radicalism was dead, and higher education was all about getting ahead in the system. At roughly the same time, in the summer of 2011, there were large youth riots in several English cities, sparked initially by an unlawful police killing, with obvious echoes of the triggers in both US and Northern Irish civil rights movements but characterised by widespread looting. These riots were widely attributed in the press to a lack of anywhere for young people to go. Economic recession was biting, and while youth clubs had been closed down, there was fresh scandal over government corruption (MPs fiddling their expenses). 'Who *does* the country belong to?' was an understandable response. "If the young are not initiated into the village, they will burn it down just to feel its warmth", was one journalist's summing up (McVeigh, 2011). While in Quebec and New York, students involved in local wings of the Occupy movement protested against the corporatisation of higher education.

## The state, education and 'located' or 'global' dissent

The causes of each of these waves of revolt are both politically circumstantial and intrinsic to the nature of higher education and its relationship with citizenship. Sectarianism is certainly involved, but rarely and never entirely the cause. Non-cohesive societies with a history of inequality can provide the fault line but unequal or clumsy interventionist policies make it worse. The ideational and physical aspects of belonging and identity appear equally implicated in the main conditions and catalysts for anti-government unrest, which combine economic disenfranchisement or inequality, political marginalisation and lack of voice, resentment of imperialist grip and perceptions of government corruption. It matters less who and what.

The complex and interwoven history of Middle East activism shows Arab and Islamic identities/causes sometimes connected, but also sometimes in opposition. In all cases, the focus of dissent is an abuse of power felt in two ways: There is not enough to go around, and there is a lack of 'right to name ourselves'. It was possible to present the Arab Spring and the Northern Ireland Troubles as sectarian-religious because it was the marginalised demographic groups who were the angriest. In the recent UK student and youth protests, a common cause can be identified in the rolling back of the state and leaving certain groups feeling disenfranchised and disempowered.

Reducing the explanatory role of sectarianism goes some way to explaining the ineffectiveness of pluralist policies that categorise, thus perpetuating sectarianism, particularly when pluralism is used to stigmatise and justify forms of social, cultural and political exclusion. In response to further recent terrorist attacks in Paris on 13 November 2015, the media comment that it happened in "assimilationist France not multi-cultural UK" (ref.), implied that assimilation was an invalid goal. However, the comment reflected a misunderstanding of terrorism as a tactic, like rioting or protest, with a long history – "the language", as Martin Luther King said, "of the unheard." In a globalised arena, it matters less (long term) which country the target was but that there are people who feel excluded enough not to be able to find any other way of engaging with the polity.

The changing focus of student activism in the 21st century in the UK provides further illustration of just how situationally defined dissent and unrest is. Immediate socio-economic contexts shape not only the focus of the dissent but also its nature and its relationship with society: dissent, unrest, disorder, revolt, alienation, revolution, activism, militancy – each word represents a subtly different response to a situationally distinct problem. While protests of the 1960s and 1970s are widely referred to as 'student consciousness', idealistic and relatively optimistic, the activism of students who had the luxury to be so – 'time out', no fees and full grants at a time when the world seemed to be opening up, the 2010–2011 protests, by contrast, appear more economically driven, less about having a voice and using it to challenge society's values, but more about self-interest and demanding 'in' to full economic share (Sloam, 2013a). Thus the student riots and the London youth riots were highly individualised, consumer-driven versions of the same anger and economic disenfranchisement that resulted from two forms of neo-liberal policy. The student protests had less in common with the kind of *social* activism in support of a wider community that had motivated the historical protests from Germany to Iran.

This analysis throws into fresh focus important distinctions between education and mere 'information' – today as in these not too distant pasts. New media provide an unprecedented availability of mere 'information' and are opening up increased means to communicate outside pre-given and state-sanctioned channels. This has implications for both what education *can* do and what, conversely, it is possible to do *outside* the control of formal education. The transnational flow of radical and revolutionary ideas that in the past linked one movement to another reminds us of young people's thirst to learn about life elsewhere, to make connections and to use those connections to challenge what they are unhappy with in their immediate surroundings. New technologically enabled means of communicating allowed student disorder to spread in the 1960s from Cuba through Europe to the US where they merged with the civil rights and free speech movements and which, in turn, influenced student-led rebellion in 1960s Northern Ireland. TV drove anti-Vietnam war protests both by bringing the war's atrocities to the attention of students ready for a cause and by disseminating this message across the country and beyond. This focus on means, then, underscores the likely *increasingly* central role of ever-greater access to information, contacts and the outside formal educational environments. The World Wide Web has not only, as we discussed earlier, made it easier to circumvent hegemonic, localised power structures but also offered a form of (apparent) anonymity that has encouraged emergent protest groups to campaign against a movable feast of things through technological means. It has also helped recent militaristic, violent so-called jihadism, which as some of the commentary has pointed out despite claims to be seeking to reinstate tradition is a very *modern* phenomenon.

What flows from this observation is a core question about the difference education (as distinct from mere knowledge exchange) *can* make to the nature of dissent and protest – to make protest more informed, and more strategically focused on the greater good rather than a mere howl of frustration. Several recent events underscore the extent to which the freer movement of ideas and people across borders makes it even more important that education promotes constructive dialogue and independent critical thinking, across and within these borders. Without this commitment to dialogue and understanding, there are multiple associated dangers. There's the danger as Soueif cautioned about the Egyptian revolution of "getting caught between . . . two enemies. The police state and the

(Muslim) Brotherhood are both hierarchical, patriarchal, militarised, centralist, dogmatic, conformist, exclusionary organisations. Both are built on obedience. Both hate critical thinking and debate" (Soueif, 2013). It is a position that many others have echoed, as we discussed in Chapter 3. There's also the danger as we have seen recently in the EU Referendum and subsequent political fallout of people using their political voice in the form of voting as a form of protest without understanding either the issues they are being consulted about, or what is in their own long-term interests. And there's the danger of not recognising extremism for what it is. While Pickles' contentious letter has its roots in the hypocritical form of conservatism that believes traditional views that just happen to be 'extreme' are fine and that it is *what* these extreme views are that matter. The more democratic view is that extremism is extremism is extremism; in contrast to reason-based 'radicalism', extremism rejects democracy and pluralism and is therefore not acceptable whatever the views are. (Murshad Ali on R4, 5:50pm, Weds, 11 March, 2015).

The related question is, Does such a form of education that *fails* to provide critical outlet actually contributing to more individualised, socially destructive dissent? Education that merely imparts information about how things are, without promoting understanding of *why*, or how to constructively *change* things, is seen across a range of accounts to be part of the problem. While dissent may be linked to *feelings* of marginalisation and deprivation, it seems that it is neither the *most* marginalised nor those most intellectually engaged in issues of inequality, who get dragged into militancy.

Anecdote after anecdote, violent extremists of the 21st century are reported to have studied engineering or computer science rather than social science (Hertog and Gambetta, 2009; Freedland, 2015; Groll, 2013). Hertog and Gambetta found that "among violent Islamists with a degree, individuals with an engineering education are three to four times more frequent than we would expect given the share of engineers among university students in Islamic countries". Of a group of 178 violent extremists whom the authors were able to trace the course of study, 78 (44 percent) were engineers. Hertog and Gambetta consider the hypothesis that "engineers are more likely to have certain personality traits that make radical Islamism more attractive to them.". However, an alternative explanation that once more underscores the vital role of education is that rather than innate personality traits, hard sciences like engineering are less likely to help intelligent people develop the critical skills necessary to challenge indoctrination and propaganda and see instead possibilities for productive, constructive ways of dealing with injustice. And in the cause of promoting peaceful resolution of conflict, this idea is far from new. The educational wing of the Peace Pledge Union, a pacifist London-based organisation with an educational wing, has been arguing this since its establishment in 1934. Prompted today by the work and rhetoric Prevent, the organisation argues that instead of surveillance and control, the educational solution is to offer more, better ideas and to encourage the sharing of information and open debate – which it does in the form of educational resources it shares, like Prison to Peace many of whose values it shares, to help pupils "learn to justify ideas with reasons" (http://www.ppu.org.uk/rtk/).

It would seem that it is not a particular ideology that attracts lost young people to violent movements, but the existence of *an* ideology – filling the gap left by risk-averse and ideologically empty state-approved forms of education. The series of alienating circumstances reported in the story of British IS~Daesh militant Mohammed Emwazi is far from unique: displacement, disillusion, a rise in extremist views and militancy. In a climate where more people are exposed to competitive marketing that promises but fails to deliver while these same people see all that others appear to have, both peaceful protest and militant groups will exploit this disillusion along with the desire of young people to belong and to have a purpose. In this sense, Roy may have a point when he argues that, "The question is not the radicalization of Islam, but the Islamization of radicalism." (Roy, 2016). A former IS imam explains,

> 'The young who came to us were not to be lectured at like witless children; they are for the most part understanding and compassionate, but misguided.' Again, there is discernible method in the Isis approach. Eager to recruit, the group may spend hundreds of hours trying to enlist a single individual, to learn how their personal problems and grievances fit into a universal theme of persecution against all Muslims.
>
> (Atran, 2015)

Many aspects of this, too, are far from new. The blood-cult ideology was central to the Easter Rising too – sacrifice as a form of rebellion against both the older generation and the establishment, with religion invoked for credibility in the way it always has been. The rallying cry of the French Revolution, too, was "liberte, egalite, fraternite ou *mort*". This preparedness to give everything for a cause, matched by the need to transcend unpleasant realities, is key to what is offered by such movements, as Salazar explains, also pointing out the similarities between the IS~Daesh phenomenon and the French Revolution in terms of the rest of the world's scathing response to the violence (Salazar, 2015).

Location in these examples is implicated in both the processes of identity construction and the resources to act on this. When people are either excluded or so displaced that they either do not know where they belong or feel their community-based identity threatened, the need to consolidate or build community and belonging can be filled by extremist groups, gangs and xenophobic protest. The sectarian-based class divide in Northern Ireland appears to have made integration much easier for the Middle Classes while the poor and marginalised – both Nationalist and Loyalist – cling to 'their' exclusionary and defensive traditions. The Northern Ireland revolt rapidly evolved into a very localised, complex yet territory-based conflict. Daesh/IS, on the other hand, has been created through a global Internet-enabled movement; are geographically, ideologically and nominally elusive; and have global ambitions. Yet there are ways in which its global reach underscores the 'located' essence of revolution. Although disembedded and borderless itself and within a broader wave of protest that is above all anti-state (as located power), seeking ironically to carve out its own state or caliphate in Iraq and Syria draws attention on to the importance of borders and boundaries. Not only does the effort to be everywhere actually underline the loss of territory (as status) grievance, but the group also needs its own territory for both pragmatic and symbolic tactical reasons: in order to isolate recruits during 'training' and in order to compete credibly with existing states. Politicians bent on military solutions are hoping that without a geographically located caliphate, this violent movement will have no more credibility than other disaffected groups have had in the past and will simply fragment.

## Education shaping citizenship – a counterpoint to violent extremism or catalyst for radical action?

So how can we best understand the role of education, good and bad, in forms of citizenship that involve (violently) challenging existing powers and structures? A mixture of education, circumstance and community provide the key to understanding the protest aspect of citizenship in today's shape-shifting world. Defined by local-temporal circumstances but universal mechanisms and processes, these examples have shared themes (territory, community, education, wisdom, leadership, social responsibility or individualism) but in different measures, while significant points of departure underscore the situational variability of dissenting and revolutionary movements. Social marginalisation and economic disenfranchisement combined with lack of opportunity for real, constructive community and political engagement provide the spur for the sense of dignity and pride that is partly provided by an identity narrative. The UK EU Referendum of 2016, the American civil rights movements, the IRA and Daesh/IS have in their time been rallying causes for those disaffected by social and political injustices and the feeling they have been forgotten. We can also see the often conflicting ways that education provides a crucible for social discontent today – ideational, demanding, controlling, an imposition, disappointing, and requiring the young to think and then to stop thinking too much. And through successive examples we have seen technologies of the day harnessed by informed and dissatisfied students to claim what they have learned are their democratic rights as national or global citizens. Whether it enlightens or merely informs, the more people are educated, the more the status quo is challenged as the exchange of ideas and information reveals cracks in which new ideas grow and take root in the further cracks revealed by social and political change.

What we have *not* done is find the right word to describe all of these examples of anti-state, local and anti-elite anger. The choice of label depends not only on the form of revolt (ballot box, peaceful rally, violent conflict or terrorism), and so on but also on the prevailing political narrative. It has been pointed out, for instance, that organisations such as the ANC, the PLO or the IRA, even of leaders such as Mandela, Palestinian leader Mahmoud Abbas or Yitzak Shamir have changed status in line with prevailing narratives:

> The sole common denominator of all these examples is not an ideology but a political grievance and a belief, right or wrong, that the odds were stacked against them and that violence was a necessity rather than a goal in and of

itself. Political violence is a tactic most often employed and frequently with success by those opposed to forces with overwhelming military might. . . . All of these men and groups who today are either respected political leaders or on their way to returning to the international fold saw political violence as a means of the underdog to secure their perceived rights and right an injustice rather than as a criminal philosophy and practice implicit in the use of the word terrorism.

(Dorsey, 2015)

That plenty of good and influential people have been 'radical', and that 'radicalising' is what critically transformative education does should add a further note of caution about inaccurate or unhelpful terminology. Applied to violent extremism, brainwashing, brutalisation and indoctrination the terms radicalisation and radicalism either confuse the issues or romanticise violence. In an inclusively democratic world, 'radicalism' should not be a problem.

Political leaders have debated the rights and wrongs of military response to a violent geographically disembedded ideological movement and its appeal to disaffected youth. The idea of bombing an ideology has been duly ridiculed. Policy actors as many have argued would spend their time better considering the causes of widespread anger and violence. Even supporters of military action against IS~Daesh have recently, if belatedly, acknowledged the need to confront ideological brainwashing through ideological engagement that attempts to draw on inclusive national and local community narratives. Truly 'inclusive' narratives are not divisive and do not polarise. Thus, answers to the questions so beloved by politicians, "What are our values?" and "What do we stand for?" are multiple. Instead of taking seeking to stamp out an official answer through successive citizenship commissions, a better question for government is surely, "How do we make sure that all citizens are included in shaping those values?"

The implications for education are clear enough: freedom without equality, understanding without the skills or means for self-determination, and knowledge and skills without understanding, are time bombs.

Every revolutionary movement has begun as a challenge to existing narratives, social systems and power structures. A far-sighted education policy would not only acknowledge but also actively embrace education's role in shaping consciousness and providing the critical skills needed to challenge indoctrination and raise awareness of the need for social change. The importance of forms of education that take seriously the responsibility to provide venue and means for inclusion and identity, structured space and support to engage with society and enact ideas, is underscored as much by its absence as by examples of when this works. It would be a policy far removed from the UK's so-called anti-radicalisation agenda, to which end purportedly 'educational' processes and instruments have been repurposed as if protecting people and institutions from challenging ideas were suddenly *the* point of education. Our schools and universities should *shape* society for the good of all rather than for some at the expense of others. They cannot do this without resisting the significant pressures to respond to either competitive markets or politics.

# 6 Feminist citizenship
## Education and change in gendered societies

In the Arab world, anti-imperialist revolt is not *all* that has been happening. The Arab region and Arab Gulf in particular are also very interesting on account of quite profound changes to the social structure and citizenship that have been happening more quietly in the background. One of these is the mass higher education of large numbers of women, many of whose mothers and grandmothers took for granted that they were excluded from many aspects of society. Chapter 2 discussed the ways that citizenship has appeared over time "as a discourse of masculinism" (Gouws, 2004). Today, it is still dismissed by feminist scholarship as part of a world shaped by male hegemony on account of the extent that women in many places are excluded or marginalised – financially, by sociocultural attitudes and by the lack of access to education and/or technology. Education's role in this hegemonic process still shifts – across the world – from providing the tools to challenge it, to reinforcing it.

But because of the way education at least opens up possibilities for citizens to challenge hegemonic knowledge and structures, this process has begun to shift the balance of power in many Arab countries. While women's voices were relatively unheard in coverage of Arab Spring unrest, there is creeping awareness that women are educated, informed and angry about social injustice on both local and global levels. There is cultural and political ambivalence; opportunity is constrained by ways in which male hegemony is educationally reinforced, education simultaneously opening up minds while impeding the exercise of freedom. Yet there are also cracks in this process, which as we have discussed provide opportunities for these women to build ". . . a new identity that redefines their position in society and, by so doing, seek the transformation of overall social structure" (Castells, 1997:8).

### Gendered citizenship, gendered space and education

Politics, power, public voice, space and representation form the centre of what can be seen as successive waves of feminist thought in varying ways. What is often called 'first-wave feminism' draws on a hegemonic theory that sees women as one class of subordinates, campaigning for women's full economic and legal citizenship in situations where they have been socio-economically marginalised. 'Second-wave feminism' focuses more on the gender-specific aspects of grass-roots and lived experiences and sees the ideal form of citizenship as fair but *gendered*, in relation to both gender essentialism and physical separateness. In terms of gender essentialism, whereas writers like De Beauvoir and Smith focused in different ways on the female *essence* (De Beauvoir, 1953; Smith, 1987), there has been more recent focus on the *individualised* experiences and struggles of women (Lewin, 2006). And in terms of the contestability of both freedom and seclusion, as we discussed earlier (Chapter 3, p.51), the first wave feminist preoccupation with equal public voice has here and there been relegated to the second wave ideal that "in . . . privacy a woman finds at least one guaranteed source of freedom" (Cusk, 2010). More recently still (but overlapping and not temporally discrete), what is sometimes called a 'third-wave feminist' approach to gender definition has drawn together elements of both of these earlier waves, challenging cultural and political hegemony that defines and reproduces social values (Butler, 1990), but using second-wave consciousness of difference and how gender can intersect problematically with other identity characteristics to demand rights and freedoms of all sorts.

The 're-gendering' (Lister, 2004) of citizenship takes something from each of these strands. The process of re-claiming citizenship, begun in earnest in the mid-1990s, to address narratives of inequality/injustice was also accompanied by some re-conceptualisation. For instance, Lister's alternative paradigm of feminist thinking about citizenship contrasted 'gender neutrality', 'gender differentiation' and 'gender pluralism' (Lister, 1997), anticipating on some lovely tidy levels Parekh's 2000 taxonomy of the relationship between the state, diversity and citizenship: 'gender neutrality' ~ 'procedural' multiculturalism; 'gender differentiation' ~ 'separatist' multiculturalism; and 'gender pluralism' ~ pluralist' multiculturalism.

The re-gendered perspective on citizenship also casts into fresh focus the classic liberal feminist paradigm. Lister associates gender neutrality with 'liberal feminism', which emphasizes equal gender rights and responsibilities. Liberal feminism sees the prioritisation of *other* aspects of diversity, such as poverty, class, disability, age or ethnicity as detrimental to the 'feminist' cause (Okin, 1999). Nussbaum, high-profile advocate of a form of liberal feminism (1999, 'A plea for difficulty', pp. 105–114 in Okin ed), compares liberal feminism to Rawlsian political liberalism, where diversities converge around a common core of strategic consensus. In turn, liberal feminism is criticised for favouring gender equality over the efforts needed to protect some gender and ethnic and other forms of diversity (Enslin, 2003). Dietz's rallying cry to reject the way that 'protective' (de-political) boundaries are drawn around the home and mothering (Dietz, 1985) has been criticised for being unrealistic, for ignoring the practical constraints that bear down on the lives of women who regardless of participative ideals simply do have second-wave dimensions to their existence and circumstances. Champions of gender 'differentiated' feminist citizenship continue to foreground women's difference in relationship primarily to their roles as mothers and to their different priorities and ways of seeking the world. For instance, there have been a series of waves of pressure for 'care' to be included in more truly inclusive definitions of citizenship that are about rights and participation, exemplifying the sorts of differentiation that liberal feminists condemn as gender segregation and more like sexual norming than equal citizenship.

And so the circular debate around the relationship between equality and difference continues, whereas on another level even to *argue* about neutrality, differentiation or pluralism is a distraction if we agree with Dietz that none of these is meaningful as long as rights and laws are enshrined *on women's behalf*, (Dietz, 1985). Thus, Kabeer (1999) offers a different categorisation of feminism based largely on fieldwork in South Asia that is concerned with the *levels* of empowerment, which she describes as 'immediate' (resources and achievements), 'intermediate' (at the level of seeing institutional rules and resources) and 'deeper' (critical engagement with underlying structural relationships between different groups of people), to become what Sen terms "dynamic promoters of social transformations that can alter the lives of both women and men" (Sen, 1999:189).

The solution, in terms of an aspirationally gendered form of citizenship with traction may lie in what Lister calls 'gender pluralism', or perhaps 'pluralist feminism', that can "accommodate the range of social divisions, such as sexuality, class, 'race', religion and age, which intersect with gender to shape the citizenship of women and men" (Lister, 2004:325). Here though, there is the same danger we found discussing *political* pluralism; representative pluralism, for which categories are essential, is criticised for not allowing fluidity, movement, for "freezing group identities (and) suppressing differences within groups" (Lister, 2004:325). Thus, Lister expounds a view of gender pluralism that "accommodate(s) the range of social divisions, such as sexuality, class, 'race', religion and age, which intersect with gender to shape the citizenship of women and men." (Lister, 2004:325). While Mouffe taps into 'labelling theory' perspectives on diversity to remind us that the feminist struggle is not one for equality as a homogenous group of something called 'women', as a discrete *category*, but a struggle against the many ways in which that very category is "constructed in subordination" (Mouffe, 1992:377). Together, these visions outline a form of liberal feminism that is based on choice with the acknowledgement that these choices are not free but shaped and constrained by other aspects of background, circumstances and identity.

The problem at the heart of each of these competing analyses is straightforward *oppression*, the pervasiveness of which is also the main preoccupation of intersectional literature, which moves away from an unwinnable argument about sameness or difference by focusing attention in a way that is especially relevant to diversifying and globalising frames of reference on how aspects of gender identity, particularly as those relate to marginsalisation, 'intersect' or are compounded by other aspects of difference or marginalisation such as race, class, age, sexuality, religion and so on (AWID, 2004). For instance, Hooks, writing about education as both oppressive (structures) and liberating (ideas) for her, reminds us that ". . . women do not necessarily claim citizenship simply as women but as, for example, Black women, disabled women or lesbian women" (Hooks, 1994). And it is a perspective that strikes a chord with Lister too, who positions herself at the interstices of multiple marginality (black, female) which, in her view, endows her with an 'Otherness' that not only makes her an object but that, by 'recentring' her identity, also enables her to have a critical distance on the society that she then discusses (Lister, 2004:325).

While, as we have seen, education's structural-political and cultural dimensions both challenge and reinforce gendered citizenship, this reading of feminism sees education as the means by women can become "informed and empowered by their very differences in order to rally about a singular commonality" (Soja and Hooper, 2002). And since the days when schools fairly automatically reinforced gendered social interaction, successive waves of feminist campaigning have been enlisting education in the cause of equal, or fairer, citizenship – but in different ways. First-wave feminism sees improved educational access as critical from both social and economic perspectives, to "mould. . . and integrate. . . the citizen into the polity" (Unterhalter, 1999:113–114). Second-wave feminism, on the other hand, has been more concerned with education's cultural and ideational function, promoting emphasis on alternative 'ways of knowing' and the 'politics of difference'. While the emphasis in third-wave feminist thought has been criticism – of the ways that education systems have helped to reproduce dominant "values, attitudes, beliefs and morality, that in various ways support the established order and the class and male interests which dominate it" (Arnot, 2002:105).

There has certainly been progress on some of these counts. The rapid international increase in numbers of women going to university and getting better degree results than men has helped provide women with radical ideas and ambitions, to make public demands and assert self-representation, and had some part in reshaping public understanding of women as citizens who can shape social discourses and values. Even Lister acknowledges that there is also a male dimension to the business of gendering and limiting roles and opportunities (Lister, 2004).

In other ways, these successive waves of educationally mediated feminist thinking and action have made little actual difference. It is clear from ongoing graduate under-employment, glass ceilings and continued ambivalence in women's public roles that their freedoms to act are still limited. The limitations have been explained by underlying hegemonic structures that are felt still predominantly male – that is the practice of excluding from aspects of what citizenship means still applies more to women than men. In terms of formal political participation, in the UK, "[b]etween 1992 and 2010 the number of women voting in general elections fell by 18%" (McVeigh and Helm, 2015:8). Yet the same Observer article notes that the number of women candidates actively involved beyond mere voting has increased. In educational institutions themselves, there is ongoing discrimination. Laments continue that the female voice is still routinely erased in American and European universities, which still reproduce gendered and unequal ideologies and practices through the "continuous privileging of men and hegemonic masculinities and devaluation of women and femininities" (Heward, 1996). Prevailing higher education discourses are condemned for erasing the (feminist) 'personal' and minimising differences (David and Clegg, 2008:491), and little appears to have changed since it was flagged up as problematic two decades ago that lower career expectations restricted women's power to participate and to shape public discourses (Morley and Walsh, 1996;).

In the circular debate about what the 'right' focus of feminist campaigning should be, artificially separating the cultural, political and socio-economic aspects of education's role in promoting equal citizenship is not very productive, as we saw earlier. In the production of knowledge, Mascia-Lees et al.'s humorously cynical appraisal of the male embrace of postmodernity points out that when "Western white males – who traditionally have controlled the production of knowledge – can no longer define the truth . . . their response is to conclude that there is not a truth to be discovered" (Mascia-Lees et al., 1989:15).

What makes this kind of feminist thinking 'radical' is the exhortation to think outside the box or existing structures, which is what education can unleash. But thinking outside the box is a tough call when the box and the centre have for so long been defined for you. Without basic socio-economic and legal citizenship *rights*, attempts to challenge hegemonic discourses, practices and epistemologies are going to be non-starters. And without education, you cannot exploit either socio-economic opportunity or the rights laws provide. As Lister argues: "citizenship as rights enables people to exercise their agency as citizens" (2004:321).

Sustaining the 'thirdspace' theme (Soja, 1999 & 2010), part of the feminist approach to citizenship seeks to 'occupy' or re-purpose spaces in a way that exploits links between ideas and physicality. Of the long-standing association between 'feminine' and 'local', Massey pointed out the way that in certain societies, historic and contemporary alike, "the mobility of women does indeed seem to pose a threat to a settled patriarchal order. Whether it be the specific fact of going out to work in nineteenth-century England . . . or the more general difficulty . . . of keeping track of women in the city" (Massey, 1994:11). Education can, as we saw in Chapters 3 and 5, bring both awareness of this fear-driven patriarchy and preparedness to challenge or subvert such hegemonically defined spatiality. Challenging is fairly straightforward, but there are more possibilities for subversions: working *around* hegemonic systems to bring "change from outside the centres of established political power" (Stromquist, 2004:36). But another is to work quietly from within – to co-opt the state structure.

## Citizenship, education, gender and space in developing countries

Yet all of this is easy to say. The gap between awareness and enabling social and political structures can be vast in countries that are 'catching up' for one reason or another. Long-standing inequalities, lack of access and inclusion, rapidly rising populations and demand for education, volatile economies, traditions that marginalise girls and women are among the additional challenges in many developing countries. In such contexts, while education can indeed open doors it is also as compromised as other social institutions by these same circumstances.

On one hand, studies have pointed to higher education having a greater impact in *developing* countries on gender equality and reshaping social norms (Oketch et al., 2014). And there have long been advocates for education as *the* solution to gender injustice. Nawal a-Sa'adawi, Egyptian human rights activist, author of a string of groundbreaking feminist books and Arab feminist symbol, became famous in the 1970s for protesting against the practice of wearing of the veil and female genital mutilation (FGM) – especially among the poor – and has never been silent since. Embracing in turn Marxism, secularism, even Islamism in the early Arab Spring days, as potential escape routes from the oppression of women, Sa'adawi has argued fiercely that the answer lies in ideas, changing people's minds, rather than diktat by the powerful. She points to the failure of Egypt's 2008 law outlawing FGM as evidence: "[I]t has stayed the same. You can't change such a deep-rooted habit by passing a law. You need education. The law was passed to satisfy the West. They wanted to cover that disgrace, not to eradicate the practice itself" (Sa'adawi, 2015:17).

These are precisely the sorts of concerns behind some key initiatives, one of which happened in Sa'adawi's home and sometime cradle of the Arab 'nation' – Egypt. The 2003 Egyptian Girls' Education Initiative (EGEI), part of the United Nations Girls' Education Initiative, developed a network of 'girl-friendly' schools that would be 92 per cent female and with an alternative educational agenda, practices and curricula that would help "getting girls into schools" (Sultana, 2007:12), where circumstances among poor communities were preventing attendance beyond puberty and, by extension, improving their life chances. It was also, its advocates report, "about the creation of a new generation of schools for a new generation of women – women who are educated, empowered, and eager to take their rightful place in society, as equal partners" (Sultana, 2007:13). Ministry-led but modelled (in both curriculum and governance) on local Egyptian 'community schools', the initiative was grounded in a commitment not to patronise or condemn communities where parents tended to keep girls at home but to work with them, "winning them over and mobilizing them behind the same ideal" (Sultana, 2007:13). Thus, they communicated closely with parents, engaging local intermediaries to talk to them about their concerns. A portfolio-based form of assessment was designed to encourage self-management skills and with an emphasis "on the child comparing herself to her own potential rather than entering into insidious competition with her classmates" (Sultana, 2007:81). Working closely with rather than in opposition to the government here in the form of being led by the National Council for Childhood and Motherhood (a provocative nod to one version of the Arab woman's 'traditional' role) does open up the core 'feminist' issue of gender differentiation or neutrality arguments. But on balance the initiative appears to have been successful on a range of counts over and above simply getting more girls to school: successfully resisting efforts to incorporate it into the public school system, prompting the ministry to rethink its approach to mainstream schooling, especially regarding community relations and teacher training (Sultana, 2007) and "reveal(ing) the power of local communities", even reportedly provoking villages to come out collectively against FGM (Khattab, 2007:9).

And yet such educational 'opportunity' has another side. Although access to digital technologies may increasingly be enabling women to bypass traditionally male hegemonic power structures. Two interesting studies, one in 1990s South Africa and the other in early-21st-century Latin America, illuminate the both the integral relationship between existing citizenship structures, ideational freedom and educationally mediated possibilities for change, and the context-specific nature of this relationship.

In South Africa, one of the battles being fought over the last few decades has been for gender equality in terms of equal presence and voice in both private and public spaces. Seeing the state as a site for the construction of citizenship, Gouws has described government attempts to involve previously excluded women in discursive struggles around legislation and policy reform. The 1990s attempt to introduce the 'National Machinery for women' was an act aimed at improving women's rights in South Africa by giving women political platform in drafting the post–Apartheid National Constitution at a time when the equality of women had become integral to rights discourses in South Africa. Customary laws concerning marriage, divorce, consent, polygamy and divorce were unequal and problematic from a late-20th-century human-rights point of view, with blatant reinforcement of patriarchal norms including the fact that married women had minority status. The process involved a Committee for Traditional Learning as an attempt to ensure structured participation in national decision-making and accountability by government to women. In this, there was a long local history of women's activism to draw on, and a Women's National Coalition formed in 1992. But these women's inability to be as involved as the state had intended meant that the initiative failed. Few responses were received to discussion paper and workshops, and briefings were poorly attended. In the end, unequal customary law was systematised into state law without the real participation of many of the women (Gouws, 2004). What this story reveals is how hard it is to disrupt hegemonic practices and norms. Here, even though the state went out of its way to make structured space for women, the attempt was undermined by these women's lack of access due to a mixture of lack of education, skills, confidence, understanding and social structures that would have made it possible for them to participate meaningfully. The business was also urban-centred, which proved an additional challenge for women restricted by means to the countryside where they lived.

The Women's National Coalition case underlines the importance of educational and public structures working alongside each other if the marginalised are genuinely to participate in shaping power and discourses and citizenship discourses and processes themselves are to escape from hegemony. As Unterhalter's work, and before hers, Sen's and Nussbaum's, has shown us that resources are no good if they are prevented, through policy-makers' lack of understanding of structural or ideational impediments, from being converted into 'capabilities' (Unterhalter, 2007). Stromquist has applied a similar argument to her criticism of classic human-rights activism insofar as it is "based on a juridical model of individual complaints against state agents for their denial of civic liberties" (2004:40). This, she argues, is meaningless in cases (developing country, indigenous communities and women) when violators are not only state agents but endemic to how society is structured. Thus democratising political structures is fruitless if people are not educated to understand their own long-term interest. The point casts a note of caution for adult and community education projects whose goals are defined by the participants/students themselves and may thus reflect only partial understandings of what is possible. The EGEI's non-competitive assessment regime, too, is in principle open to the same charge: How can these girls know what they are capable of unless they see what others have achieved?

The impact of grass-roots (non-formal) education in Latin America, on the other hand, is linked to its role in the Women's Movement – a campaign to reform legislation on 'women's issues' such as instance abortion rights, domestic violence and rape. As in the Popular Administration Porto Alegre project, non-formal education is characterised by a commitment to working with the poor and marginalised and participatory pedagogies, explicitly linking education to social action. Discussing three women-led organisations involved in this movement, in Peru and the Dominican Republic, where women's movements are largely middle class and non-violent, Stromquist notes the advantage of non-formal (or popular) education over formal education systems, whose "limitations regarding their potential for transformative knowledge" relate to their enlistment and history as part of the hegemonic modernist project (Stromquist, 2004). By contrast, a critical pedagogy-oriented form of non-formal education enabled women to focus on working (and working around) the system to achieve "new legislation on family violence, rape, father's child support, access to land titles, training of police and judges to implement feminist laws, increase in the political representation of women via electoral quotas, incorporation of feminist ideas in educational plans . . . (and) . . . formation of national alliances to work on minimum plans of action . . ." (Stromquist, 2004:49).

The different outcomes in these latter two stories underlines the two main imperatives needed to address adequately such endemic inequalities; flexible modes of delivery to accommodate women's commitments and structural barriers to access are indeed necessary, but so, too, is an understanding of the difficult transition between ideational oppression and enlightened political participation. They also focus our attention on space. It is often pointed out that supposedly 'liberating' movements fall into the classic differentiated feminist or pluralist trap of actually reinforcing segregation. As Stromquist partly acknowledges, "[t]he link between the women-led NGOs in the study and economically marginalised women shows a path that has shifted from seeking to work in coordination with men . . . to women working by themselves" (Stromquist, 2004:47). Whether this is oppression or freedom, freely chosen or imposed, depends on how *different* (perhaps competing) freedoms are prioritised, but it also depends on how one understands the nature of a social structure that *makes* such isolation preferable.

## The Arab Gulf

This ambivalence is central to the ways in which women in the Arab Gulf have been engaging with education, using it to challenge their relationships with and roles in wider society. Notwithstanding its recent wealth and influence, the Arab Gulf is part of the wider Arab world, where enlightened political participation may still be problematic but where feminist tradition is steeped in long-standing regional links among politics, education and protest and in aspirations for lives changed in more than economic terms. We can see this on one level in the ways that Sa'adawi's literary focus mirrors debates around oppression in Egypt and the wider Arab world: moments of revolutionary hope in the 1970s and the Arab Spring, interwoven with anti-FGM campaigning and anti-extremism.

And the close political feminist links with *education* go back at least to the early 20th century when Egyptian women challenged political and domestic patriarchy and fought admission to the new Egyptian (subsequently Cairo) University, becoming politically active secularising force and challenging prevailing systems of patriarchy.

On the other hand, citizenship and education in this region have distinct developing country characteristics, not limited to the ways that postcolonial and religio-political resistance to perceived Western imperialism has formed a crucible that vies with pro-democracy as an ideological focus for change movements. And this tension has been played out in the social and citizenship aspects of education. The dominant models of citizenship in the Gulf as in other Arab states are strongly patriotic, though not ethnonationalist, with both pan-Arab and Islamic dimensions. Thus, as far as many schools are concerned, 'citizenship' refers to "the individual's loyalty in serving its country to the extent to the self-sacrifice when needed" (Rayan, 1993:3) and governments' generous provision of services and authority. A review of Egyptian school textbooks found that the least frequent associations with citizenship were most commonly used in relation to the government providing services, then national symbols such as flags, then tourism, and then authority. The least frequent associations with citizenship were social justice, political participation and the rule of law (Baraka, 2008:12). And in Arab countries with very large expatriate communities, such as the Gulf states, citizenship is furthermore a marker of those who are protected by included in the national distributive system, while those without 'citizenship' have to fend for themselves.

However, there is also growing government awareness across the Arab world of the need to promote an inclusive, constructively politically, economically and socially engaged citizenship among youth, and a model of citizenship education that draws inspiration from US civic education programmes. What seems to be emerging in the Gulf is a prevailing mix of liberal (individual rights) and communitarian concepts of citizenship, mostly nation-state framed but with Arab and Islamic dimensions. In Bahrain, for example, a ministerial committee formed in 2004 to look into Citizenship education in secondary schools produced a model influenced by the British one, in keeping with the long political ties between the countries. Yet like the UK model, it was also condemned as mostly "confused", not least because of its failure to address the ethnic mix of Bahrainis and the associated tensions in terms of community and equality (Selaibeekh, 2009). So there is awareness on one level at least of schools' responsibilities in addressing the challenges of pluralism: ". . . if citizenship education in Bahrain is to be a liberal education, it has to either acknowledge all the different communities living in Bahrain, by teaching pupils about each community's culture or else it should not teach about any culture at all" (Selaibeekh, 2009:4).

A high proportion of university students across the Arab world today are women, and an ongoing raft of initiatives, such as but not limited to The Girls' Education Initiative, has been spurred by greater contact with transnational organisations and international institutional links to redress socio-economic gender inequalities. Yet 'feminism' as a discursive currency remains compromised by reservations about the lack of representativeness, cultural imperialism and essentialist subjugation, which makes even women wary of adopting it explicitly (al-Ali, 2000:47). As I found in ethnographic fieldwork I conducted between 1999 and 2012 – from PhD work on the nation-building role of higher education in the United Arab Emirates (UAE), Bahrain and Kuwait, to a shift of focus in 2009 to the role of higher education in a 'feminist' social change project, which explored how Gulf women students, graduates and academics were situating themselves against available feminist narratives; how they were seeing themselves as citizens and political actors; and how higher education's spaces and constraints were mediating these processes (Findlow, 2012). Both projects also drew on my personal experience living and working in Egypt, Kuwait, Bahrain and the UAE, including roundtable discussions, a student survey, interviews with Gulf women academics and several ongoing conversations.

While graduate students and academic women I talked to in 2009 mostly described themselves in feminist terms in their personal lives and careers, they agreed that the term *feminism* has no currency. While most Gulf women I have met during this period and since are comfortable discussing political matters, there are definite no-go areas. Bringing the personal into the public is one of these areas. Gulf women would like an increased voice in government, better jobs that enable them to balance work with family responsibilities, and cultural change in order to provide more options for education, work and marriage/family. They would like it to be easier to combine family and work. Across the Gulf, but again especially in Saudi Arabia, it is the support of family that makes the difference to whether or not you can do this. However, there is a reluctance to link these desires to 'feminism'. There still seems to be a sense in which cultural and gender essentialism mix, to produce arguments that the difference between men and women is greater in the Arab world. More than one woman from more than one Gulf country has suggested that concerns about gender equality in the Gulf are rather imperialistic: "We are equal but different. I mean, we have our rights, but our rights are different from the men's rights" (Findlow, 2012).

Yet while the term *feminism* has had even less currency in the Gulf than in other Arab countries, large numbers of Gulf women are entering higher education and are increasingly publicly visible, and there has been indication for some time now that Gulf women are challenging the status quo (Findlow, 2012). Clearly not all Gulf countries are the same, and in the *small* Gulf states women have traditionally had more freedom and status than in Saudi Arabia. But everywhere, against the cultural norm that places women inside the home and publicly invisible, there is evidence of changing attitudes. This includes prolific official support for female empowerment and achievement, the establishment in each of these countries of special councils for women with the declared intention of both documenting and creating opportunities for greater equality and, more significant, grass-roots women's movements that embrace the political. While Kuwaiti women's activism has had a narrower focus on *gender* equality and UAE women's activism has been relatively embryonic, the vocal women's movement in Bahrain represents women as one category of oppressed people and has called not for *tinkering* with 'family law' but for equality for every category of oppressed citizen – in law, the economy and politics. Prominent Bahraini female activists Maryam and Zainab al-Khawaja are among those who go further to argue that sectarianism in Bahrain is not only a symptom of underlying inequalities, as in Northern Ireland, but actually a convenient way of deflecting attention from the fact that power and privilege are concentrated in the hands of a very small group of powerful people.

Across the Gulf women have obtained the right to both vote and seek election to parliament despite Islamist opposition. In Kuwait, Bahrain, Qatar, the UAE and Saudi Arabia, women now hold public office including – in some cases – ministerial roles. Even in arch-conservative Saudi Arabia, where public policy has been drawn up to reflect a view of women as weaker than men, where women still cannot drive, are not allowed to appear alone in public or to travel, conduct business or obtain identity cards without their male guardians, women are challenging society to recognize them as citizens. Saudi women were recently given the right to vote and stand for public office and are continuing to campaign for the equal right to drive, to take part in sports and for the system of guardianship to be removed.

This increased awareness, and attainment, of rights in the Gulf is linked fairly clearly to the widespread reduction of poverty. But it can also be traced, at least partly, to access to higher education. This has been a major thread of public policy in all the Gulf countries for the last few decades, central to both infrastructure needs and individual governments' desires to internationally competitive on both economic and political terms (Findlow and Hayes, 2016). From a time in the mid-20th century when state education was reserved for the male elite, the realisation in the 1960s of the need to educate an indigenous workforce saw new national constitutions quickly emphasising the right of free education to *all* citizens. Since then, specific policies including systems of overseas scholarships and projects to help eradicate illiteracy and social seclusion have focused on female education. In time, modern schools grew into technical colleges and then many into universities – to which women were granted immediate access, in contrast to the UK, where women were only admitted to degrees in Cambridge in 1948. Since then, numbers of women students have increased rapidly, enabled by the expansion of local higher education institutions, distance-learning and women-only colleges. While there are many higher education institutions across these states today, the flagship national universities provide reasonable indications of gender balance. Today about 75 per cent of Kuwait University's students are women, and in 2012, 61 per cent of students at the University of Bahrain were women, while in the UAE, new female enrolments exceeded male ones four years after its first university was founded in 1977, and by 1999 the student body was approximately 80 per cent women. Women and girls outnumber and outperform men and boys at all educational stages, and there is a disproportionately rapid rise in female literacy rates. In Saudi Arabia women with higher degrees now outnumber men.

As in the early days of the Egyptian University, being highly educated can promise a way out of oppression of all sorts. Gulf women, like women elsewhere (Heward and Bunwaree, 1999), have non-instrumental rationales for educational choices. My 1999 survey snapshot found that only 35 per cent of UAE women compared to 77 per cent of men had chosen their degree subject for career-related reasons. Fatima, a UAE-national lecturer studying for a PhD in England, explained their choice as a matter of identity and finding out where they fit in the world – an opportunity both for conscientisation and to build some individual capital:

> "[F]or our women . . . They see this as the only way out if, for example they never get married or they do get married, they have something there. Otherwise . . . Most of our women they move from parents to husbands. They don't have a transition of really finding out where they are themselves. So I think it's time at college, it gives them that little bit of time to just reflect on their own identity, on who they are as people. So I don't think they have a choice. Whereas with men it's very very different, they have more options. But none of these options are available for women so they only have to go for higher education.
> (Findlow, 2012)

In 1999, three times the number of female than male university students cited self-improvement as their educational goal, and *all* the women I talked to from 1999 to 2011 insisted that education was indeed helping them make choices and challenge expectations. Some students contrasted their own choices with those their mothers had made: "[Y]ou know, . . . I'll finish my education before *I* get married!" (Findlow, 2012).

Yet progress in the empowerment of women as citizens equally able to shape society continues to be hampered by a couple of weak links: continued gender segregation and the related problem of weak linkage between education and employment. Space is key to persistent gender inequality in the Arab world. Centrally important in the Arab political and cultural imaginations, from the macro-level of crusades, empire and the carving up of kingdoms to the more micro-level and recent disputes over territories, buildings and localities, space is at the root of regional politics, identity and society. While obviously hard to generalize when a lot happens behind closed doors, the traditional distribution of gender roles, where men do not do housework and women tend not to participate in major decisions or public life, seems still to be a persistent model (Al-Kubaisi, 2010). Outside the home, a recent report about the strategy of female street children pretending to be boys in order to survive underlines the fundamental nature of this divide:

> For some, the aim is not just to avoid sexual assault, but to feel more at home in public space, which in Egypt is traditionally seen as a male domain. It allows girls to smoke, shout, or simply sit in the street, actions that boys can easily do without reproach, but girls can't. Amira El Feky, a former academic who has researched this topic, explains: "All the privileges that men have – they can have them. They mock the whole idea of gender, they say: 'Oh you think women are weak? Well I'm just not going to be a woman any more.'"
> (Kingsley, and Patrick, 2015:35,)

Like racial segregation, gender segregation in the Arab world works through a mixture of official and non-official structures. The veil and hijab are visible symbols of separation, worn for a mixture of reasons, by conservative women or women from conservative backgrounds. Acknowledging its complex symbolism, Sa'adawi, for instance, dismisses its resurgence as a "fashion" (Sa'adawi, 2015). Other women believe that its symbolic segregating function is ethical and honourable, and far from subjugating women provides a bulwark against the temptation to flaunt beauty and distract from the important things in life. Furthermore, others argue that actual physical segregation is not a problem, that we are wrong to suppose that the 'real' world is the more public one experienced by men. Tapping into essentialist, gender differentiated, forms of feminist thought, these women argue that liberal feminism is not only politically and culturally inappropriate for the Arab world, but it threatens to actually curtail women's rights (Talhami, 1996:135).

Today, most arguments in the Gulf for empowering women and girls through gender segregation emphasize not *difference* but secure, non-distracting *environments*. Always fairly central to Kuwait's modern identity, pressure to segregate in Bahrain is relatively new, brought in by the recent political changes that have seen increased alignment with the more conservative codes in neighbouring countries, while in the UAE rapid economically driven internationalisation-modernisation has seen the opposite process. Across the Gulf, state schools tend to be gender-segregated while private schools make policy on the basis of their different markets. University level policies respond to a super-complex range of drivers. Kuwait University has always been partially segregated. Politically backed proposals in 2005 to introduce segregation at Bahrain University were challenged and abandoned. In the large and complex UAE, higher education–sector segregation policies are applied, relaxed and removed as a solution to diverse and changing demands (Findlow, 2008). The segregation issue goes deeper than mere arguments for and against mixing genders. The prevalent view in the early days of higher education that that many subjects were not suitable for women to study was quickly overturned by weight of demand. But residues of gender stereotyping remain, not least in the differential levels of prestige accorded to women-only institutions and their mixed counterparts in the something-for-everyone UAE higher education system (Findlow, 2012).

This concern to protect separateness spills over into thoughts about space and segregation. Most of the women I have spoken to since 2006 have spoken of single-sex institutions as spaces for young women to develop senses of self and society and to be open in ways that the presence of men in patriarchal family settings might otherwise prohibit. When Zayed University in the UAE was planning to admit men, an assertive unveiled young student there lamented that this space, "to explore what it means to be a woman without the insecurity of . . . men", would be lost (Findlow, 2012). The same argument has long been applied to single-sex colleges and schools in the UK, and whether it is right or wrong appears to depend on what it is you are looking for. On the other hand, there is disdain for the limiting of choices that often flow from segregation. Thus, in 2009 when Zayed University was still all-female, one student I spoke to decried the "emphasis on family, family sciences and . . . there's still an emphasis on women as domestic" and the hypocrisy: "On one hand you're told to be global leaders and on the other hand you're not allowed to leave the campus unless you have permission from your parents. . . . But what kinds of messages are you sending to these girls?" (Findlow, 2012).

In this sense, segregation has the same dual function as restrictive dress codes for women. In 2008, Kuwait's two female government ministers made news by refusing to wear the hijab, but head scarves and veils have also been adopted by well-educated women out of a feeling that these afford them some invisibility that allows them to take more risks in male-dominated workspaces and to challenge other more pressing inequalities. Whereas even a *strategic* rationale for covering your hair as subtle subversion can be seen as submission to constraint (after all, sacrificing visibility for the right to be heard would not be necessary in an equal system), the *hijab* is also worn by well-educated Gulf women studying in 'Western' countries in order to challenge assumptions and assert their Muslim identity in a highly religiously politicised environment. There are many reasons for both wearing and not wearing the *hijab*; Al-Sa'adawi may be right that fashion is one of those, in some cases, but so is challenging norms.

Gendered spaces, on the other hand, also impact directly on the complex connections between higher education and employment. From a state point of view, the economic rationale for women's independence is stronger than the ideological one. The shift from public- to private-sector employment in all three countries has helped broaden the range of jobs women can and will do. Emphasis from the 1960s on the importance of women teachers has eased the path for the professionals in education, medicine, civil servants and academics. UNDP (United Nation Development Programme) rankings show apparently rapid rises in female–male labour force participation ratios in the Gulf (UAE 32nd of 169 countries, Bahrain 37th and Kuwait 49th, UNDP, 2010). Yet the economic rationale for higher education is undermined by a series of cultural factors that make the link between university and work seems to be less strong than governments would like. While it is an often repeated truism that in the Gulf, '[m]en can get jobs without a degree anyway' the substantial gap between numbers of female graduates and rates of female graduate employment is influenced by residual glass ceilings for women and by the reluctance of women graduates to take jobs that do not require graduate-level entry qualifications. In stark contrast to the high female–male higher education participation ratios, local sources in Kuwait cite the female graduate employment rate as 40 per cent, and in the UAE individual institutions' female graduate employment rates of around 50 per cent are presented as a success. Social attitudes combined with economic prosperity have meant that "employment is a matter of choice, rather than of necessity" (UAE Ministry of Information and Culture, 2001). Bahrain, on the other hand, has a lower female higher education participation rate than the other two countries, but women have long been an integral part of the workforce at all levels.

Despite apparent freedoms then, it is possible to see the powerful hand of Gulf governments still dictating what women should be doing and where. Certainly, more Gulf women today are permitted to research, write and present at international conferences on gender issues; there is not as much state censorship and sensitivity as there was ten years ago. But in terms of the deeper levels of empowerment that allow *free* choice, not (as Hall pointed out in 1988) between options that have been *made* available, the hefty residues of gendered structures that inevitably shape women's choices can be seen in the way, for instance, money is distributed for overseas scholarships. In order to meet the high demand for higher education, especially for higher degrees, Gulf governments have regularly sent students abroad, increasingly more women than men. Yet in Saudi Arabia women have been restricted from entering studies in engineering, journalism, pharmacy and architecture; accordingly, sponsorship has been allocated to areas where their domestic roles can be extended including education, health services and public administration (Baki, 2004). And while women's opportunities across the region are broader today, the majority of funding for women to study abroad is still allocated in fields of health and social services, as well as education. Even Bahrain recently announced a shift in sponsorship away from humanities and social sciences towards health care and education services on the basis that women were felt most likely to be able to take up jobs in these areas (Secretariat General of the Higher Education Council, 2012).

Certainly, sponsorship structures like these tell a story where women's 'freedoms' in the Gulf are still dependent on hegemonic systems, and public rhetoric across the region as in Egypt tends to conflate discussion of gender with 'family' issues and tradition (Findlow, 2012). Freedoms are 'afforded', 'offered', 'provided' and 'encouraged'. Bahrain's National Action Charter, according to the Supreme Council for Women, has "safeguarded (women's) rights, stipulating that the country would promulgate laws that would defend women and protect families; All citizens are equal before the law in terms of rights and duties, without discrimination amongst them because of sex" (Supreme Council for Women, 2011). But what is seen by many as tokenistic representation is manifest in a disproportionately large presence of ruling family members among the number of female ministers and members of bodies such as the UAE Women's Federation and Bahrain's Supreme Council for Women, while the UAE's now-female-populated Federal National Council is merely consultative, and public debate continues in Kuwait about whether it is right for women to be in the judiciary.

It is these kinds of things that provoke cynicism. While some of the Bahraini and UAE women endorsed official assessments of society's readiness to change, stressing the need for what is often called 'gradualism': "Our society is still developing!", official 'equality' structures like women's councils were felt, as one UAE PhD student explained in 2009, to be window dressing:

> The things happening in our society claiming to give women more rights are mostly just cosmetic things, you know, we have a couple of female ministers and, there's all this rhetoric about women's leadership . . . but when you come to the actual mentality, what people believe in, there's gross gender stereotypes among the people that are at the highest level of society I think.
> (Findlow, 2012)

118  *Feminist citizenship*

Others feel that the increasing number of female members of government in the Gulf "are really puppets," and point to the disproportionately high ruling-family connections of women in political high office. In Saudi Arabia, opinion is divided about whether the current ruler is committed to working within conservative structures to actually bring about change.

Across the Gulf, in contrast to South Africa, it is widely said to be culture, or social structures, in the Arab Gulf case that lag behind educational opportunity and uptake. The official line in the Arab Gulf has been that women's equality is central to modernisation. Thirty-six years ago, in the earliest days of UAE nation-state building, the state presented itself as the progressive partner, dealing with 'the family' and "backward and inhuman ideas about women in the home" (Emirates, 1980). However, an alternative explanation focuses on the residual patriarchy and argues that this has been actually *strengthened* by collision between tradition and modernity to produce a "conservative, relentless male-oriented ideology, which tend(s) to assign privilege and power to the male at the expense of the female" (Sharabi, 1988:33). It is alleged that higher education has been co-opted this system, and used as a further means for the entrenchment of "domination and subordination . . . (flimsily disguised by) . . . notions of citizenship and participation" (Mazawi, 2007:79 & 90).Inconsistency and dissonance between women's espoused radical ideals and strategic collusion can be explained by the constraining impact of the underlying structural relationships. It is possible to detect a broadly 'feminist' movement at work, with education at its core, contesting injustices and generally helping increasing numbers of women see themselves as equal citizens in social, economic and even political terms. Yet in terms of the ability to shape public discourses, a sense of social responsibility is mixed with skepticism about what young women can actually do in the circumstances and how prepared they would be anyway. As a UAE student explained to me in 2011,

> They've been given these opportunities and . . . especially among some of the students that are going to the more liberal universities, I think they're starting to feel like they want to make a difference. It's more than just rhetoric, it's a real desire, and commitment to do something. But in terms of practice, I think they still haven't hit reality yet.
>
> (Findlow, 2012)

There is awareness of powerful structures and the need to work strategically against, or more usually around, those. Most women not protected by connections proceed carefully through a unique mix of gradualism, networking, determination and waiting for the right opportunity. Increasing numbers of educated women opinion leaders share their critiques of society at international and regional conferences. But while, publicly, such critiques are aimed at increasing political representation among under-represented groups, political hypocrisy is cited privately.

And yet. In an interesting recent development, the Emirati government has begun to train well-educated young Emirati women as *muftiyas*, Islamic scholars, in order to share their learning with local women via a telephone hotline

(Ghafour, 2016). This development can be regarded as a re-shaping of the state's relationship with religion, understandable at a time of widespread religious misinformation. But it is also an instance of women's distinctive voices being involved at a state level in shaping what citizens think, in shaping the law, and in shaping the state's relationship with religion, providing hopeful contrasts to the 1990s South African failure to involve women in state-driven decision-making and opinion-shaping, due to the women's lack of education.

## Education for full and equal citizenship? Ideals and realities

This chapter has drawn on a range of developing country snapshots of the ways that education has mediated citizenship as social and political equality, on both official and grass-roots levels, in some developing country contexts. And especially in the way the Arab Gulf case differs from the Egyptian, South African or Latin American ones, it has revealed ambivalence and some apparent contradictions around how equality is envisaged and how education is used as a vehicle for challenging the powerful definition of structures and cultures.

Across the world, flexible modes of education have been established to accommodate girls' and women's commitments, and both cultural and structural barriers to access. These are necessary and represent progress in terms of 'getting the girls to school', as do the evident links with community. But they also detract from other aspects of 'equality', and can fall into the trap of reinforcing segregation. Moving from ideational and socio-economic oppression towards enlightened political participation, we have seen both what happens when attempts at reform are top-down and neither grounded in lived, gendered realities nor supported by education (as in the South African attempt), and the ways that higher education can promote awareness among women of how these realities can constrain and shape their choices. In the Arab Gulf, higher education has also been a vehicle and focus for challenging these realities, working both within and outside existing structures and helping some women to make public demands and assert their ambitions. However, these freedoms are still limited by underlying gender capital imbalances, and the impact of public support, flagship legislative changes and venues for exercising a political voice are compromised by traditions that mean women still have to fight to be heard without being *too* visible.

Regarding the currency of feminist citizenship ideals, it is possible to detect rhetorical oscillation across a range of cases between 'women are different' gender essentialism and liberal feminist demands for equality, with a particularly spatial application. It is clear that there are different forms of segregation and that segregation can be seen as either oppression or freedom. There is a still prevalent view in the Arab Gulf that women are "'a discrete category" (Mouffe, 1992:377); women are not embarrassed to proclaim this view, while governments try more awkwardly not to offend. Yet there is also resistance to "the many ways in which that very category is "constructed in subordination" (Mouffe, 1992:377). In the Gulf, this takes the form of resistance to categorisation – by outsider assumptions as much as by local male structures. Well educated Gulf women want to speak for themselves, clearly valuing, for instance, the *option* of separation or seclusion even though they can see it is only necessary because of underlying social and political structures, hence their caution about embracing the term '*feminism*'. While glocalisation (R.Robertson, 1995) has created awareness of broader contexts, it has also created a heightened need to take a position, to claim distinctiveness, to reject assumptions and to have 'the right to name (them)selves', challenging both local power and global cultural hegemony to dictate their choices.

And what about citizenship as awareness of structural inequalities and the right to (re)shape society? For instance, do the opportunities for *some* Gulf women to achieve political and economic voice reflect a widespread understanding of the deep structures of inequality and the nature (possibilities and implications) of 'free' choice that it is argued are key to 'deeper' levels of empowerment (Kabeer, 1999)? And what about links between such awareness and radical *action* for change? On both counts, there is some ambivalence – between deep understanding of specific forms and manifestations of gender capital imbalance and a failure, for various reasons, to trace those to underlying hegemonic power structures, or at least to challenge these structures directly. Gulf women see hypocrisy, superficiality and tokenism, and understand their struggle as part of larger ones for social and political equality both locally and globally. But for every one woman who like the Khawaja sisters openly challenges local injustices, there are many more who approach the issues more selectively, strategically and pragmatically, using spaces created by official ambivalence to challenge the mis-use of power. So while the radical consciousness-raising function of education as we have seen here across international examples - promoting first knowledge, then voice, then empowerment and structural change - would seem inexorable, we can also see that there the ways and speed in which this translates into direct challenge depends on local circumstances. After all, there are many struggles to be had and, increasingly, many ways of engaging with struggle, with and against the state.

# 7 Ecological stakeholder citizenship
## Educating for sustainability

There is one dimension of the citizenship~space~education relationship we have not discussed in detail yet but which captures the ecological core of all that has been said so far. While 'sustainability' has been a fairly high-profile public agenda for some time now, its cultural, critical or radical and anti-individualistic aspects are less clearly articulated. In fact, there are ways in which sustainability is properly seen as the cornerstone of a place-based concept of citizenship. If equal share and ownership of resources is a stakeholder citizenship issue, and global citizenship means being responsible for not only yourself but also other people in other societies, we have to engage with critical arguments about the *un*sustainability of 'development' and capitalism, which are essentially competitive. Recent global economic meltdown and the waves of discontent and violence that have followed should be enough to alert us to the interconnectedness of everything. Seen in these terms, sustainability and ecology actually provide the *widest* lens for looking at citizenship. Furthermore, accepting these principles mandates a form of education that promotes a politics of equal responsibility, an understanding of sustainability that is not only about our physical environment and using fewer resources but also about equal sharing of those resources, and develops the cultural capital and capabilities societies need to manage natural capital.

### Sustainability and education for sustainable development

Sustainability has long been a radical agenda, and traditionally linked to activism. Yet the focus of recent *official* sustainability discourse has been conservation and climate change. With seeds of awareness planted in the 1970s, today's bubble of sustainability rhetoric has produced broad policy commitment to 'sustainability' principles and promising measures to reduce consumption. But there is less evidence of this filtering down into actual practice on either individual or collective levels, and a lot of unevenness across the world in terms of how this issue is seen as an aspect of (already-ambiguous) citizenship.

As for its links with education, again there is widespread awareness across the world, with Education for Sustainable Development (EDS) national coordinating bodies becoming the norm. But there is a huge variance in terms of how this agenda is linked to others. In a few countries, sustainable development is a central strand of *citizenship* education, with policy and curriculum framed around the idea that young people should understand critical issues facing the planet and how they can play a part in shaping its future. Elsewhere, however, sustainability tends still to be seen as either the preserve of geographers, economists and environmentalists or a matter of 'green citizenship', good householder behaviour and redolent of the responsibilising tones of 'active citizenship' (Gorham, 1992; Furedi, 2005).

However, sustainability agendas are beginning to coalesce around the rejection of the false dichotomy between 'politics' (people, ideas) and 'environment' (space, nature). For instance, arguments in favour of a shift from global oil-driven economies to local, more resilient ones are also based on the idea of this shift being *fairer*. That is, exploiting natural resources wherever they are found for as little money as possible is unethical in human as much as environmental terms. Fair trade, for instance, is an accessible champion of socio-economic justice with *just enough* environmental baggage to be absorbed, as *one* message, and have popular currency. This humanity–environment conflation has a consistent policy pedigree. According to the widely cited 'Brundtland definition' produced in response to the 1983 World Commission on Environment and Development, sustainable development is that which "meets the needs of the present without compromising the ability of future generations to meet their own needs" (United Nations, 1987). And there has been a fairly consistent trend towards policy guidance on the basis of this broad definition. Thus, the global blueprint for sustainability in the 21st century produced by the 1992 UNCED 'Earth Summit' in Rio de Janeiro fed into the UNDP coordinated Millennium Development Goals (MDGs) in 2000, in which education, poverty, gender, health and sustainability form part of the same broad anti-poverty agenda:

Goal 1: Eradicate extreme poverty and hunger
Goal 2: Achieve universal primary education
Goal 3: Promote gender equality and empower women
Goal 4: Reduce child mortality
Goal 5: Improve maternal health
Goal 6: Combat HIV/AIDS, malaria and other diseases
Goal 7: Ensure environmental sustainability
Goal 8: Develop a Global Partnership for Development

This led fairly swiftly to a 'plan of implementation', agreed on at World Summit on Sustainable Development, held in Johannesburg in 2002, which led to the UN-declared Decade of Sustainable Development', 2005–2014. And in August 2015 the 2030 Agenda for Sustainable Development replaced the MDGs with 17 'Sustainable Development Goals', intended to "build on the Millennium Development Goals and complete what they did not achieve" and explicitly rejecting what they argue is a false division between human and environmental: "They are integrated and indivisible and balance the three dimensions of sustainable development: the economic, social and environmental" (UN, 2015:1). So even within this emerging paradigm, sustainability is emphatically not just about the physical environment but about balancing "people, . . . planet, . . . prosperity, . . . peace, . . . partnership" (UN, 2015:2).

If sustainability is not only about our physical environment and using fewer resources but also about equal sharing of those resources, this gives education a distinctive set of responsibilities. Instead of equipping the young for competitive capitalism and to master technologies that have limited shelf lives, education would facilitate a new way of thinking about their relationship with the world they live in that promotes collective and long-term good and intergenerational equity. And it would develop the cultural capital and capabilities needed to understand "the underlying factors that provide human societies with the means and adaptations to maintain themselves in their environment" (Cochrane, 2005:318). This is the central position of Education for Sustainable Development (ESD) exponents:

> Education for sustainable development is a vision of education that seeks to balance human and economic well-being with cultural traditions and respect for the Earth's natural resources. It emphasizes aspects of learning that enhance the transition towards sustainability including future education; citizenship education; education for a culture of peace; gender equality and respect for human rights; health education; population education; education for protecting and managing natural resources; and education for sustainable consumption.
>
> (Wals and Kieft, 2010:7)

A 2007 publication spree forced UNESCO's hand in clarifying the differences and connections between Education for International Understanding (EIU), Environmental Education and ESD. UNESCO chose ESD as the umbrella term (UNESCO-APCEIU, 2007) and held a World Conference on ESD in 2009 that produced the Bonn Declaration that urged universities to "mobilise (their) core functions . . .: teaching, research and community engagement to strengthen global and local knowledge of ESD . . ." (UNESCO, 2009).

The importance of this educational role has been fairly consistently acknowledged by educational policy actors, writers and NGOs. In 1990, signatories to the Talloires Declaration exhorted university leaders to establish programmes for "environmentally responsible citizenship' and teaching 'environmental literacy to all . . . students" (ULSF, 2001). And in 1992 the Rio Earth Summit identified education as "critical for promoting sustainable development and improving the capacity of people to address environmental and development issues", defining the development ESD priorities as improving access to education and reorienting education towards sustainability (UNCED, 1992). In 1993 the International Association of Universities adopted the Kyoto Declaration on Sustainable Development, agreeing to develop university capacity to teach, research and take action according to 'sustainable development principles. . .'. By 1994 the Association of European Universities had signed on behalf of its 305 members the COPERNICUS University Charter for Sustainable development, which obliged universities to "incorporate an environmental perspective in all their work and set up environmental education programmes involving teachers and researchers as well as students – all of whom should be exposed to the global challenges of environment and development, irrespective of their field of study . . ." (CRE-COPERNICUS, 1994:2). Declarations of commitment have appeared on a regular basis since, including in 1996 the formation of the Environmental Association of Universities and Colleges, and between 2000 and 2003 the Higher Education Partnership for Sustainability.

And the fundamental position that it is the business of schools and universities to engage with, and lead on, the 'big' issues/problems of our time has shaped, equally, the campaigning work of organisations such as the World Universities Forum and academics' critical thinking about the role of higher education (Naidoo, 2011; Nixon, 2011). The academic field of 'sustainability science' has also emerged, aimed at developing "a comprehensive, holistic approach to identification of problems and perspectives" relating to intergenerational equality or justice (Komiyama and Takeuchi, 2006).

But what does it mean to be 'sustainable' or not? These policy interventions tend not to interrogate compatibility between the vision and the current global econo-political landscape. It has been argued that even on its own terms, the Bonn Declaration failed "to challenge the political economy, specify philosophic values, offer theoretical models, counter current economic rationalism or productively apply critical approaches and empowerment" (Ellis, 2016:37). And while the Brundtland definition goes *so* far towards addressing the issue of intergenerational equality, a slight shift of emphasis towards the future and *well-being*, reveals that the core of the problem is what Jones et al. call 'interconnectivity': "Sustainability represents a condition or set of conditions whereby human and natural systems can continue indefinitely in a state of mutual well-being, security and survival" (Jones et al., 2010:19). It has long been argued that the interdependence of economic, social and political freedoms are the route to global wellbeing – that they have to 'develop' *together* (Sen, 1999). And this premise, of fundamental interconnectedness, is what lies at the base of arguments that political 'sustainability' rhetoric is too narrow, superficial and/or hypocritical to be effective. Sustainability as ecology, on the other hand, redirects our attention to the global inequalities that accompany the essentially competitive nature of development.

That capitalism is unequal, exploitative, unethical and unsustainable is perennially revisited, in The New Left Review, for instance, and in a number of new books (Piketty et al., 2014; Mason, 2015; Stiglitz, 2015), is a fundamental Marxian tenet. For instance, Marx said the following about credit:

> In its beginnings, the credit system sneaks in as a modest helper of accumulation and draws by invisible threads the money resources scattered all over the surface of society into the hands of individual or associated capitalists. But soon it becomes a new and formidable weapon in the competitive struggle, and finally it transforms itself into an immense social mechanism for the centralisation of capitals.
>
> (Marx, 1867, Vol. I, Ch. 25, Section 2, pg.687)

Explaining competitive capitalism as gambling, Marx also showed us long ago how it stops people caring for others:

> In every stock-jobbing swindle everyone knows that some time or other the crash must come, but every one hopes that it may fall on the head of his neighbour, after he himself has caught the shower of gold and placed it in safety.
> (Marx, 1867, Vol. I, Ch. 10, Section 5, pg.296)

All these framings of sustainability are premised, at least broadly, on the idea of equality, which occupies a proportionally bigger space the more politically critical the framing. The financial crash of 2009 witnessed talk that capitalism has had its day, and some consideration of the idea that inequality (its basis) was not only bad for the poor but bad also for growth itself; junk bonds, unaffordable house prices, interest payments instead of investment – it suddenly appeared that the inequalities these produce might be unsustainable distortions to both society and the economy. Thus, 'development', the constant quest for improvement fundamental to capitalism, is also unsustainable – since resources are finite, one person's 'development' will always be at the expense of another person's stagnation or backtracking. And we have seen in this recent phase of economic instability and the widespread unhappiness, violence and injustice that followed some of the ways that economic stability is linked to society, culture and politics. Yet, while minor political actors such as the UK Green Party ground their message in precisely these concerns, it is quite widely claimed that powerful decision-making continues to contribute to unsustainability. For instance, Monbiot argues that vast amounts of public money are spent each year on policies and work that make household flooding inevitable. While UK experts have for decades been sent to remote hill communities to advise on how to prevent their villages being swept away, he calls it "destructive perversity" that "they forgot to bring their lessons home" (Monbiot, 2014). It is an argument that has led to the occasional use of the alternative acronym 'Education for Sustainability' (EfS), which dispenses with the contested 'development'. But with none of the political and economic investment in ESD's effective *norming* of the goal of 'development', it has had little traction and remains largely an aspirational term of resistance.

## Sustainability, citizenship and stakeholding

Sustainability can be seen as the core of citizenship in several distinct but compatible ways. Seeing sustainability in this ethical way highlights the 'stakeholder' aspect of being a citizen, and facing the fact that we all have a stake in our planet is the essence of a place-based concept of citizenship. Furthermore, the business of mutual respect and relations between communities, and challenging exploitation, it brings us back to what has been called 'cultural citizenship' (Stevenson, 2011). And finally, challenging competitive, exploitative, individualistic policies is also the essence of a feminist citizenship. While 'sustainability' rhetoric has begun to prioritise gender equality – the UN Sustainable Development Resolution, for instance, explains the indivisibility of the Goals initially in terms of "the human rights of all and . . . gender equality and the empowerment of all women and girls" (UN, 2015:1) – sustainability has long been a central moral and political issue to feminist citizenship: "In a time of ecological crisis, ecofeminists worldwide have become agents of history/nature. They give voice to subversive politics, aware of its own situatedness and transitionality" (Salleh, 1997, preface). A feminist reading of *global* citizenship means being responsible not only for yourself but also for other people in other societies, and not only now but also in the future: "Bringing ecology, feminism, socialism and indigenous politics together means giving up the Eurocentric lens for a genuinely global one" (Salleh, 1997:103).

This broad commitment to ecology understood as interdependence underpins much of the work of grass-roots movements. The Transition movement, whose cultural and radical aspects we have already discussed, was influenced by the work of Richard Heinberg (2004) on oil-stock depletion and the need to prepare for life afterwards. Aiming initially at encouraging behaviour change to reduce energy consumption, it has since expanded its scope to target environmental and economic sustainability more widely. It sees the solution to oil stock depletion as intrinsically local, community-based 'cultural citizenship' "empower(ing) ordinary citizens in the politics of climate change" (Stevenson, 2011:75). Its fundamental commitment to human equality is explicit in the principle that "there is no room for 'them and us' thinking in the challenge of energy descent planning", and in its rejection of centralised control, it also seeks to model "the ability of natural systems to self organize" (Transition United States, 2013, the US national hub of the international Transition Network, http://transitionus.org/transition-town-movement).

Although it has been argued that the focus of the Transition Movement is not so much about distribution, more about feeling and participation (Stevenson, 2011), this approach to ecological sustainability helps us to see stakeholder citizenship as 'sharing' on a deeper level. It also forces us to engage head-on with several tensions between individualist or competitive and communal or democratic models of stakeholding. For instance, Stevenson notes the "disconcerting language of certitude" (2011:76), and while movements like Transition may be grass roots there is still a good deal of powerful/hegemonic linguistic norming going on. Stevenson also points out the lack of *real* attention to socio-economic class in dominant sustainability discourses. And he argues that there is still work to be done, in movements such as Transition, to "convert life politics not only into public questions but also into forms of public power" (Stevenson, 2011:77). Stevenson is pointing out a lack of radical democracy, then, at the levels of ideas, socio-economic inclusion and political voice.

It is a problem that has also been discussed in a slightly different way, contrasting stakeholder citizenship in its ideal form as collectivism with its practical neoliberal meaning. Looking critically at household sustainability (as 'green/active citizenship'), it has been argued that in its responsibilising emphasis on changing oneself, in privileging private morality and 'virtue' over collective action, this discourse *prevents* communal engagement on political issues that need rectifying

(Scerri, 2012). Scerri argues that this allows the hegemonic de-coupling of 'sustainability' from competitive growth, and, it might be added, the norming process helps to tip the business of 'being green' into competitive individualism: 'I can do this "sustainability" thing better than others'. It is a problem that should be familiar; it is central as we discussed in Chapter 1 to policy conceptions of 'citizenship' per se. By way of contrast, to achieve an ecological "politics of shared and not personal responsibility" (Scerri, 2009:480) and to avert the danger of stakeholder citizenship being *subverted* into competitive individualism (Scerri, 2009:473), we are once more back at the importance of citizenship of collective, radical action.

## Who is responsible? Educating for ecological stakeholder citizenship

Ecological campaigners like Monbiot and Klein emphasize the disproportionate role of the most economically wealthy and competitive societies in producing the ecological problems they then profess to be committed to solving (Monbiot, 2014). This campaigning literature is simultaneously a rallying cry for grass-roots activism and for a reorientation of education, especially as it has been pointed out that

> [i]t is worth noting that (the destruction of the planet) is not the work of ignorant people. Rather it is largely the results of work by people with BAs, BScs, LLBs, MBAs, and PhDs . . . Education can equip people to be more effective vandals of the earth. If one listens carefully, it may even be possible to hear the Creation groan every year in late May when another batch of smart, degree-holding, but ecologically illiterate, Homo sapiens who are eager to succeed are launched into the biosphere.
>
> (Orr, 1994:52)

This view is reflected across the grass-roots and sub-political movements we have discussed. For instance, the '7 Guiding Principles of Transition' (in the US movement) are fundamentally about education. The first, 'Positive Visioning', focuses on "[t]he generation of new stories and myth"; the second, 'Education and knowledge', on promoting awareness of environmental and economic issues in a "non-directive" way; the third is 'Dialogue'; and the seventh, 'Subsidiarity', is focused on principles of open and inclusive dialogue (Transition United States, 2013). And the way in which Transition UK envisages 'community' as the solution to the ecological crisis is through grass-roots education, "engaging their communities in home-grown, citizen-led education, action, and multi-stakeholder planning to increase local self reliance and resilience." The shared learning package produced and disseminated by the first badged 'transition town', Totnes, shows the way this dissemination process works (https://www.transitionnetwork.org/support/; http://www.transitionstreets.org.uk/).

But the long pedigree of critical pedagogues whose work we have drawn on in this book would also argue that this is *the* point of education per se – to engage with and help define (through discussion and the imparting and exercise of wisdom) the important issues of our time and, hopefully, the future. And if ecological sustainability is as core as it appears to citizenship, it follows that this should be a central focus of education. The demands of a world interconnected in the ways we have seen demand a transformative vision of education that is not about equipping the young for competitive capitalism but for a new way of thinking about their relationship with the world and other people. This is the position that Freire moved towards in his later years, that "[e]cology has to be present in every radical practice" (Freire, 2000:66).

Far from the isomorphic *following* of market-oriented institutional norms that is now firmly established as the modus operandi for educational policy, practice and governance (Meyer and Rowan, 2006), part of this involves unpicking, as many have argued, the diktat of hegemonic discourses, the "popular forms of common sense" that neo-liberal forms of globalisation have helped to construct (Stevenson, 2011:67). And one of the first things that need unpicking is the educational prioritisation of competitive neo-liberal market principles, which are produced by reductive, competitive forms of education itself – challenging, that is, an economically globalised education system that "attempt(s) to harness education to the rapid and competitive growth and transmission of technologies and knowledge linked to the national competitiveness of nations within the global economy" (Ozga and Lingard, 2007b:70). Indeed, critiques of the way that globalisation prioritises individual competition over equality is beginning to run through some of the sustainability literature, in the Swedish International Development Cooperation Agency (SIDA), for instance:

> For instance, the glorification of the knowledge society and the commoditization of education in general and higher education in particular tend to favour the creation of a global economy with a mobile, resilient and 'lifelong learning' workforce who also play the role of eager consumers of universal products at the expense of local identities, critical thinking and values alternative to material ones.
> (Wals and Kieft [citing Raven 2001], 2010:22)

An ecologically focused form of education, by contrast, would focus on the importance of 'wisdom' (rather than the ability merely to manipulate lots of information) in facilitating the ability of humans to live together in peace and harmony. Just as Freire coined the term *conscientisation*' to denote the way that re-seeing one's relationship with the world can open up possibilities of acting on and changing it for the better, the term consilience has been applied to a form of all-encompassing wisdom, understanding of the interdependence of everything that both the unity and the precariousness of the world itself demands (Wilson, 1999:306–307). That such thinking, against the arbitrary divisions between disciplines in pursuit of understanding that leads to appropriate action in overcoming a great danger, so closely echoes Lindsay's mid-20th-century rationale for the Keele experiment further underscores the interconnectedness of environmental and human perspectives on ecology.

A strategy for ecological citizenship education (or what has been called 'sustainable citizenship education'; Warwick, 2012) would first be characterised, therefore, by a sustained and coherent view of sustainability as ecology, as cultural citizenship – in which structure, mutual respect and understanding are integrally connected and essential to making positive change in a world in which we all have an equal share and responsibility to keep whole. The critical dimension of such a curriculum would involve interrogating and challenging 'development' and competition as goals, individually and collectively. It would teach about education's role in both causing ecological harm and in shaping a more just society. And it would shift the current emphasis away from householder virtue towards enlightened political participation and activism.

In terms of precisely *how* education can be reshaped towards this end, there are clear challenges and some acknowledgement of the impact of local circumstances:

> The often forgotten 'E' in ESD can be conceptualized in different ways, depending on the amount of space there is for participation, self-determination and autonomous thinking. When this space is narrow, a more transmissive version of ESD is likely to result with a strong emphasis on instructional forms of teaching and knowledge transfer. When this space is broad, then ESD will emerge that is characterized by higher levels of participation, self-determination, autonomous thinking and knowledge co-creation. The latter, more transformative, versions of ESD require alternative teaching and learning strategies that also allow for the development of new competences. A country's tradition in governance might affect what a country emphasizes; a more pedagogical orientation towards ESD consequently implying (social) learning, participation and capacity-building or a more instrumental orientation that emphasizes a change in people's behaviour.
>
> (Wals and Kieft, 2010:7)

But within these variable parameters, ecological or sustainable citizenship education would definitely not be shoved into special 'extra' slots to be taught by teachers with neither interest in nor understanding of these issues. Such a version of transformative education, once more, requires both adequate training, education and incentivising of teachers, as well as a shift in policy away from reductive and competitive curricula and testing regimes that get individuals, institutions or states further forward only at the expense of others. In terms of how it would actually look, the 'critical literacy' (reflexivity), 'creative thinking' (thinking beyond predetermined solutions) and 'active learning' (participation) elements of such an approach have been written about (Warwick, 2012:135–138). As we saw in Chapter 3, Warwick's exposition of dilemma-based learning in the context of OSDE (open space for dialogue and enquiry) methodology was grounded in educating for sustainability citizenship (Warwick, 2012). However, the desirability of an overall democratic approach notwithstanding, part of this is a matter of curriculum content, where the experience, the history and the politics of the ecological problem are explained and illustrated on both local and global scales. This – not shying away from imparting knowledge – was, after all, a feature of the

Citizen School Project; it was not about action without content. Allowing the young to learn by seeing (after all, the technology and removal or porosity of so many previously opaque boundaries allows this today) combined with the provision of safe spaces and tools for open dialogue, is more likely than the prevailing current policy of relying on ever-changing political messages about 'priorities' to lead to grass-roots collective ownership of what is in the collective long-term interest. Opportunities for ensuing action should include actual political space and connections with actors outside the school or university, and *assume* the possibility of structural change to flow from that action.

## The application (or not) of ecological citizenship education principles

Despite today's overwhelming competitive educational focus, there are examples of education policy that addresses these sorts of links between (in)equality, capitalism, development, competition and sustainability. The more explicitly (or less *conflicted*) values-based educational approach in Australia promotes a 'national' identity in which the goals of equality and 'the common good' are prioritised over 'development':

> Civics and citizenship education promotes students' participation in Australia's democracy by equipping them with the knowledge, skills, values and dispositions of active and informed citizenship. It entails knowledge and understanding of Australia's democratic heritage and traditions, its political and legal institutions and the shared values of freedom, tolerance, respect, responsibility and inclusion.

In this, sustainability is integrally linked with intercultural understanding and appreciation of cultural diversity (de Leo, 2012). Recently, more centrally coordinated, the new curriculum now has sustainability firmly in the 'Civics and Citizenship' curriculum, in the 'Citizenship, Diversity and Identity' thread, the other two being: 'Government and Democracy' and 'Law and Citizens' (ACARA, 2015). While previous versions of Australia's curriculum tended to switch between the acronyms ESD and EfS (ACARA, 2012), the new curriculum relies less on labels, and instead teaches the material as core ecological knowledge. For instance, a lower-middle/secondary lesson in the unit called 'For the Good of All: Understanding the Common Good in Australian Democracy' has as its aims "[f]or students to investigate a significant civics and citizenship education issue, and apply their understanding of the 'common good' to the challenges of climate change and sustainability" (ESA, 2015). And giving the lie to the 'post-materialist' thesis (that environmentalism is really only an option for the rich), Tongan education is aimed at teaching the young how to live sustainably (*nofo fakapotopoto*, literally 'intelligent living'). And as an exemplar of place-based citizenship education, it grounds this in the ways that different physical environments, cultures, political systems and educational traditions mandate distinct approaches (Thaman and Thaman, 2009:65).

Closer to home, the idea of interdependence has appeared belatedly in ACT literature, under the heading, 'Diversity and values':

> Interdependence . . . enables pupils to consider how their thinking progresses from the local to the global in relation to everyday things at their school and home; the air miles for food, climate change, energy security, migration and immigration and war. It can enable for example powerful questions about child labour and the clothes pupils wear, the price paid for them, the denial of education to child labourers, and the connections between high street vendors and factories in Bangladesh.
>
> (ACT, 2014)

Yet in this, the perennial 'something-for-everyone' UK~English approach to citizenship education persists; many boxes are ticked (communities, environment, financial education, economic development, Active Citizenship, reuse and recycle . . .) without being integrated around a unifying core – with the result that it is not at all clear how sustainability is being conceived:

> Sustainable living: This concept revolves around needs, wants and the notion of living in a fair and equitable way for all. It is about how communities resolve future needs in a more sophisticated way; understanding the interconnection between the social, economic and environmental spheres and considering probable and preferable futures and how to achieve the latter. As Citizenship includes financial education, this is also an opportunity to appreciate that economic development is only one aspect of quality of life and that this needs to be balanced to meet the conflicting and competing demands of varied communities across the globe. There is much opportunity in exploring this concept to engage in active Citizenship projects. If these use the reduce, reuse and recycle mantra they should relate strongly to wider political aspects of Citizenship; about how communities make decisions on sustainable living and who influences those with power.
>
> (ACT, 2014)

By contrast, some examples of devolved education policy do a better job. The Welsh newly 'national' education policy was conceived with "education for sustainable development and global citizenship" at its core: "Wales is . . . one of the few world nations with sustainable development at the heart of government" (Wales, 2012).

A really good example of integrated work on citizenship, understanding sustainability is seen a core part of global citizenship – more collaborative and integrated across its public services and policy than England, and as young people's *right*: "Young people have a right to understand the crucial issues facing the planet and know how they can personally play a part in helping shape the future" (Wales, 2012). While in Scotland, there is quite an emphatic focus on the environmental aspect, especially saving water. While this emphasis is redolent of top-down discourse definition, on the plus side, 'EDS' was changed in 2015 to 'EfS' and is dealt with (on a policy level at least) as one of three key 'themes across learning' – along with global citizenship and entrepreneurship, "an ideal vehicle for interdisciplinary learning":

> Learning for sustainability (LfS) is an approach to learning, life and work. It enables learners, educators, schools and their wider communities to build a socially-just, sustainable and equitable society. An effective whole school and community approach to LfS weaves together global citizenship, sustainable development education, outdoor learning and children's rights to create coherent, rewarding and transformative learning experiences.

Though this commendably broad ecological framing is undermined by a cover picture of young children looking at bugs through a magnifying glass (Education Scotland, 2015)!

In England, however, there has been a consistent tendency for bandwagon rhetoric to be unsupported by policy, and to dissolve on probing. For instance, although skills for sustainable development were said over a decade ago to be a "vital national asset" (DfES, 2003:8), and to amount to more than green householding:

> Sustainable development is a way of thinking about how we organize our lives and work – including our education system – so that we don't destroy our most precious resource, the planet . . . It must be much more than recycling bottles or giving money to charity. It is about thinking and working in a profoundly different way.
>
> (DfES, 2006:6)

Again this hint at holism has been repeatedly undone by a return to the very unimaginative activities that might promote such an aim, as we see in OFSTED's (Office for Standards in Education, Children's Services and Skills) evaluative criteria, which come down to good behaviour and responsibility, in terms that are un-interrogated: "The most successful schools were able to show that an increased appreciation of the need to care for the environment also led pupils to take greater pride in the local environment." But it gets worse: the same 2009 report, when it eventually, reluctantly, gets to defining 'sustainability' reveals nothing more than the old preoccupation with litter, recycling and saving energy (OFSTED, 2009). Promising sentences like "The most successful work on sustainability linked learning to action, so that pupils knew how they could make a difference" (OFSTED, 2009:13) lose impact when it is revealed that the *ways* students are encouraged to 'act' are ones that will make no 'difference' at all: "The pupils looked at a bag of rubbish and discussed what could be recycled or composted. To test the comparative biodegradability of paper and plastic, they buried bags in the soil for four weeks and compared the results" (OFSTED, 2009:13). At best, this is green householding; at worst risible, and *nothing* to do with challenging inequality and competitiveness.

And so it has continued. In 2012, for instance, another promising-sounding opening to OFSTED's Guide for Inspectors, "While sustainable development is often thought to focus on environmental challenges, it actually focuses on . . ." is immediately undercut with the reductive backtracking in the second half of the sentence: "maximising social and economic outcomes as well as environmental ones. Sustainable development has a broad focus, including health, well-being and sustainable communities, as well as issues like waste management, energy use and resource management" (OFSTED, 2012).

In English *higher* education, the key policy awareness moments discussed above have resulted in some institutional and strategic initiatives, such as in 2005 the Higher Education for England's (HEFCE's) Sustainable Development in Higher Education consultation document, outlining a vision where sustainability forms a central part of HEFCE's strategy for future development. While still using the contested 'development' term, this document does at least acknowledge that higher education has contributed to unsustainable scenarios: "Few students graduate with an understanding of how to make a specific contribution to future social and economic development in a sustainable way" (HEFCE, 2005a:7). The solution is seen as a mixture of knowledge and skills: "the greatest contribution education has to make to sustainable development is by enabling students to develop new skills and knowledge" (HEFCE, 2005a:14), though the nature of this knowledge and these skills are not developed. Subsequent reviews and strategic action plans do little more beyond continuing to state the importance of 'sustainable development' and (interchangeably) 'sustainability', and calling for institutional champions (HEFCE, 2005b, 2008 & 2009). The UK's Higher Education Academy's (HEA's) 2011 pilot change programme, 'Green Academy', superficially reflected a view of sustainability that blended human and environmental aspects of ecology, aiming to enhance graduates capabilities "to contribute to sustainable and just societies" (HEA, 2011). But again this nod to issues of equality was not sustained; its 2012–2016 Strategic Plan reverts to a pragmatic view of the challenges as "satisfying greater expectations with less resource, flexible delivery, equality and diversity, assessment and feedback, education for sustainable development, reward and recognition, employability and internationalisation." A planned collaboration with the non-profit Forum for the Future failed to get off the ground as objectors cited the principle of "non-intrusion into the affairs of notionally independent tertiary institutions" (Jones et al., 2010:4). One critic of this new agenda, the vice-chancellor of the University of Central England, explained his objection in terms of academic freedom:

> [The HEFCE] circular on sustainable development . . . is one of the most pernicious and dangerous circulars ever to be issued. . . . The issue here is not whether sustainable development is a good or bad idea. It is about the basic rights and responsibilities of universities and the need to safeguard academic freedom. It is not the job of universities to promote a particular political orthodoxy; it is their role to educate students to examine critically policies, ideas, concepts and systems, then to make up their own minds.
>
> (Knight, 2005)

On one level, this is reminiscent of criticisms of Prevent. Yet the important difference is that sustainability or ecological citizenship education does not 'other' particular categories of people, nor are academics and teachers asked to enlist as informers.

HEIs themselves are also beginning to engage with the sustainability agenda in a variety of ways, including the supposed 'greening' of campuses, the creation of 'sustainability czars', sustainability symposia and hosting sustainability SRHE network events. The University of Plymouth Centre established a Centre for Sustainable Futures in 2005, the University of Bradford an 'Ecoversity' in 2006, and Keele University gave a nod to its radical roots in electing Jonathan Porritt, sustainability champion and 1996 founder of Forum for the Future as chancellor in 2012, the university's symbolic half-centenary. In keeping with this symbolism, Keele then embedded through its 2015 Strategic Plan its 'Deep Green' policy and commitment to 'Greening the Curriculum'. This is reflected in its balanced mission: to contribute "positively to social, environmental, and economic agendas locally, nationally and internationally"; its values: "The University is committed to . . . environmental and economic sustainability"; the fifth of its Strategic Aims: "To develop an environmentally aware and sustainable outward facing campus community"; and its strategic objectives: "To provide models of innovation and good practice in environmental sustainability through all our activities". Continued effort to sustain awareness of these aims and objectives has included holding a 'sustainability forum', making "[a]n appreciation of the social, environmental and global implications of your studies and other activities, including recognition of any ethical implications", the fifth of Keele's Distinctive Graduate Attributes statements, and the badging of 'Keele citizens'. But what is *more* indicative of levels of awareness and understanding is how these issues are reflected in spontaneous conversation. The 'greening' of campus was the main point of contention, for instance, in a 2015 public row about campus car parking. The popular email debate captured the 'development' dilemma at the heart of higher education today. More parking facilities were needed, it was argued, for more students. Growth was needed in order to be able to compete in the market through economy of scale. The conclusion was that economic sustainability was only achievable at the cost of environmental and ethical sustainability.

The economic and competitive pressures on schools and universities look likely to continue to constrain any room for principled thinking, when this is not economically remunerative. It is hard to see ways in which formal education might really encourage new ways of thinking about our relationship with the world and other people that promotes collective and long-term good and causes no harm. It is hard to see any formal education-mediated real change in terms of making the world more equal and sustainable. And it is hard to shake the view that, even in their own limited terms, few if any of these initiatives are more than tokenistic. Curriculum change, at best, has largely been limited to 'sharing best practice'. Yet it has been suggested that it may, ironically, be the market itself that challenges inertia – that this cause will be the new face of student activism as graduates are faced by very different conditions than those of a generation ago and will need understanding, outlooks and skills necessary to cope with conditions of uncertainty, complexity and rapid change. And as employer demand for 'sustainability-literate' graduates and 'future-proof' skills rises, apparently), students may seek universities that reflect good sustainability practices (Business in the Community, 2010; Bone and Agombar, 2011).

## Conclusion

This chapter has considered relationships between (in)equality, capital, capitalism and competition, asking how these relationships reflect ecological citizenship principles and what a real commitment to citizenship as sustainability say would say about the role of education. Seeing the world as interconnected in the ways we have discussed underscores the importance of teaching ecological and cultural sustainability, not as green housekeeping and not 'along with' citizenship – but as central to citizenship and therefore as central to the curriculum. Tokenistic and narrow definitions of sustainability will lead to the same shoddy pedagogy that we have seen in much 'citizenship education'. Ecologically focused curricula across educational levels would be a far more systemic matter. Far from taking the kids out to sow seeds, it would interrogate and challenge 'development' and competition as goals, and instead focus on new ways of thinking about their relationship with the world and other people that promotes collective and long-term good and causes no harm. They would do this through content, ideology, pedagogy and links with communities outside school. Curriculum content would examine the problem on both local and global scales, exploring it from historical, political and philosophical perspectives. Schools and universities would provide safe spaces and tools for open dialogue leading to grass-roots collective ownership of action in the collective long-term interest. Opportunities for that action would include political space (and connections with actors outside school) for structural change to flow from that action.

The chapter has also looked for forms and approaches to education that both challenge competitiveness and prioritise values and behaviours, including activism, that fight against unequal distribution and exploitation of both human and natural capital. There is widespread rhetorical acknowledgement of the importance of both a commitment to sustainability and 'transformational' education, and rhetorical readiness to assume the mandate for change. But long with Ellis, we have to conclude that "micropolitics has failed to challenge macropolitics . . . preventing . . . ESD and citizenship studies from uniting educationally moral purposes of social justice with radical democracy" (Ellis, 2016:37). While competitive capitalism gets us nowhere in terms of providing better for all, a collective form of stakeholder citizenship grounded in a politics of equal responsibility and thus education appears to have little traction for policy-makers and practitioners locked into a cycle of fearful competition. Far from taking responsibility, including for its own part in getting us to this sad state through isomorphic aping rather than agenda setting, education's reluctance to challenge power and underlying structures leaves 'sustainability' largely at the householder virtue level.

However, the ways in which policy, curricular and pedagogic approaches to sustainability and ecology vary in different places do three things. To our theoretical understanding of place-based citizenship, they underscore the extent to which place matters – the same ingredients, in different measures. The policy lesson is therefore, again, that genuine engagement with local communities and grass-roots movements is more likely to lead to positive change. And third, they illustrate the *scope* there *is* to do make such change. From the Welsh case of a newly 'national' or devolved education policy conceived with "education for sustainable development and global citizenship" at its core (Wales, 2012) through to Tongan education as an exemplar of fit between education's purpose and local culture, these differences underscore the ineffectiveness of blanket definitions and solutions that are dictated by those in powerful positions and which become 'policy'. We have seen in repeated examples the lack of impact of policy that is unconnected to real lives and real needs.

# Final thoughts
## The educational mandate for boundary-crossing in an interdependent world

Neither 'global citizenship' or 'citizenship education' as badges nor as educational frameworks are fit for the purpose of inspiring and shaping productive change amid the shifting and unpredictable flows that are produced by the processes of re-scoping. Boundaries are being broken and crossed, there are multiple and diverse challenges to state power, traditional political lines are crumbling and nations are dividing in a complex shattering of identity, ideological and social structures. Yet competitive capitalism combined with increasing censorship means more inequality and less freedom to challenge injustices that are also produced. Viewing education as both problem and solution, this book has explored three things: first, the dimensions of a radical, ecological, stakeholder, critically multicultural, community-based form of citizenship that addresses this context; second, some of the ways that education *has* promoted, facilitated and mediated the shaping and exercise of citizenship through and some different ways in which education can be seen as *the* space for radical thinking, for transformative learning grounded in the ideals of encounter, for struggle, for crossing boundaries, and for taking social, political and ideational risks and radical thinking; and third, therefore, how we *should* think of education's place in a world attempting to ride the choppy waters of combined globalisation, localism, anti-state revolt and xenophobia.

Describing the context in such terms also underscores the importance of place and localism, in the sense that re-scoping and boundary crossing can lead, as we have seen, to increased need for "the right to name ourselves" (Harstock, 1987:196). We have also seen various ways in which claiming this right *need not* be ethnonationalist and exclusivist but be based on living together in the same place, involved in community relations within and across boundaries.

Attempting to understand how local and global perspectives interact in this picture, without, as Massey and Said separately argued, attempting to "institute horizons, to establish boundaries . . . to stabilize the meaning of particular envelopes of space-time" (Massey, 1994:5) in a categorising and controlling way, we have seen locally differentiated forms of glocalisation. Through looking at phenomena from both global and local (including some 'national') *perspectives*, we have seen clearly that these do not contradict each other. Debating, which is the more important aspect of citizenship, therefore, is founded on false alternatives. We have seen that, *however*, 'the nation' is drawn into this project, doing so in a 'fundamental British values', top-down and exclusionary sense is unproductive. A grass-roots 'place-counts' invocation of 'the national', on the other hand, as one of several meaning-bestowing spaces is more conducive to the active shaping of citizenship by communities of people living together in the same place, a more genuinely productive framework for "a renegotiated and inclusive national identity" (Meer and Modood, 2012:190) and a truer representation of how citizenship is actually experienced. Glocalising processes are unpredictable and situationally specific, as illustrated, for instance, by the ways that Arab Gulf women are assigning meaning to global influences and acting on existing structures in somewhat unexpected ways, including some that appear to entrench gender differences, or, for a more historical example, by the dramatically different evolutions of the US and Northern Ireland civil rights movements. As Robertson warned us, homogenisation and heterogenisation *absolutely* coexist (R. Robertson, 1995), and this fusion is producing really interesting forms of citizenship.

Of pluralism, assimilation and integration as approaches to managing this diverse, fluid and shifting world, their shortcomings revealing them more as slogans rather than offering ways to promote inclusive bonding over shared purpose. *If* we need labels to inspire the right sorts of policies, structures, actions and understandings, then 'critical multiculturalism' and 'ecological' are as good as any, insofar as the focus attention on important debates, facilitate engagement with people across boundaries, and remind us that the world is interconnected – in all of its dimensions. This is a fairly radical citizenship agenda, asking fundamental questions about the sustainability of development and competitiveness and the *desirability* in an interdependent world of everyone being in competition with each other.

However, understanding citizenship as equal share, equal freedom, equal stake in the world and equal responsibility for both the present and the future across boundaries requires education. Furthermore, as I have argued, it requires an approach to education that focuses on the acquisition of 'wisdom', – a *transformative* form of education that is not about equipping the young for competitive capitalism, but for a new way of thinking about their relationship with the world and other people. It demands a form of education not for a dumbed-down form of 'democratisation' but for the Deweyan 'democratic ideal'. To commit seriously to both reflecting and *shaping* society fit for the next century if we are to make sure that the boundaries being broken, crossed and reshaped are done for the greater good requires far-sighted education policies that not only acknowledge but actively embrace education's role in shaping consciousness and providing the critical skills needed to challenge indoctrination and raise awareness of the need for social change. Instead of promoting divisive competition, this form of education would educate *about* citizenship in its various forms, encourage young people to value community (within and across boundaries that while not defining or categorising nonetheless provide frameworks and meaning) and promote the sorts of open and radical thinking that can help them to cross ideological and physical borders and use their voice in line with their own (and others') real, long-term interests.

Understanding citizenship in this way also requires readiness to confront power and injustice. The examples discussed here underline the importance of a form of conscientising' education that takes seriously its responsibility to shape and channel productive social and political action. We have discussed ways in which education has mediated (through omission, through ad hoc efforts, through 'safe spaces' and through different and distinct approaches to policy) enlightened and un-enlightened political participation, community building, the challenging of power and its exercise. To re-embrace their transformative social and critical role, education systems, institutions and curricula need actively to help the young navigate our changing world to make it a better one.

Again, the issues are global but responses local. Locatedness, the demand to 'listen to us, here!', is an increasingly prominent feature of grass-roots demands for democracy. The spatial forms of education are also diverse and multiple: a disembedded process, phenomenon, flow of consciousness, resource for exploring diversity, site for seeing society in action, site of struggle or in an institutional sense in terms of structures and governance.

As we have seen here, across the UK, the US and the Arab Gulf well-educated people are demanding equality. But schools and universities understood as either *sites* for the construction of citizenship or *communities* of actual citizens, are located in specific places. The movements, policies, stories and projects discussed here are all different, grounded in local experiences and local needs and varying according to local space, local interpretations, local culture and local challenges. We should, therefore, as Giroux cautioned, "resist the recuperation of (for instance) Freire's work as an academic commodity, a recipe for all times and places" (Giroux, 1992b). But at their best, the citizenship work of educational institutions is not limited by their boundaries. We can, and should, learn from examples of what is possible and from the history of what happens when we do not learn.

Yet we have found problems with the perfunctory ways in which this happens in *formal* education settings. Risk-averse, competitive and responsibilising policies and forms of education will not do the trick. Recent events have brought equality, voice and identity into fresh focus. While isolationism is futile, increased access to information about life elsewhere feeds anger at inequalities. Political elites need to realise this and shift from remote politics that ignore local needs for equality, voice and belonging. But they also need to understand that complaining about people not understanding the world and not using their votes properly is unjustified if they are not educated to do so. We should not be surprised that risk-averse, competitively focused education that allocates a resource-draining yet undervalued hour or so per week for politically correct responsibilising classes produces disengagement, confusion and an inability to understand one's own long-term interests or the connections between people in fluid communities. Yet seen against what is possible, these manifest inadequacies themselves show how education can be used to change the world for the better. To re-embrace their transformative social and critical role, education systems, institutions and curricula need to both instruct and mobilise for collective action that helps the young navigate our changing world to make it a better one. The resources that education provides need to be used to at least attempt to right wrongs.

# References

Abbas, Al-Murshid, 'Protests in Bahrain are about citizen rights not identity politics', Arab Reform Initiative, email 11/3/11

ACARA (The Australian Curriculum, Assessment and Reporting Authority), 2012, 'The Shape of the Australian Curriculum: Civics and Citizenship', http://www.acara.edu.au/

ACARA (The Australian Curriculum, Assessment and Reporting Authority), 2015, 'Tracked changes to F-10 Australian Curriculum', http://www.acara.edu.au/verve/_resources/Changes_to_the_F-10_Australian_Curriculum.pdf

ACT, 2014, e-news, 18 December 2014, citing Edward Timpson MP, Parliamentary Under-Secretary of State for Education, 27th/11/2014

ACT, 2015, http://www.teachingcitizenship.org.uk/about, accessed 19/6/15

ACT, 2015i, http://www.teachingCitizenship.org.uk/resource/global-learning-programme-and-citizenship

ACT, 2015ii, 'The Prevent Duty and Controversial Issues', email 15/12/15

Adams, Tim, 2015, 'Art gets things out in the open' – young British Muslim artists tell their stories', *The Observer*, The New Review, 12/4/15:12

Agnew, John A., 1989, 'The devaluation of place in social science', in Agnew J., and Duncan J. (9–29)

Agnew, John A. and James S. Duncan (eds.), 1989, *The Power of Place: bringing together the geographical and sociological imaginations*, Boston: Unwin Hyman

Ajegbo, Keith, 2007, 'Curriculum Review: diversity and citizenship', http://resources.cohesioninstitute.org.uk/Publications/Documents/Document/DownloadDocumentsFile.aspx?recordId=48&file=PDFversion

al-Ali, Nadja, 2000, *Secularism, Gender and the State in the Middle East*, Cambridge: Cambridge University Press

Alexiadou, Nafsika, 'The Europeanization of Education Policy: Researching Changing Governance and 'New' Modes of Coordination', *Research in Comparative and International Education*, 2:2, 102–116

Al-Kubaisi, Fatima, 2010, 'Partnership in the Qatari family' (in Arabic), Doha: Supreme Council for Family Affairs

Anderson, Benedict, 1991, *Imagined Communities: reflections on the origin and spread of nationalism*, London: Verso

Apple, Michael, 1993, 'The politics of official knowledge: Does a national curriculum make sense?', *Teachers College Record*, 95:2, 222–241

Apple, Michael, 1993/2000, *Official Knowledge: democratic education in a conservative age*, Abingdon: Routledge (2nd ed.)

Apple, Michael, 2003, *The State and the Politics of Knowledge*, New York: RoutledgeFalmer

AQA, 2013, 'GCE AS and A Level Specification, Citizenship Studies: For exams from June 2014 onwards; For certification from June 2014 onwards', Manchester: AQA

Arnot, Madeleine, 2002, *Reproducing Gender? Essays on Educational Theory and Feminist Politics*, London: RoutledgeFalmer
Arthur, James, 2005, 'Introduction to Arthur and Bohlin', in James Arthur and Karen Bohlin (eds.), *Citizenship and Higher Education: the role of universities in community and society* (135–157), London: RoutledgeFalmer
Arthur, James and Hilary Cremin (eds.), 2012, *Debates in Citizenship Education*, Abingdon: Routledge
Atran, Scott, 2015, 'Mindless terrorists? The truth about Isis is much worse', *The Guardian*, 15/11/15, http://www.theguardian.com/commentisfree/2015/nov/15/terrorists-isis
AWID, 2004, 'Intersectionality: a tool for gender and economic justice', *Women's Rights and Economic Change*, 9/08/04, http://www.awid.org/sites/default/files/atoms/files/intersectionality_a_tool_for_gender_and_economic_justice.pdf
Back, Les, Keith, Michael, Khan, Azra, Shukra, Kalbir and Solomos, John, 2002, 'New Labour's White Heart: Politics, multiculturalism and the return of assimilation', *The Political Quarterly*, 73:4, 445–454
Baki, Roula, 2004, 'Gender-segregated Education in Saudi Arabia: Its Impact on Social Norms and the Saudi Labour Market', *Education Policy Analysis Archives*, 12:28. http://epaa.asu.edu/epaa/v12n28/
Ball, Stephen, 1994, *Education Reform: a critical and post-structural approach*, Buckingham: Oxford University Press
Banaji, Shakuntala and David Buckingham, 2013, *The Civic Web: young people, the internet, and civic participation*, Cambridge, MA: MIT Press
Banks, James A., 2001, 'Citizenship Education and Diversity: implications for teacher education', *Journal of Teacher Education*, 52:5, 5–16
Baraka, Pakinaz, 2008, 'Citizenship education in Egyptian Public Schools: what values to teach and in which administrative and political contexts?', *Journal of Education for International Development*, 3:3 (online journal: http://www.equip123.net/jeid/articles/7/Baraka-CitizenshipEducation.pdf)
Bates, Richard, 2012, 'Is global citizenship possible, and can international schools provide it?', *Journal of Research in International Education*, 11:3, 262–274
Bauböck, Rainer, 2005, 'Expansive Citizenship: Voting beyond Territory and Membership', *Political Science and Politics*, 38:4, 683–687, American Political Science Association, http://www.jstor.org/stable/30044350
Bauböck, Rainer, 2007, 'Stakeholder Citizenship and Transnational Political Participation: A Normative Evaluation of External Voting', *Fordham Law Review*, 75:2393, http://ir.lawnet.fordham.edu/flr/vol75/iss5/4
Bauböck, Rainer, 2008, 'Stakeholder citizenship: an idea whose time has come?', Washington, DC: Migration Policy Unit, http://www.migrationpolicy.org
Baumann, Gerd, 1996, *Contesting Culture: discourses of identity in multi-ethnic London*, Cambridge: Cambridge University Press
BBC, 2013, 'Viewpoint: How should radicalisation be tackled?', BBC News, 29/5/13, interview with Brooke Rogers, Kings, London
BBC, 2014, 'The Moral Maze', *Radio 4*, 26/11/14
BBC, 2015, 'We British', *Radio 4*, 8/10/15
Bell, 2005, 'Citizenship through participation and responsible action', speech, 15/11/2005, http://www.ofsted.gov.uk
Benhabib, Seyla, 1992, 'Models of public space, Hannah Arendt, the liberal tradition and Jurgen Habermas', in Craig Calhoun (ed.), *Habermas and the Public Sphere* (73–98), Cambridge, MA: MIT Press

Bennett, W. Lance, 2007, 'Civic Learning in Changing Democracies: Challenges for Citizenship and Civic Education', in P. Dahlgren (ed.), *Young Citizens and New Media: learning and democratic engagement* (59–77), New York: Routledge

Bernstein, Basil, 1975, 'Class and Pedagogies: visible and invisible', *Educational Studies*, 1:1, 1

Bernstein, Basil, 1977, *Class, Codes and Social Control*, Boston and London: Routledge

Blake, Nigel, Richard Smith and Paul Standish, 1998, *The Universities We Need*, London: Kogan Page

Bleiklie, Ivar, 2000, 'Universities as sites of citizenship', *Report Submitted to the Working Party*, CC-HER, Council of Europe

Bleiklie, Ivar, 2012, 'Universities as Sites of Citizenship and Civic Responsibility Project Proposal', *Higher Education, Civic Responsibility and Democracy*, NSF Pilot Project Proposal, International Consortium

Bone, Elizabeth and Jamie Agombar, 2011, 'First year attitudes towards, and skills in, sustainable development', York: Higher Education Academy

Bourdieu, Pierre, 1991, *Language and Symbolic Power*, Cambridge: Polity Press

Bourdieu, Pierre, 1990, *Reproduction in Education, Society and Culture*, London: Sage Publications

Breslin, Shaun, Richard Higgott and Ben Rosamond, 2002, 'Regions in Comparative Perspective', Introduction in Breslin Shaun et al. (eds.), *New Regionalisms in the Global Political Economy: theories and cases* (1–19), Abingdon: Routledge

Brett, Peter, 2007, 'Endowing participation with meaning': citizenship education, Paulo Freire and educating young people as change-makers', http://www.citized.info/pdf/commarticles/Endowing%20Participation%20Peter%20Brett.pdf

Brown, Roger and Helen Carasso, 2013, *Everything for Sale? The Marketisation of UK Higher Education*, Abingdon: Routledge

Business in the Community, 2010, '*Leadership skills for a sustainable economy*' (online), http://www.bitc.org.uk/our-resources/report/leadership-skills-sustainable-economy

Butler, Judith, 1990, *Gender Trouble: feminism and the subversion of identity*, New York: Routledge

Bynner, John Peter Dolton, Leon Feinstein, Gerry Makepeace, Lars Malmberg and Laura Woods, 2003, 'Revisiting the benefits of higher education: a report by the Bedford Group for Lifecourse and Statistical Studies', London: Institute of Education

Cahn, Steven, 1997, *Classic and Contemporary Readings in the Philosophy of Education*, Oxford: Oxford University Press

Cameron, David, 2011, 'Prime Minister's speech at 47th Munich Security Conference', National Archives, 5/2/2011, http://webarchive.nationalarchives.gov.uk/20130109092234/http://number10.gov.uk/news/pms-speech-at-munich-security-conference/

Campus Compact, 2012, http://www.compact.org/wp-content/uploads/2009/02/Presidents-Declaration.pdf

Cappellano, Luiz Carlos, 2013, 'The Sociology classroom: critical, transformative, radical? Part 3 – Radical Pedagogy and Practice', *Sociology Lens – The Society Pages*, https://thesocietypages.org

Castells, Manuel, 1997, *The Power of Identity*, Oxford: Blackwell

Castells, Manuel, 2008, 'The New Public Sphere: Global Civil Society, Communication Networks, and Global Governance', *The ANNALS of the American Academy of Political and Social Science*, 616:1, March 2008, 78–93

CBI (Confederation of British Industry), 2009, 'Stronger together – businesses and universities in turbulent times', http://www.abdn.ac.uk/cad/documents/6_CBI_HE_taskforce_report_Ensuring_students_have_the_skills_to_succeed.pdf

Chakrabortty, Aditya, 2013, 'Why this year's freshers are just part of a failed experiment', *The Guardian*, 23/9/2013, https://www.theguardian.com/commentisfree/2013/sep/23/freshers-failed-experiment-higher-education

Chatterjee, Partha, 1993, *The Nation and Its Fragments: colonial and postcolonial histories*, Princeton, NJ: University of Princeton Press

Citizenship Foundation, 2003, 'Teaching about controversial issues: guidance for schools', http://www.Citizenshipfoundation.org.uk/lib_res_pdf/0118.pdf

Citizenship Foundation, 2012, 'What is citizenship education?' http://www.citizenshipfoundation.org.uk/main/page.php?286, accessed 23/1/12

Citizenship Foundation, 2015a, 'Our work', http://www.citizenshipfoundation.org.uk/main/page.php?402

Citizenship Foundation, 2015b, 'What is citizenship education?' (http://www.citizenshipfoundation.org.uk/main/page.php?286, accessed 30/5/15

Citizenship Foundation, 2015c, 'Teachers concerned about exploring controversial issues in class', *News Item*, 4/6/2015

Citizenship Foundation, 2015d, 'Prevent Duty on schools: citizenship classes are key, says Government', http://www.citizenshipfoundation,org.uk/main/news.php?ptype=n1144, *News Item*, 9/7/2015

Cochrane, Phoebe, 2005, 'Exploring Cultural Capital and its Importance in Sustainable Development', *Ecological Economics*, 57:2, 318–330

Cogan, John J. and Ray Derricott, 1998, *Citizenship for the 21st Century: an international perspective on education*, London: Kogan Page

Cohen, Nick, 2015, *The Observer*, 7/6/15, p.33

Collini, Stefan, 2013, 'Sold Out', *London Review of Books*, 35:20, October 2013, 3–12

Connolly, Paul, Alan Smith and Berni Kelly, 2002, 'Too young to notice? The cultural and political awareness of 3–6 year-olds in Northern Ireland', Belfast: The Community Relations Council

Crane, Andrew, Dirk Matten and Jeremy Moon, 2004, 'Stakeholders as Citizens? Rethinking Rights, Participation, and Democracy', *Journal of Business Ethics*, 53:1–2, 107–122

CRE-COPERNICUS, 1994, COPERNICUS – THE UNIVERSITY CHARTER FOR SUSTAINABLE DEVELOPMENT, Geneva, May 1994, http://www.iau-hesd.net/sites/default/files/documents/copernicus.pdf

Crick, Bernard, 1999, *National Curriculum Citizenship*, http://www.publications.parliament.uk/pa/cm200607/cmselect/cmeduski/147/14705.htm

Crick, Bernard, 2002, 'Education for Citizenship: the Citizenship Order', *Parliamentary Affairs*, 55, 488–504

Curtis, Will and Alice Pettigrew, 2009, 'Learning and identity in a multicultural community', in Curtis and Pettigrew (eds.), *Learning in Contemporary Culture* (Chapter 7), Exeter: Learning Matters

Cusk, Rachel, 2010, 'The female eunuch, 40 years on', *The Guardian*, 20/11/2010, https://www.theguardian.com/books/2010/nov/20/rachel-cusk-the-female-eunuch

D'Alessio, Simona and Amanda Watkins, 2009, 'International comparisons of inclusive policy and practice: Are we talking about the same thing?', *Research in Comparative and International Education*, 4:3, 233–249

Davies, Ian, Mark Evans and Alan Reid, 2005a, 'Developing citizenship through international exchanges', in Arthur and Bolin (eds.), *Citizenship and Higher Education:*

*The role of universities in community and society*, Chapter 9 (135–157), London: RoutledgeFalmer

Davies, Ian, Mark Evans and Alan Reid, 2005b, 'Globalising citizenship education? A critique of 'global education' and 'citizenship education'', *British Journal of Educational Studies*, 53:1, 66–89

De Beauvoir, Simone, 1953, *The Second Sex*, New York: Knopf

de Leo, Joy M., 2012, *Quality Education for Sustainable Development*, Australia: UNESCO-APNIEVE

DfE (Department for Education), 2003, 'Twenty-first Century Skills: realising our potential, individuals, employers, nation', London: Treasury

DfE (Department for Education), 2006, 'Education for Sustainable Development. An Expert Review of Processes and Learning', London: Treasury

DfE (Department for Education), 2011, National Archives, http://webarchive.nationalarchives.gov.uk/20130401151715/http://www.education.gov.uk/publications/standard/publicationdetail/page1/DFES-00045-2007, accessed 20/2/11

DfE (Department for Education), 2013, 'Citizenship programmes of study: key stages 3 and 4 national curriculum in England', https://www.gov.uk/government/uploads/system/uploads/attachment_data/file/239060/SECONDARY_national_curriculum_-_Citizenship.pdf, Sept 2013

DfE (Department for Education), 2014, 'Promoting fundamental British values as part of SMSC in schools, Departmental advice for maintained schools', November 2014

DoE (Department of Education for Northern Ireland), 1998, 'Towards a Culture of Tolerance: integrating education', Bangor: DoE

DoE (Department of Education for Northern Ireland), 1999, 'Towards a culture of tolerance: educating for Diversity', Bangor: DoE

Deuchar, R. and Bhopal, K. (2013) 'We're still human beings, we're not aliens': promoting the citizenship rights and cultural diversity of Traveller children in schools: Scottish and English perspectives. *British Educational Research Journal*, 39:4, 733–750

Dewey, John, 1916, *Democracy and Education*, New York: MacMillan

Dewey, John, 1927, *The Public and its Problems*, New York: Holt Publishers

Dewey, John, 1937, 'Democracy and Educational Administration' ('On Democracy', extract), *School and Society*, 45, 457–467

Dewey, John, 1938, *Experience and Education*, New York: Simon & Schuster.

Dietz, Mary, 1985, 'Citizenship with a feminist face: the problem with maternal thinking', *Political Theory*, 13:1, 19–37

DIUS (Department for Innovation, Universities and Skills), 2007, 'Promoting good campus relations, fostering shared values and preventing violent extremism in the name of Islam in universities', London: Department for Innovation, Universities and Skills

Dorsey, James M., 2015, 'Political Violence: retiring the word Terrorism', my email of this date, *RSIS blog* – 101, 27/4/15

Doshi, Vidhi, 2016, 'They are trying to erase dalit history: This death is a martyrdom, a sacrifice', *The Observer*, 24/1/16, p.2

Douglas, Mary, 1992, *Risk and Blame: essays in cultural theory*, New York: Routledge

D'Souza, Dinesh, 1991, *Illiberal Education*, New York: The Free Press

Durkheim, Emile, 1957, *Professional Ethics and Civic Morals*, New York: Routledge

Durkheim, Emile, Everett K. Wilson and Herman Schnurer, 1961, *Moral Education: a study in the theory and application of the sociology of education*, New York: Free Press

EC (European Commission), 2005, 'Working together for growth and jobs: a new start for the Lisbon Strategy'
Education Scotland, 2015, 'Learning for sustainability', http://www.educationscotland.gov.uk/learningandteaching/learningacrossthecurriculum/themesacrosslearning/sustainability/index.asp
Eisenstadt, Shmuel Noah, 2003, *Comparative civilizations and multiple modernities*, Vols 1 and 2, Leiden, Netherlands: Brill Publishers
Ellis, Maureen, 2016, *The Critical Global Educator: global citizenship as sustainable development*, London: Routledge
Emerson, Lesley, Karen Orr and Paul Connolly, 2014, *Evaluation of the Effectiveness of the 'Prison to Peace: learning from the experience of political ex-prisoners' educational programme*, Belfast: Centre for Effective Education, Queen's University Belfast
Emirates, 1980, 'New education policy under discussion', *Emirates: UAE Embassy Magazine*, 39
Enslin, Penny, 2003, 'Liberal feminism, diversity and education', *Theory and Research in Education*, 1:1, 73–86.
Entrekin, J. Nicholas, 1989, 'Place, region and modernity', in John Agnew and James S. Duncan (eds.), *The Power of Place: bringing together the geographical and sociological imaginations*, Chapter 3 (30–43), Boston: Unwin Hyman
ESA (Education Services Australia), 2015, http://www.civicsandcitizenship.edu.au/cce/discovering_democracy_curriculum_resources,9067.html
Evans, Mary. 2004, *Killing Thinking: the death of the universities*, London: Continuum
Fieldhouse, Edward, Mark Tranmer and Andrew Russell, 2007, 'Something about Young People or Something about Elections? Electoral Participation of Young People in Europe: Evidence from a Multilevel Analysis of the European Social Survey', *European Journal of Political Research*, 46, 797–822
Findlow, Sally, 2008, 'Islam, Modernity and Education in the Arab States', *Intercultural Education*, 19:4, Special Issue on religion, 337–352
Findlow, Sally, 2012, 'Higher education and feminism in the Arab Gulf', *British Journal of Sociology of Education*, 34:1, 112–131
Findlow, Sally and Aneta L. Hayes, 2016, 'Transnational academic capitalism in the Arab Gulf: balancing global and local, and public and private, capitals', *British Journal of Sociology of Education*, 37:1, 110–128
Fiske, John, 1992, 'British Cultural Studies and Television', in Allen (ed.), *Channels of Discourse Reassembled: television and contemporary criticism*. Chapel Hill, NC: University of North Carolina Press (292–329)
Freedland, Jonathan, 2015, 'Isis lures 'Jihadi John' and all those who crave certainty', *The Guardian*, 28/2/15, p.35
Freire, Paulo, 1970, *Pedagogy of the Oppressed*, London: Continuum
Freire, Paulo, 1973 (2009, Continuum), *Education for Critical Consciousness* (including 'Education as the Practice of Freedom' and 'Extension or Communication'), New York: Seabury
Freire, Paulo, 2000, *Pedagogia da indignação, Cartas pedagógicas e outros escritos*. São Paulo: UNESP
Furedi, Frank, 2005, 'Citizens can't be made in class', *Daily Telegraph*, 3/2/05, http://www.telegraph.co.uk/education/3349433/Citizens-cant-be-made-in-class.html
Gallagher, Tony and Alan Smith, 2002, 'Attitudes to academic selection, integrated education and diversity within the curriculum', in A. Am Gray, K. Lloyd, P. Devine, G. Robinson and D. Heenan (eds.), *Social Attitudes in Northern Ireland: The Eighth Report* (120–137), London: Pluto Press

Gandin, Luis Armando, 2007, 'The Construction of the Citizen School Project as an Alternative to Neoliberal Educational Policies', *Policy Futures in Education*, 5:2, 179–193, http://dx.doi.org/10.2304/pfie.2007.5.2.179

Gandin, Luis Armando, 2009, 'The democratization of governance in the Citizen School Project: building a new notion of accountability in education', in Apple, Ball and Gandin (eds.), *The Routledge International Handbook of the Sociology of Education*, Chapter 31 (349–357), Abingdon, UK: Routledge

Gandin, Luis Armando and Michael Apple, 2003, 'Educating the State, Democratizing Knowledge: the Citizen School Porject in Porto Alegre, Brazil', in Apple (ed.), Chapter 8

Gault, Stephen, 2012, 'Love across the divide', *The Guardian*, 3/11/12

Gellner, Ernest, 1983, *Nations and Nationalism*, Oxford: Basil and Blackwell

Ghafour, Hamida, 2016, 'Please hold the line', *The Guardian* magazine, 20/8/16, pp. 30–41

Gholami, Reza, (in press), 'The Sweet Spot between Submission and Subversion: Diaspora, Education and the Cosmopolitan Project', in D. Carment and A. Sadjed (eds.), *Diaspora as Cultures of Cooperation: Global and local perspectives*, Basingstoke, UK: Palgrave

Giroux, Henry A., 1981, *Ideology, Culture and the Process of Schooling*, Philadelphia, PA: Temple University Press

Giroux, Henry A., 1988, *Teachers as Intellectuals*, New York: Bergin & Garvey

Giroux, Henry A., 1992a, *Border Crossings: cultural workers and the politics of education*, New York and London: Routledge

Giroux, Henry A., 1992b, *Paulo Freire and the Politics of Postcolonialism*, http://www.henryagiroux.com/online_articles/Paulo_friere.htm, reprinted in 1992

Giroux, Henry, 2014, *Neoliberalism's War on Higher Education*, Chicago: Haymarket Books

Gogolin, Ingrid, 2002, 'Linguistic and Cultural Diversity in Europe: a challenge for educational research and practice', *European Educational Research Journal*, 1:1, 123–138

Gorham, Eric B., 1992, *National Service, Citizenship and Political Education*, New York: SUNY

Gouws, Amanda, 2004, 'The politics of state structures: Citizenship and the national machinery for women in South Africa', *Feminist Africa: National Politics*, 3, http://www.feministafrica.org/

Green, Andy, 1997, *Education, Globalization and the Nation-State*, London: Palgrave Macmillan

Grillo, Ralph, 1998, *Pluralism and the Politics of Difference: state, culture and ethnicity in comparative perspective*, Oxford: Clarendon

Groll, Elias, 2013, 'There's a Good Reason Why So Many Terrorists Are Engineers', *Foreign Policy*, http://foreignpolicy.com/ . . . /theres-a-good-reason-why-so-many-terrorists-are-e . . . 11/7/2013

Grosvenor, Ian, 1997, *Assimilating Identities: Racism and educational policy in post 1945 Britain*, London: Lawrence and Wishart

Habermas, Jurgen, 1995, 'Reconciliation through the public use of reason: Remarks on John Rawls' political liberalism', *Journal of Philosophy*, 92:3, 109–131

Hall, Stuart, 1980, 'Encoding/decoding', *Culture, Media, Language: Working papers in cultural studies, 1972–79* (128–138), London: Hutchinson

Hall, Stuart, 1982, 'The rediscovery of "ideology": Return of the repressed in media studies', in Gurevitch, Michael, Tony Bennett, James Curran and Janet Woollacott (eds.), *Culture, Society and the Media* (Part 1, 'Class, Ideology and the Media'), London: Methuen

Hall, Stuart, 1988, 'The toad in the garden: Thatcherism among the theorists', in Cary Nelson and Lawrence Grossberg (eds.), *Marxism and the Interpretation of Culture*, Urbana: University of Illinois Press

Hall, Stuart, 1996, 'When was the 'post-colonial'? Thinking at the limit', in I. Chambers and L. Curtis (eds.), *The Post-Colonial Question* (242–260), London: Routledge

Hall, Stuart, 2000, 'The multi-cultural question', Chapter 10 in Hesse, Barnor (eds.), *Un/settled Multiculturalisms: diasporas, entanglements, 'transruptions'* (209–241), London: Zed Books

Hall, Stuart, Chas Critcher, Tony Jefferson, John Clarke and Brian Roberts, 1978, *Policing the Crisis: mugging, the state, and law and order*, London: Macmillan

Hansard, 2016, 'Petition debate on the exclusion of Donald Trump from the UK', http://www.publications.parliament.uk/pa/cm201516/cmhansrd/cm160118/halltext/160118h0002.htm

Harari, Yuval Noah, 2014, *Sapiens*, London, UK: Vintage

Harstock, Nancy, 1987, 'Rethinking modernism: minority versus majority theories', *Cultural Critique*, 7, 187–206

Hays, Samuel P., 1967, 'Political parties and the community-society continuum', in W. N. Chambers and W. D. Burnham (eds.), *The American Party Systems: stages of political development* (152–181), New York: Oxford University Press

HEA, 2011, 'Green Academy', HEA Strategic Plan 2012–2016

HEA, 2013, 'Social science strategic priorities 2013–14'

Heater, Derek, 2004, *Citizenship: the civic ideal in world history, politics and education*, Manchester: Manchester University Press (3rd ed.)

HEFCE, 2005a, 'Sustainable development in higher education', http://www.hefce.ac.uk/pubs/hefce/2005/05_28/

HEFCE, 2005b, 'Strategic Statement and Action Plan', Bristol: HEFCE

HEFCE, 2006, 'Strategic Plan, 2006–2011', Bristol: HEFCE

HEFCE, 2008, 'Strategic Review of Sustainable Development in Higher Education in England', Bristol: HEFCE

HEFCE, 2009, 'Updated Strategic Statement', Bristol: HEFCE 03/2009

Heinberg, Richard, 2004, *Powerdown: Options and actions for a post-carbon world*, Gabriola Island, Canada: New Society Publishers

Held, David, 1989, 'The decline of the nation state', in S. Hall and M. Jacques (eds.), *New Times* (191–204), London: Lawrence and Wishart

Herbrechter, Stefan and Michael Higgins, 2006, *Returning (to) Communities: Theory, Culture and Political Practice of the Communal*, New York and Amsterdam: Rodopi

Hertog, Steffen and Diego Gambetta, 2009, 'Tinker, tailor, engineer, jihadi: can university subjects reveal terrorists in the making?', *New Scientist*, 202:2712, 26–27

Heward, Christine, 1996,'Women and careers in higher education: What is the problem?', in L. Morley and V. Walsh (eds.), *Breaking boundaries: Women in higher education* (11–23), London: Taylor & Francis

Heward, Christine, and Sheila S. Bunwaree, 1999, *Gender, Education and Development: beyond access to empowerment*. London: Zed Books

Hobsbawm, Eric J., 1977, *The Age of Capital: 1848–1875*, London: Abacus

Hooks, Bell, 1994, *Teaching to Transgress*, London: Routledge

Hughes, Joanne and Rebecca Loader, 2015, ''Plugging the gap': shared education and the promotion of community relations through schools in Northern Ireland', *British Educational Research Journal*, 41:6, 1142–1155

Huntington, Samuel, 1996, *The Clash of Civilizations and the Remaking of World Order*, New York: Simon & Shuster

Illich, Ivan, 1970, *Deschooling Society* (46–47), London: Marion Bowyars
Iliffe, Alan H., 1968, 'The Foundation Year in the University of Keele', *The Sociological Review* Monograph, 12/7/1968
Inglehart, Ronald and Christian Welzel, 2005, *Modernization, Cultural Change and Democracy: The Human Development Sequence*, Cambridge: Cambridge University Press
Iqbal, Karamat, 2013, *Dear Birmingham*, Bloomington, IN: Xlibris
Isin, Engin F. and Bryan S. Turner, 2003, *Handbook of Citizenship Studies*, London: Sage
Isin, Engin, Peter Nyers and Bryan S. Turner, 2008, *Citizenship between Past and Future*, London: Routledge
Jameson, Fredric, 1984, 'Postmodernism, or the cultural logic of late capitalism', *New Left Review*, 146, 59–92
Jenson, Jane, 2000, 'Restructuring citizenship regimes: the French and Canadian women's movements in the 1990s', in J. Jenson and B. de Sousa Santos (eds.), *Globalizing Institutions: case studies in regulation and innovation*, Hampshire: Ashgate
Jones, Paula, David Selby and Stephen Sterling, 2010, *Sustainability Education: perspectives and practice across higher education*, London: Earthscan
Kabeer, Naila, 1999, 'Resources, Agency, Achievements: Reflections on the Measurement of Women's Empowerment', *Development and Change*, 30, 435–464
Kaldor, Mary, 2003, *Global Civil Society: an answer to war*, Maldon, MA: Polity
Keating, Avril, 2009, 'Educating Europe's citizens: Moving from national to post-national models of educating for European citizenship', *Citizenship Studies* 13:2, 135–151
Keating, Avril, 2014, *Education for Citizenship in Europe: European policies, national adaptations and young people's attitudes*, Basingstoke: Palgrave MacMillan
Keating, Avril, Debora Hinderliter Ortloff and Stravroula Philippou, 2009, 'Introduction: Citizenship education curricula: the changes and challenges presented by global and European integration', *Journal of Curriculum Studies*, 41:2, 145–158
Kerr, David, Eleanor Ireland, Joana Lopes, Rachel Craig and Elizabeth Cleaver, 2004, 'Making citizenship education real: citizenship education longitudinal study', 2nd annual report, NFER
Khattab, Moushira, 2007, 'Foreword' in Sultana
Kingsley, Patrick, 2015, 'The streets where girls pretend to be boys', *The Observer Magazine*, 12/7/15, pp. 28–35
Klein, Naomi, 2015, *This Changes Everything*, London: Penguin
Knight, Peter, 2005, 'Unsustainable Development', *The Guardian*, 8/2/05, https://www.theguardian.com/education/2005/feb/08/highereducation.administration
Kolbert, John M., 2000, *Keele, the First Fifty Years: a portrait of the university 1950–2000*, Keele: Melandrium Books
Komiyama, Hiroshi and Kazuhiko Takeuchi, 2006, 'Sustainability science: building a new discipline', *Sustainability Science*, 1:1, 1–6
Kowalewski, David, 1982, 'Student and non-student protest in Japan and the USSR: some commonalities', *Higher Education*, 11, 51–65
Langran, Irene, Elizabeth Langran and Kathy Ozment, 2009, 'Transforming today's students into tomorrow's global citizens: challenges for US educators', *New Global Studies*, 3:1, http://www.bepress.com/ngs/vol3/iss1/art4
Leighton, Ralph, 2004, 'The nature of citizenship education provision: an initial study', *The Curriculum Journal* 15:2, pp. 167–181
Leighton, Ralph, 2012, *Teaching Citizenship Education: a radical approach*, London: Continuum
Levinson, Meira, 2002, 'Dilemmas of Deliberative Civic Education', *Philosophy of Education Yearbook*, 262–270

Lewicka-Grisdale, Katarzyna and Terence H. McLaughlin, 2002, 'Education for European Identity and European Citizenship', in Jose Ibanez-Martin and Gonzalo Jover (eds.), *Education in Europe: politics and policies* (53–81), Dordrecht: Kluwer

Lewin, Ellen (ed.), 2006, *Feminist Anthropology: a reader*, Wiley-Blackwell

Lindsay, Alexander D., 1957, *Selected Addresses*, Painswick: K. R. Webb Printing Company

Lister, Ruth, 1997, *Citizenship: feminist perspectives*, London: MacMillan

Lister, Ruth, 2004, 'Citizenship and Gender', in Kate Nash and Alan Scott (eds.), *The Blackwell Companion to Political Sociology*, Chapter 33 (323–332), Oxford, UK: Blackwell

Macedo, Stephen, Yvette Alex-Assensoh and Jeffrey M. Berry, 2005, *Democracy at Risk: how political choices undermine citizen participation, and what we can do about it*, Washington, DC: Brookings Institution

MacKinnon, Dolly and Catherine Manathunga, 2003, 'Going Global with Assessment: What to do When the Dominant Culture's Literacy Drives Assessment', *Higher Education Research and Development*, 22:2, 131–144

McGearty, Sean and Margie Buchanan-Smith, 2012, 'From prison to peace: Final evaluation', European Union, European Regional Development Fund

McGowan, Tristan, 2009, *Rethinking Citizenship Education: A curriculum for participatory democracy*, London: Continuum

McVeigh, Tracy, 2011, 'The message when youth clubs close is: no one cares', *The Observer*, 14/8/11, p.19

McVeigh, Tracy and Toby Helm, 2015, 'Female candidates are on the rise – but why aren't women voting?', *The Observer*, 8/3/15, p.8; British Election Study, http://www.britishelectionstudy.com/, accessed 18/11/2015

Manchester, Helen and Sara Bragg, 2013, 'School Ethos and the Spatial Turn: "Capacious" Approaches to Research and Practice', *Qualitative Inquiry*, 19:10, 818–827

Marginson, Simon, 2007, 'The Public/Private Divide in Higher Education: A Global Revision', *Higher Education*, 53, 307–333

Marsh, David, Therese O'Toole and Su Jones, 2007, *Young People and Politics in the UK: Apathy or Alienation?*, Palgrave Macmillan

Marshall, Thomas H., 1949/50, *Citizenship and Social Class*, Cambridge: Pluto Press

Marx, Karl, 1857, *Grundrisse*

Marx, Karl, 1867, *Das Capital*

Mascia-Lees, Frances E., Patricia Sharpe and Colleen Ballerino Cohen, 1989, 'The postmodern turn in anthropology: cautions from a feminist perspective', *Signs*, 15:1, 7–33

Mason, Paul, 2015, *Postcapitalism*, Allen Lane

Massey, Doreen, 1994, *Space, Place and Gender*, Cambridge: Polity Press

Massey, Doreen, 2005, *For Space*, London: Sage

May, Stephen (ed.), 1999, *Critical Multiculturalism: rethinking multicultural and antiracist education*, London: Falmer Press

May, Theresa, 2011, Secretary of State review of 'Prevent Strategy', https://www.gov.uk/government/uploads/system/uploads/attachment_data/file/97976/prevent-strategy-review.pdf

Mazawi, Andre E., 2007, 'Besieging the King's tower? En/gendering academic opportunities in the Gulf Arab states', In C. Brock and L.Z. Levers (eds.), *Aspects of Education in the Middle East and North Africa* (77–98), Oxford: Symposium Books

Meer, Nasir, 2010, *Citizenship, Identity and the Politics of Multiculturalism*, Basingstoke, UK: Palgrave

Meer, Nasir and Tarek Modood, 2012, 'Assessing the Divergences on Our Reading of Interculturalism and Multiculturalism', *Journal of Intercultural Studies*, 33:2, 233–244

Meredith, Robbie, 2015, 'Stranmillis proposes universities move to its Belfast site', *BBC News Northern Ireland*, 12/3/2015, http://www.bbc.co.uk/news/uk-northern-ireland-31841172

Meyer, Heinz-Deiter and Brian Rowan, 2006, *The new institutionalism in education*, Albany: SUNY Press

Meyer, John W., 1977, 'The effects of education as an institution', *American Journal of Sociology*, 83:1, 55–77

Meer, Nasir and Tarek Modood, 2013, 'The "civic re-balancing of British Multiculturalism" and beyond', in Raymond Taras (ed.), *Challenging Multiculturalism: managing diversity in Europe* (75–96), Edinburgh: Edinburgh University Press

MoE, 2014:5, 'Singapore Primary School Education: preparing your child for tomorrow', Singapore: Ministry of Education

Mok, Ka Ho, 2012, CHES seminar at IoE, 13/3/12, 'Bringing the State Back in: Privatisation or Restatisation of HEd in China?' CHES in conjunction with the Centre for Learning and Life Chances in Knowledge Economies and Societies (LLAKES)

Monbiot, George, 2014, 'Drowning in money: the untold story of the crazy public spending that makes flooding inevitable', *The Guardian*, online, 13/1/14

Morgan, W. John and Alexandre Guillerme, 2014, *Buber and Education: dialogue as conflict resolution*, London: Routledge

Morley, Louise and Val Walsh, 1996, *Breaking boundaries: women in higher education*, London: Taylor & Francis

Morris, James, 2015, 'Central Foundation Boy's School pupil was accused of extremism', *Islington Gazette*, 1/10/2015, http://www.islingtongazette.co.uk/news/education/central_foundation_boy_s_school_pupil_was_accused_of_extremism_1_4254097

Mouffe, Chantal, 1992, in Butler, Judith, Joan Scott and Joan Wallach (eds.), *Feminists Theorize the Political* (377), New York: Routledge

Myers, John P., 2010, 'To Benefit the World by Whatever Means Possible': Adolescents' Constructions of Global Citizenship', *British Educational Research Journal*, 36:3, 483–502

Myers, John and Husam A. Zaman, 2009, 'Negotiating the global and national: Immigrant and dominant-culture adolescents' vocabularies of citizenship in a transnational world', *The Teachers College Record*, 111:11, 2589–2625

Naidoo, Rajani, 2011, 'Higher Education, the Competition Fetish and the Construction of Values', in H. Aittola and T. Saarinen and Jyvaskylan Yliopisto (eds.), *Kannataako Korkeakoulutus*

National Foundation for Educational Research (NFER), 2010, 'The Citizenship Education Longitudinal Study, 2001–2010', http://www.nfer.ac.uk/research/projects/cels/research-design-and-data.cfm

Nawaz, Aatif, 2016, 'Not all British Muslims think the same, whatever Channel 4 might claim', *The Guardian*, 15 April 2016, http://www.theguardian.com/commentisfree/2016/apr/15/channel-4-islamophobic-bandwagon-british-muslims

Nicholson, James, 2012, 'The summer riots, 2011', *Teaching Citizenship*, ACT, 34, 24–27

Nixon, Jon, 2011, *Higher Education and the Public Good: imagining the university*, London: Continuum

Noddings, Nel (ed.), 2005, *Educating Citizens for Global Awareness*, New York: Teachers College Press

NICC (Northern Ireland Curriculum Council), 1990, 'Cross-curricular Themes – Guidance Materials', Belfast: NICC

Norris, Pippa, 2002, *Democratic Phoenix: reinventing political activism*, New York, NY: Cambridge University Press

OFSTED, 2009 'Education for Sustainable Development: improving schools – improving lives', 12/2009, http://webarchive.nationalarchives.gov.uk/2014112 4154759/http://www.ofsted.gov.uk/sites/default/files/documents/surveys-and-good-practice/e/Education for sustainable development.pdf

OFSTED, 2012, 'Sustainable development in learning and skills inspections: Guidance for inspectors', Manchester http://efsandquality.glos.ac.uk/toolkit/OFSTED_Inspections_2012.pdf

Ohmae, Kenichi, 1994, *The Borderless World: power and strategy in the interlinked economy*, London: Harper Collins

Ohmae, Kenichi, 1996, *The End of the Nation State: the rise of regional economies*, London: Harper Collins

Oketch, Moses, Tristan McCowan and Rebecca Schendel, 2014, *The Impact of Tertiary Education on Development: a rigorous literature review*, Department for International Development

Okin, Susan M., 1999, *Is Multiculturalism Bad for Women?*, Princeton, NJ: Princeton University Press

Ong, Aihwa, 1999, *Flexible Citizenship: the cultural logics of transnationality*, Durham: Duke University Press

Orr, David, 1994, 'What is Education For?', In Context#27, 'The Learning Revolution: education innovations for global citizens', http://www.context.org/iclib/ic27/

Osler, Audrey, 2005, 'Education for democratic citizenship: New challenges in a globalised world', in Osler and Starkey (eds.), *Citizenship and Language Learning: international perspectives*, Chapter 1 (3–22), Stoke on Trent: Trentham Books

Osler, Audrey, 2008, 'Citizenship education and the Ajegbo report: Re-imagining a cosmopolitan nation', *London Review of Education*, 6:1, 11–25

Osler, Audrey and Hugh Starkey, 2001, 'Young people in Leicester (UK): Community, identity and citizenship', *Interdialogos*, 2, 48–49

Osler, Audrey and K. Vincent, 2002, *Citizenship and the Challenge of Global Education*, Stoke-on-Trent: Trenthamnew

Oxley, Laura and Paul Morris, 2013, 'Global citizenship: A typology for distinguishing its multiple conceptions', *British Journal of Educational Studies*, 61:3, 301–325

Ozga, Jenny and Bob Lingard, 2007a, *The RoutledgeFalmer Reader in Education Policy and Politics*, Abingdon: RoutledgeFalmer

Ozga, Jenny and Bob Lingard, 2007b, 'Globalisation', in Ozga and Lingard (eds.), *The RoutledgeFalmer Reader in Education Policy and Politics*, Chapter 5 (65–82), Abingdon: RoutledgeFalmer

Paige, Jonathan, 2013, 'British public wrong about nearly everything, survey shows', *The Independent*, 9/7/13, http://www.independent.co.uk/news/uk/home-news/british-public-wrong-about-nearly-everything-survey-shows-8697821.html

Parsons, Talcott, 1951, *The Social System*, New York: Free Press

Parsons, Talcott (ed.), 1965, *Theories of Society: foundations of modern sociological theory*, New York: Free Press of Glencoe

Piketty, Thomas and Arthur Goldhammer, 2014, *Capital in the Twenty-First Century*, Cambridge, MA: Harvard University Press

Polychroniou, C. J., 'Neoliberalism and the Politics of Higher Education: An Interview With Henry A. Giroux', Truthout | Interview, Tuesday, 26/3/2013, http://www.truth-out.org/news/item/15237-predatory-capitalism-and-the-attack-on-higher-education-an-interview-with-henry-a-giroux

Potter, John, 2002, *Active Citizenship in Schools: a good practice guide*, Abingdon: RoutledgeFalmer

## 152  References

Pratt, Mary Louise, 2002/1991, 'Modernity and periphery: toward a global and relational analysis', in E. Mudimbe-Boyl (ed.), *Beyond Dichotomies: histories, identities, cultures and the challenge of globalization* (21–48), Albany: State University of New York

Pring, Richard, 2002, 'Education, pluralism and the teaching of values', in Jose Ibanez-Martin, and Gonzalo Jover (eds.), *Education in Europe: politics and policies*, Chapter 4 (83–96), Dordrecht: Kluwer

Puolimatka, Tapio, 1996, 'Democracy, Education and the Critical Citizen', *Philosophy of Education*, 329–338; His footnote refs – Israel Scheffler, 1985, *Of Human Potential*, London: Routledge & Kegan Paul

QCA (Qualifications and Curriculum Authority), 1998, *Education for Citizenship and the Teaching of Democracy in Schools: final report of the advisory group on Citizenship*, The Crick Report, 22/9/1998, London: QCA

QCA (Qualifications and Curriculum Authority (QCA), 2007, 'Citizenship Programme of study for key stage 3 and attainment target', London: QCA

Ramesh, Randeep and Josh Halliday, 2015, 'Student accused of being a terrorist for reading a book on terrorism', *The Guardian*, 24/9/2015

Rancière, Jacques, 1995, *Disagreement: politics and philosophy*, Minneapolis: University of Minnesota Press

Rawls, John, 1993, *Political Liberalism*, New York: Columbia University Press

Rayan, Fekry Hassan, 1993, *Al Tadris Wa Ahdafouh, Ossosouh, Assalibouh, Takween Nataegahou, Wa Tatbeekatouh* (Teaching, its objectives, principles, evaluation of its results, and applications), Cairo: World of Books

Ricouer, Paul (trans.), 1984, *Time and Narrative*, Chicago: University of Chicago Press

Rimmerman, Craig A., 1998, *The New Citizenship: unconventional politics, activism and service*, Boulder: Westview Press

Robertson, Roland, 1995, 'Glocalization: Time-space and Homogeneity-heterogeneity', in Mike Featherstone, Scott Lash and Roland Robertson (eds.), *Global Modernities* (25–44), London: Sage

Robertson, Susan, 2007, 'Globalisation, Rescaling National Education Systems and Citizenship Regimes', in Roth and Burbules (eds.), *Changing Notions of Citizenship Education in Contemporary Nation States*, Rotterdam: Sense Publications online paper: https://susanleerobertson.files.wordpress.com/2009/10/2007-roth-rescaling-citizenship.pdf

Robertson, Susan, 2007/8, 'Embracing the Global: Crisis and the Creation of a New Semiotic Order to Secure Europe's Knowledge-based Economy', in N. Fairclough, R. Wodak and B. Jessop (eds.), *Education and the Knowledge-Based Economy in Europe* (89–108), Rotterdam: Sense Publishers

Robertson, Susan, 2009, 'Spacialising' the sociology of education: Stand-points, entry-points, vantage-points', in Ball, Apple and Gandin (eds.), *The Routledge International Handbook of Sociology of Education* (15–26), London and New York: Routledge

Robinson, William I., 2004, *Theory of Global Capitalism: production, class and state in a transnational world*, Baltimore, MD: John Hopkins Press

Rogers, Carl, 1969, *Freedom to Learn*, Columbus: Merrill

Rosaldo, Renato, 1999, 'Cultural Citizenship, Inequality and Multiculturalism,' in R.D. Torres (eds.), *Race, Identity and Citizenship*, Oxford: Blackwell

Rose, Neil, 2011, *The Guardian*, 18/1/11, http://www.theguardian.com/politics/2011/jan/18/citizenship-education-integral-big-society

Ross, Alistair, 2015, 'Young People's National and European Identities in Scandinavia', First lecture in Lecture Series, 'Constructing identities in Western Europe', 2/6/15, London: Metropolitan University

Runnymede, 2000, Summary', 5, http://www.runnymedetrust.org/uploads/publications/pdfs/ACommunityOfCommunitiesAndCitizens-2000.pdf).
Roy, Olivier, 2016, 'The Islamization of radicalism', Eutopia: Institute of Ideas, 14 Jan 2016, http://www.eutopiainstitute.org/2016/01/the-islamization-of-radicalism/
Sa'adawi, Nawal al-, 2015, interviewed'New Review', in *the Observer*, 11/10/15, p.17
Said, Edward, 1993a, *Culture and Imperialism*, New York: Vintage
Said, Edward, 1993b, 'Holding nations and traditions at bay', 2nd Reith Lecture of his series, 'Representations of the Intellectual'
Said, Edward, 1995, *Orientalism: Western conceptions of the Orient*, New Delhi: Penguin Books
Salazar, Philippe-Joseph, 2015, *Paroles armees: comprendre et combattre la propagande terrorist*, Paris: Lemieux Editeur
Salleh, Ariel, 1997, *Ecofeminism as Politics*, London: Zed Books
Sandel, Michael, The Reith Lectures, BBC Radio 4, June 2009
Santos, Boaventura de Sousa, 2010, 'The university in the twenty-first century: toward a democratic and emancipatory university reform', in Michael W. Apple, Stephen J. Ball and Luis Armando Gandin (eds.), *The Routledge International Handbook of the Sociology of Education* (274–282), London and New York: Routledge
Scerri, Andy, 2009, 'Paradoxes of increased individuation and public awareness of environmental issues', *Environmental Politics*, 18:4, 467–485
Scerri, Andy, 2012, *Greening Citizenship: sustainable development, the state and ideology*, New York: Palgrave Macmillan
Schattle, Hans, 2008, 'Education for global citizenship: Illustrations of ideological pluralism and adaptation', *Journal of Political Ideologies*, 13:1, 73–94
Schattle, Hans, 2009, 'Global citizenship in theory and practice', in R. Lewin (ed.), *The Handbook of Practice and Research in Study Abroad: Higher education and the quest for global citizenship* (3–18), New York: Routledge
Scheffler, Israel, 1985, *Of Human Potential*, London: Routledge & Kegan Paul
Secretariat General of the Higher Education Council, 2012, 'Future Skills and Preparing Graduates for the 21st Century', Bahrain: Ministry of Education, accessed 26/10/2015, http://moedu.gov.bh/hec/UploadFiles/reportr/Future%20skills.pdf
Selaibeekh, Lubna, 2009, 'Diversity in Bahrain and its implications for citizenship education: Policy and practice', unpublished conference paper https://www.surrey.ac.uk/cronem/files/conf2009papers/Selaibeekh.pdf
Sen, Amartya, 1999, *Development as Freedom*, New York: Anchor Books
Shain, Farzana, 2013, 'Race, nation and education: an overview of British attempts to 'manage diversity' since the 1950s', *Education Inquiry*, 4:1, 63–85
Sharabi, Hisham, 1988, *Neopatriarchy: A theory of distorted change in Arab society*, Oxford: Oxford University Press
Shariatmadari, David, 2015, 'If you want young people to vote, give them the handbook', *The Guardian*, 1/11/15
Shaw, Martin, 1997, 'The state of globalisation: towards a theory of state transformation', *Review of International Political Economy*, 4:3, 497–513
Sherwood, Harriet, 2016, 'Mosques open doors for tours, talks and tea', *The Guardian*, p.11, 6/2/16, http://www.theguardian.com/commentisfree/2015/nov/01/young-people-vote-political-education
Shiels, Chris, 2009,'20 May, Global Perspectives in Higher Education ', email 8/5/9, IoE?/SRHE?
Skutnabb-Kangas, Tove, 2000, *Linguistic Genocide in Education – or Worldwide Diversity and Human Rights?*, Mahwah, NJ: Lawrence Erlbaum Associates
Sloam, James, 2013a, 'Voice and Equality': Young People's Politics in the European Union', *West European Politics*, 36:4, 836–858

Sloam, James, 2013b, 'The "Outraged Young": How Young Europeans are Reshaping the Political Landscape', *Political Insight*, 4:1, 4–7

Smith, Alan, 2003, 'Citizenship Education in Northern Ireland: beyond national identity?', *Cambridge Journal of Education*, 33:1, 15–31

Smith, Dorothy, 1987, *The Everyday World as Problematic: A feminist sociology*, Boston: Northeastern University Press

Smith, Graham and Roger Otewill, 2007, 'Teaching Citizenship in Higher Education', Occasional paper, PSA

Smith, Michael B., Rebecca S. Nowacek and Jeffrey L. Bernstein, 2010, 'Introduction: Ending the Solitude of Citizenship Education', in Michael B., Smith Rebecca S. Nowacek and Jeffrey L. Bernstein (eds.), *Citizenship Across the Curriculum*, (1–12), Bloomington: Indiana University Press

Smyth, Marie, 1994, 'Borders within borders: material and ideological segregation as forms of resistance and strategies of control', Derry: Templegrove Action Research

Smyth, Marie, 1995, 'Sectarian Division and Area Planning: a commentary on "The Derry Area Plan 2011: Preliminary Proposals"', Derry: Templegrove Action Research

Smyth, Marie and Ruth Moore, 1996, 'Researching Sectarianism', Derry: Templegrove Action Research

Soja, Edward, 1996, *Thirdspace: journeys to Los Angeles and other real-and-imagined places*, Malden, MA: Blackwell

Soja, Edward, 1999, 'Thirdspace: Expanding the scope of the geographical imagination', in D. Massey, J. Allen and P. Sarre (eds.), *Human Geography Today* (260–278), Cambridge: Polity

Soja, Edward, 2010, *Seeking Spacial Justice*, Minneapolis: University of Minnesota Press

Soja, Edward W. and Barbara Hooper, 2002, 'The spaces that difference makes: some notes on the geographical margins of the new cultural politics', in Michael Dear, and Steven Flusty (eds.), *Spaces of Postmodernity: readings in human geography*, Chapter 32 (378–389), Oxford: Blackwell

Soueif, Ahdaf, 'Egypt after the Revolution: curfew nights and bloodstained days', *The Guardian*, 23/8/13, p. 3

Spannring, Reingard, Günther Ogris, and Wolfgang Gaiser (eds.), 2008, *Youth and Political Participation in Europe: results of the comparative study of EUYOUPART*, Opladen: Barbara Budrich

Steiner-Khamsi, Gita and Thomas S. Popkewitz, 2004, *The Global Politics of Educational Borrowing and Lending*, New York: Teachers College Press

Stephens, Closs A., 2013, *The Persistence of Nationalism: from imagined communities to urban encounters*, London: Routledge

Stevenson, Nick, 2011, *Education as Cultural Citizenship*, London, UK: Sage

Stevenson, Nick, 2012a, 'Localization as subpolitics: The Transition Movement and cultural citizenship', *International Journal of Cultural Studies*, 15:1, January 2012, 65–79

Stevenson, Nick, 2012b, 'Cosmopolitan education and cultural citizenship: a critical European perspective', *Cultural Sociology*, 6:1, 113–128

Stiglitz, Joseph, 2015, *The Great Divide*, London: Allen Lane

Stromquist, Nelly P., 2004, 'The educational nature of feminist action', in Griff Foley (ed.), *Dimensions of Adult Learning*, Chapter 3, Oxford University Press

Stromquist, Nelly P., 2006, 'Gender, education and the possibility of transformative knowledge', *Compare: A Journal of Comparative and International Education*, 36:2, 145–161

Sugden, John and Alan Bairner, 1993, *Sport, Sectarianism and Society in a Divided Ireland*, Leicester: Leicester University Press

Sultana, Ronald, 2007, *The Girls' Education Initiative in Egypt*, New York: UNICEF
Supreme Council for Women, 2011, 'Studies and research: Women in decision-making, Bahrain', accessed August 2011, http://www.scw.gov.bh/default.asp?action=article&ID=838
Tabouret-Keller, Andrée, 1998, 'Language and Identity', in Florian Coulmas (ed.), *The Handbook of Sociolinguistics* (316–326), Oxford: Blackwell
Talhami, Ghada H., 1996, *The Mobilization of Women in the Muslim World*, Gainesville: University of Florida Press
Tawney, Richard H., 1922, *Secondary Education for All*, London: Bloomsbury
Tawney, Richard H. and Edward S. Cartwright, 1908, *Oxford and Working Class Education*, Oxford: Oxford University Press
Taylor, Rupert, 1988, 'The Queen's University of Belfast: The liberal university in a divided society', *Higher Education Review*, 20:2, 27–45
Taylor, Rupert, 2006, 'The Belfast Agreement and the Politics of Consociationalism', *The Political Quarterly*, 77:2, 217–226
Taylor, Sandra and Miriam Henry, 2007, 'Globalization and Educational Policymaking: A Case Study', in Jenny Ozga and Bob Lingard (eds.), *The RoutledgeFalmer Reader in Education Policy and Politics* (101–116), Abingdon: Routledge
Teague, Matthew, 2015, 'Ahmed Mohamed is tired, excited to meet Obama – and wants his clock back', The Guardian, http://www.theguardian.com/us-news/2015/sep/17/ahmed-mohamed-is-tired-excited-to-meet-obama-and-wants-his-clock-back
Thaman, Konai H. and R. R. Thaman, 2009, 'Pacific island principles: learning to live wise and sustainable lives', in P. B. Corcoran and P. M. Osano (eds.), *Young People, Education, and Sustainable Development* (63–75), Wageningen, The Netherlands: Wageningen Academic Publishers
Tonge, Jonathan and Andrew Mycock, 2009, Youth Citizenship Commission Report: Making the Connection: Building Youth Citizenship in the UK, London: Stationery Office
Torney, Kathryn, 2012, 'The religious divide in Northern Ireland's schools', *The Guardian*, 24/11/2012, http://www.theguardian.com/news/datablog/2012/nov/24/religious-divide-northern-ireland-schools
Townsend, Mark, 2015, 'Amir Khan: UK Muslims must denounce ISIS', *The Observer*, 12/4/15, p.6
Transition United States, 2013, 'The US national hub of the international Transition Network', http://transitionus.org/transition-town-movement
Turner, Brian S., 1993, *Citizenship and Social Theory*, London: Sage
UCU, 2015, 'Senior Academics oppose counter-terrorism bill', http://www.ucu.org.uk/counterterrorismbillletter, 2/2015
ULSF (University Leaders for a Sustainable Future), 2001, 'Talloires Declaration', http://www.ulsf.org/programs_talloires_implement.html
UN, 2015, 'Transforming our world: The 2030 agenda for sustainable development', General Assembly, 21/10/2015, Seventieth session, Agenda items 15 and 116, Resolution adopted by the General Assembly on 25/9/2015
UNCED, 1992, 'Promoting Education, Public awareness and training', Earth Summit in Rio de Janeiro 1992, Chapter 36 of Agenda 21, http://www.sustainable-environment.org.uk/Action/Agenda_21.php
UNDP, 2000, *Millenium Development Goals*, http://www.undp.org/content/undp/en/home/sdgoverview/mdg_goals.html
UNESCO, 2009, 'World Conference on education for sustainable development', 31/3/09–2/4/09, Bonn, Germany

## 156  References

UNESCO-APCEIU, 2007, 'Two concepts, one goal: education for international understanding and education for sustainable development', Bangkok: UHA

Ungar, Sanford J., 2010, 'The New Liberal Arts', *The Chronicle of Higher Education*, 28/2/2010

UNICEF, 1989, 'UN Convention on the Rights of the Child', London, http://www.unicef.org.uk/Documents/Publication-pdfs/UNCRC_PRESS200910web.pdf

United Nations, 1987, 'Report of the World Commission on Environment and Development', General Assembly Resolution 42/187, 11/12/1987

Unterhalter, Elaine, 1999, 'Citizenship, difference and education: Reflections inspired by the South African Transition', in Nira Yuval-Davis and Pnina Werbner (eds.), *Women, Citizenship and Difference* (100–117), Surrey, UK: Zed

Unterhalter, Elaine, 2003, 'The capabilities approach and gendered education', *Theory and Research in Education*, 1:1, 7–22

Unterhalter, Elaine, 2007, 'Gender equality, education and the capability approach', Chapter 5 in Walker, Melanie and Elain Unterhalter (eds.), *Amartya Sen's Capability Approach and Social Justice in Education*, Chapter 5 (87–107), London: Palgrave Macmillan

U.S. Department of Education, 2010, 'Civics Framework for the 2010 National Assessment of Educational Progress', NAEP Civics Project National Assessment Governing Board

Usher, Robin and Richard Edwards, 1994, *Postmodernism and Education: different voices, different worlds*, London: Routledge

Vertovec, Steven, 2007, 'Super-diversity and its implications', *Ethnic and Racial Studies*, 30:6, 1024–1054

Wales, 2012, 'Education for Sustainable Development and Global Citizenship', www.esd-wales.org.uk

Waller, Chris, 2013, 'Citizenship remains in new English National Curriculum', 8/2/2013, http://ACT@cmp.ctt-news.org

Wals, Arjen E. J. and Geke Kieft, 2010, *Education for Sustainable Development: research overview*, Stockholm: SIDA, Edita

Ward, Victoria, 2015, 'Children 'profiled' with 'counter extremism' questionnaire', *The Telegraph*, 28/5/2015

Warwick, Paul, 2012, 'Climate Change and Sustainable Citizenship Education', in James Arthur and Hilary Cremin (eds.), *Debates in Citizenship Education*, Chapter 11, Abingdon: Routledge

Wattenberg, Martin, 2003, 'Electoral Turnout: The New Generation Gap', *British Elections and Parties Review*, 13:1, 159–731

Wilson, Edward Osborne, 1999, *Consilience: the unity of knowledge*, New York: Vintage

Wirth, Louis, 1938, 'Urbanism as a way of life', *American Journal of Sociology*, 44, 1–24

Whelan, Dave, 2013, 'Irish language classes on everyone's lips', Belfast Telegraph, http://www.belfasttelegraph.co.uk/news/northern-ireland/irish-language-classes-on-everyones-lips-29553329.html

Woodward, Will and Rebecca Smithers, 2003, 'Clarke Dismisses Medieval Historians', *The Guardian*, 9/5/2003, http://www.theguardian.com/uk/2003/may/09/highereducation.politics

WUF (World Universities Forum), 2009, World Universities Forum, http://2009.ontheuniversity.com/, accessed January 31, 2009

Yepes, César de Prado, 2006, 'World regionalization of higher education: policy proposals for international organizations', *Higher Education Policy*, 19:2, 111–128

# Index

active citizenship xii, 5, 10–11, 26–27, 41, 46, 122, 126, 131
activism (political) x, 48, 50, 55, 93–94, 96, 97–98, 112, 121, 129
Ajegbo Commission/Report, Sir Keith Ajegbo, Diversity and Curriculum Review ix, xii, 6, 44, 68, 69, 77, 78, 79
alternative citizenship xii, 10, 27
America (North, US and Canada) 12, 15, 16, 76, 94–95
American University of Beirut (AUB) 96
Anderson, Benedict 23, 24, 29
Apple, Michael xii, 25, 50, 91, 92
Arab (Middle East) xiii, 79, 95–96, 107–8
Arab feminism 107–120
Arab Gulf xiii, 103, 110–120, 138, 139
the Arab Spring 92, 96, 97, 108, 110
assimilationist/ism 64, 70, 72, 88
Association for Citizenship Teaching (ACT) 7, 11–12, 17–18, 30, 45, 46, 52, 77, 91, 131
Australia 130

'banking education' 46
Bernstein, Basil 25
Beyond the Youth Citizenship Commission (BTYCC) 27
Bloody Sunday 93, 94–95
Blunkett, David 3
borders & boundaries: challenging, crossing & re-shaping ix, 21, 32–33, 34, 38, 40, 47, 57, 60–61, 78, 87, 137–139; the importance of, shifting/porous 'borderless world'? ix, xii, 2, 19, 26, 34–39, 56, 58, 59, 61, 62, 137
British history 78

British National Party (BNP) 65
Britishness 29, 63–65, 68
Brundtland (definition of sustainable development) 122, 124
Butler Act 81, 94

Cameron, David 1
Campaign for the Public University 15, 57
Campaign for Social Science 15, 57
the 'capability approach' 47
Catholic(s) 80–87, 94–95
Charter for Citizenship for Further and Higher Education 14
the Citizen School Project, Porto Alegre 48, 57, 78
citizenship as political consciousness 15, 45–49, 54–61; as political participation 41–43, 45–49, 55, 106, 118–120; as political representation 118–120; as resistance 14, 50, 55–61, 119; as shared/collective responsibility xiv, 121–136, 138; as socio-economic participation 14–15, 23–24, 113, 116
citizenship education/curriculum 4, 9, 54
Citizenship Education Longitudinal Study (CELS) 8, 9
Citizenship Foundation 7, 12, 30, 43, 52–54, 84
citizenship policy x
citizenship studies x, 39
citizenship test 3
civics/civic education (US) x, 4, 5, 12–13, 14, 32, 111
civil rights (movement) xiii, 78, 79, 82, 93, 94–5, 96, 101, 138
'clash of civilisations' 64, 66

158  *Index*

collectivism/collective action 56, 108, 126–128
communities ix, 37, 62–89, 139; shifting 62
community citizenship xiii, 62–89, 137
competitition/competitive ix, xii, xiii, 138; capitalism vi, 121, 123, 124–125, 135, 138
Competition and Marketing Authority (CMA) 51
conflict, disruption & struggle (political and ideological) ix, xii, 30, 37–38, 48, 49–50, 60–61, 73, 85, 104–105, 137
'conscientize/conscientization' 40, 46, 49, 60, 91, 114, 128, 139
'contact zones' 67, 78
cosmopolitan(ism) xi, 36, 38
cosmopolitan citizenship xi
Council for the Defence of British Universities 15
Council of Europe on Education for Democratic Citizenship 16
Creative Partnerships 79
Crick, Sir Bernard ix, 4–6, 7
Crick Commission, Crick Report, Advisory Group on the Teaching of Citizenship in 'critical education for citizenship' ix, 2, 30, 41, 68, 69, 72
critical multiculturalism x, xi, 62–89, 137
critical pedagogy/pedagogies x, 45–49
Cuban Revolution 93, 98
cultural citizenship x, 41
cultural diversity xiii
cultural learning 55–56

debate/debating (the importance of/controversial topics) 44–45, 137
'deliberative democracy' 40–43, 73
democracy 40–61
'the democratic ideal' 40–43, 48, 138
democratic learning 45, 48
Department for Education (DfE) 12, 17–18
Derry/Londonderry 80, 81–82, 94–95
Derry Citizens Action Committee (DCAC) 82, 94–95
Devlin, Bernadette 94
Dewey, John 41–43, 63, 66–67, 72, 94, 138
dialogic (inquiry/governance/pedagogies/multiculturalism) 44, 57, 58, 61, 71

Dietz, Mary 104–105
'dilemma-based learning' 44, 129
diversity/diverse communities 62–89, 72–74, 77–89
Durkheim, Emile 25

the Earth Summit, Rio de Janeiro 122
ecological xi, 121, 137
ecological stakeholder citizenship xiv, 121–136
the Education Act (1870) 41
the Education Act of Northern Ireland 81
Education for Mutual Understanding 84
Education for sustainable development (ESD) xiv, 121–136; *versus* Educating for Sustainability (EfS) xiv, 121–136
Education Reform Order (NI) 83
Egypt 98, 107–108, 110, 111
the Egyptian Girls' Education Initiative 108, 111
the Egyptian Revolution 98
the Egyptian University 113
'enlightened political participation' xiii, 40, 43, 44, 51, 53, 60, 91, 110, 119, 129, 139
the Enlightenment 91
environmentalism 26
'environmentally responsible citizenship' (Talloires Declaration) 123
equality (and inequality/ies) ix, x, 62–89, 138; of opportunity 73, 74
Equality Commission (NI) 82
ethnic identity 23
ethnonationalism 33, 86, 137
Eurocentric/ism 24, 25, 77, 126
Europe 55
European citizenship 33–34
European Commission 32, 33
European Declaration on Human Rights 17
European Union (EU) 3, 32
European Union (EU) | Referendum 2016 33, 40, 42, 63, 76, 101

the Far Right 55
feminism(s) 103–106; in developing countries 107–120
feminist citizenship xii, xiii, 10, 25, 27, 28, 103–120, 125–126
'flexible citizenship' 34
France 69, 74, 97
freedom 51, 74–75; of ideas, speech, language xiii, 40, 74–75; *versus* equality 75

Free Speech Movement 93
French Revolution 100
Friere, Paulo 43, 44, 46, 47, 48, 57, 60, 92, 94, 128, 139
'fundamental British values' (FBV) 9, 29, 61, 138
Furedi, Frank 27

gender: differentiation 104; essentialism xiii, 104; neutrality 104; pluralism 104
gender differentiated feminist citizenship 104
gendered citizenship 103–104
gendered society/ies 103
gendered spaces 114–118
Germany 92
Giroux, Henri xii, 14–15, 34, 47, 48, 49–50, 92, 139
global and local ix
global citizenship 2
global education 2
globalisation ix, xi, 2, 3, 37–38
Global Learning Project/Global Learning and Citizenship 17, 45
'global society' 29
glocalisation xi, xii, 34, 36, 61, 138
the Good Friday Agreement (GFA) 81–86
Gramsci, Antonio xii, 49
grass roots 36, 40, 58, 88, 138; democracy 40, 90–102; education 110; mobilisation 69, 90–102
'green citizenship' 122
Gulf Corporation Council (GCC) 32

Hall, Stuart 37, 46, 55, 64, 69
hegemony/hegemonic x, 46–47, 49–50, 73, 103, 106, 107
heterotopia(s)/heterotopic 74, 78
the 'hidden curriculum' 46
Higher Education Academy (HEA) 16, 132
Higher Education Funding Council for England (HEFCE) 14, 133
Higher Education Partnership for Sustainability 124
Hobsbawm, Eric 23
homogenisation and heterogenisation 36, 138
household sustainability (as responsibilisation) 126–127
Human Rights Act 17
Hume, John 82, 94
hybridity(ies) 38, 64, 68, 71
'hyperspace' 36, 60

identity (politics/and belonging) viii, x, xi, xii, 1, 3–6, 8, 19–20, 21–24, 28, 29, 34, 37–39, 62, 63, 66; European 32–33; national 29; and place 37
'imagined communities' 29
inclusion ix, xiii, 63
individualism 19, 59, 63, 127
integrated schooling/education xiii, 83–84
integration 33, 34, 35, 54, 64, 69, 71, 73, 84, 86–87, 95, 100, 138
interdependence 17, 36, 77, 124, 126, 128, 131, 138
internationalisation 35
Irish Free State 80
Irish Republican Army (IRA) 95, 101
'Islamic extremism' 1
Islamic State/Daesh 63, 76, 99, 100–101
Islamism 96
'the Islamization of radicalism' 100
Islamophobia xiii, 62, 64–65, 87

Keele University 59–60, 134
King, Martin Luther 13, 75, 93, 94, 97

language/linguistic xiii, 33; diversity/death/genocide 72–74; shared 23, 85, 88
Latin America Women's Movement 108–110
Lawrence, Stephen 4
Lebanon 79, 96
liberal arts 58
liberal feminism xiii, 104
liberalism/political liberalism 69–71, 104
liberal multiculturalism 26
liberating 91
Lindsay, Lord 59–60
Lisbon Strategy 32
Lister, Ruth x, 25, 27, 104–107
localism/'the local'/localities/locatedness/localization ix, x, xi, xii, xiii, 2, 4, 11, 17, 21–39, 56–57, 62, 77, 97, 100–101, 139; 'the re-localisation of citizenship' x
Loyalist 86, 87, 99, 100

Maastricht Treaty 32
Marshall, T. E. 24, 25
Marx, Karl/Marxist/m 15, 36, 70, 108, 124–125
Massey, Doreen 21, 36–38, 137
The Middle East 55, 96, 97

migration 23, 62–64
the modernist education project 21, 22–24, 25, 61
moral cosmopolitanism 26
multicultural(ism) 1, 6, 16, 53, 62–89; critical multiculturalism x, xi, xii, xiii, xiv, 62–89; liberal multiculturalism 26, 70; 'multicultural' *versus* 'multi-cultural' 69; pluralist multiculturalism 70, 71; procedural multiculturalism 104; separatist multiculturalism 104
'multiple identities' 38, 69
Muslim (identity/community/ies) x, 53, 64–66, 68, 74–76, 79, 96
Muslim Brotherhood 98–99
the Muslim Council of Britain 78

'(the) nation' xii, 62
'the national' ix, 23, 29, 138
National Assessment of Educational Progress (NAEP) 12
National Curriculum 4, 5, 6, 7, 8, 30; for Citizenship 11–12, 17–18, 27, 77, 84, 85
National Foundation for Educational Research (NFER) 8, 9
national identity 1, 29, 34
nationalist/ism 28, 29, 31, 100
nationality 1, 3, 65, 80
National Machinery for Women (South Africa) 109
National Union of Teachers (NUT) 52, 53, 56
Nazi student fraternities 93
neo-liberalism 26
new citizenship 2, 10, 27
Northern Ireland xiii, 80–89, 94–95, 100, 113, 138
Northern Ireland Civil Rights Association (NICRA) 82, 94–95
Northern Ireland Council for Integrated Education (NICIE) 83

Occupy (movement) 31, 55, 57, 60, 97
'official knowledge' 30, 46–47
'official nationalism' 23
OFSTED 11–12, 132
One nation 21
Open space for dialogue and enquiry (OSDE) 44, 78, 129
'the other'/othering/'otherness' 62, 64, 76–77, 83, 91, 105

Parekh Commission/Report ix, 6, 29, 70–72, 104
Paris Spring 93
Parsons, Talcott 62
patriotism 29
Peace Pledge Union 99
Phillips, Andrew 7
Physical, Social and Health Education (PSHE) 9, 20
pluralism/pluralist 69, 74, 80, 83, 86, 88, 95, 97, 99; categorical pluralism 86, 105; gender pluralism 105; pluralist feminism 105; representative pluralism 105
'The policy problem' xii
political education 4, 25, 32, 41, 46
political liberalism 70, 71, 104
political literacy ix, 5, 6, 8, 10, 12, 13, 25, 40, 41, 61, 72
political participation/engagement (citizenship as) 41–43, 45–49, 55, 106, 118–120
political representation (citizenship as) 118–120
Political Studies Association (PSA) 14, 33, 42
'the politics of difference' 2, 106
Politics Online Learning and Citizenship Skills (POLiS) 14, 16
Porto Alegre, Popular Administration Project 48, 78, 110
'post-colonial' 37
Prague Spring 93
prevent strategy/duty/guidance ix, 30, 51–56, 65, 66, 79, 99
Prison to Peace 85, 100
'problem-posing education' 43, 47
progressive education/school(ing) 56–57, 60
protest (politics, movements, citizenship) xiii, 12, 28, 31, 36, 40, 42, 55, 57, 58, 63, 90–102
Protestant 80–87

Qualifications and Curriculum Authority (QCA) 4
Queens University/College 81, 94–95

Race Relations Act 4
racism/racist ix, xiii, 64
radical/radicalism xiii, 40, 54–55, 99–102, 107, 137, 138; as action for change 120; as boundary crossing 55
radical democracy/radical democratic citizenship xi–xii, 60

radical education (as consciousness-raising) 56, 119–120
radicalisation xiii, 40, 53, 55, 62, 102
Rancière, Jacques xii
Rawls, John 70, 71, 104
the Really Open University 57, 60
the Reform Act 1867 40
regional citizenship xii
regionalism 21
re-scoping xi, 34
revolt 91
'the right to name ourselves' 28, 63
risk (and risk aversion/avoidance) xiv, 40, 45, 46, 54, 58, 83, 91, 92, 100, 116, 137, 139
Robbins, Lord/the Robbins Report 50
The Roman Empire 22
'ruling ideas' 46

safe spaces xiii, 51, 135
Said, Edward 25, 37–38, 137
schools ix, xii, 4–6, 9
Scotland 31, 32, 35, 42, 131–132
Scottish Independence Referendum/campaign of 2014 31–32, 35, 42
Scottish National Party 31–32
Sectarian(ism) 79, 80, 81, 82, 83, 85, 96, 97
segregation 83, 86, 93, 105, 114–118; and seclusion (gendered) 104, 114–118
separatist/separatism 35, 86, 104, 119
Shared Education Programme 84
Singapore 73–74
'sites for citizenship' 66–67
social marginalisation xiii
Society Counts 15
Soja, Edward 56, 59, 106, 107
South Africa 108–109, 119
sovereignty 23
space(s) xi, xiii, 15, 21, 23, 31, 32, 33, 36–39, 60, 114–116, 121–136
'the spatial turn' xi, 37
'spiritual, moral, social and cultural education' (SMSC) 11
stakeholding/stakeholder citizenship xi, 19, 121–136, 137
'state multiculturalism' 1
Stromquist, Nelly 47, 107, 109–110
student consciousness/riots/protests/activism xiii, 96–98

'Students for a Democratic Society' 93
sub-politics/political xii, xiii, 55, 56, 57, 60–61, 82, 127
subversion 19, 107, 116
Summerhill 56
sustainability xiv
Sustainable Development Goals 122
Swann Report 72
'symbolic violence' 47

teachers as agents of change 47
'Teaching about Controversial Issues' 12
Tehran University 96
'thirdspace(s)' 56, 61, 78
Tonga(n ecological education) 130, 136
Transition (movement) 31, 57, 60, 126, 127
transnational(ism) xii, 4, 34, 61, 68, 69, 98; competition xii; terrorism 4
'the Troubles' 80, 97
Trump, Donald 65, 75–77, 93
Turkey/the Turkish state 79, 93
TV 94

UK Independence Party (UKIP) 65
UN Convention on the Rights of the Child 17, 43
union(s) 55–56
Unionist (NI) 86
United States (US) xiii, 16, 32, 33, 55, 69, 73, 74, 76, 94–95, 98, 135, 138, 139
university/universities (& higher education) 15, 50–51, 54, 57, 59–60, 81, 94, 112–116, 133–135, 139

values (shared, collective) 11, 23, 75
Vietnam (anti war protest) 94, 98
Voting Rights Act (US) 93

Wales 73, 131, 136
workforce, labour force 14–15, 23–24, 113, 116
World Summit on Sustainable Development 122
World Universities Forum (WUF) 15, 57

Youth Citizenship Commission xii, 6, 30
youth disaffection xiii, 40